Point Taken

Point Taken
Collected Poems 2014-2020

Don Gutteridge

First Edition

Hidden Brook Press
www.HiddenBrookPress.com
writers@HiddenBrookPress.com

Copyright © 2020 Hidden Brook Press
Copyright © 2020 Don Gutteridge

All rights for poems revert to the author. All rights for book, layout and design remain with Hidden Brook Press. No part of this book may be reproduced except by a reviewer who may quote brief passages in a review. The use of any part of this publication reproduced, transmitted in any form or by any means, electronic, mechanical, photocopied, recorded or otherwise stored in a retrieval system without prior written consent of the publisher is an infringement of the copyright law.

Point Taken: Collected Poems 2014-2020
by Don Gutteridge

Cover Design – Richard M. Grove
Layout and Design – Richard M. Grove
Cover Image – Happy Person: Impressionistic City, watercolour.
    from Shutterstock

Typeset in Garamond
Printed and bound in USA
Distributed in USA by Ingram,
    in Canada by Hidden Brook Distribution

Library and Archives Canada Cataloguing in Publication

Title: Point taken : collected poems, 2014-2020 / Don Gutteridge.
Other titles: Poems. Selections (Hidden Brook Press)
Names: Gutteridge, Don, 1937- author.
Identifiers: Canadiana 20200213717 | ISBN 9781927725726 (softcover)
Classification: LCC PS8513.U85 A6 2020 | DDC C811/.6—dc23

For Anne
in loving memory.

Point Taken

List of books

– The Way it Was – *p.1*
– Tidings – *p.28*
– Peripheries – *p.54*
– Inundations – *p.83*
– The Blue Flow Below – *p.121*
– The Sands of Canatara – *p.151*
– Inklings – *p.180*
– Cameron Lake: A Suite of Poems – *p.201*
– Home Ground – *p.219*
– Night Skating – *p.251*
– Days Worth the Telling – *p.278*
– The Breath of My Being – *p.305*
– The Star-Brushed Horizon – *p.316*
– Foster's Pond – *p.387*
– Mara's Lamp – *p.417*
– Inking the World – *p.453*
– Village Dreaming – *p.503*
– Recent Work – *p.541*

A Short Autobiographical Story – *p.569*
An Essay on Don Gutteridge's "Big Book" *Point Taken* – *p.579*

The Way it Was

Friesen Press
2014

BLUE-EYED
For my Grandmother: 1888-1957

My grandmother: shaking
dust-bunnies out of her mop
in a willing wind, and me,
at five, hopping in a one-
footed dance at her side,
the serene sun alive
in her hair as together
we breathe easy in the April
air, crisp clouds
clustered above: her glance
a blue-eyed barometer
of her love.

UNISON

Grace and I skating
on Leckie's farthest field:
our fingertips a millimetre
apart as stride by rhythmic
stride we ride the Earth's
perimeter on a thin inch
of ice in effortless motion
under a moon-blooming sky
instilled with stars,
until out of breath and wonder
we yield our hearts to the grip
of gravity.

LETTERS
For my Grandfather: 1892-1955

I am now the last one
who will remember my grand-
father, and so it is
I try again to catch
that fleeting face in the prism
of a poem, to see it
again with the clarity of crystal
and feel that benign smile
in the serendipity of a simile,
knowing that he will survive
as long as these letters
linger and thrive.

DUNES AT CANATARA

It took a million years
to sculpt these dunes,
grain by grain of wave-
washed sand whipped
by seasoned winds into
voluptuous curves
and bevelled runes.
It took my pals and me
an afternoon to put
our imprimatur upon
the shimmering concavities,
our bodies pressing
their wry signatures deep
deep into the sun-stunned sand,
feeling the heat of a hundred
centuries oozing through.

THE ZOO

We sing our way to the zoo,
forty cub scouts
on a blue bus that masters
the many miles to Detroit,
where they stuff untameable
beasts in soul-corroding
cages, I watch tigers
pawing to and fro
with all the monotony
of a muffled metronome,
I peer into the lion's eyes
and see the wide savannah
home he's been torn out of,
while the elegant elephants
amble in a parody of their
jungle trundle, and the chimps
scramble from limb to limb
as if these stunted trees
were soaring eucalyptus,
and on the long ride back
no voices are lifted
in celebratory song.

GRINNING

One wild winter
when the snows heaved up-
wards of three feet,
my grandfather built
us a snow-slide
on the backyard hill,
and sailing down we went
as ardent as Argonauts,
our scarves spinning out
behind us and our eyes
as wide and thrilled as a
hummingbird's flutter,
while high on the hill,
his own eyes alight,
my Grandpa – grinning.

STEEPLES

My Grandmother didn't fancy
the Church of England or
any other steepled
edifice for that matter;
she spent each Sabbath
morning, pewless,
baking raisin pies
for Grampa's workaday
lunches and cooling
Jello on the side
verandah, but God,
if He's still with us,
would have danced a duet with her
and all those like her.

BOWER

Mrs. Bray among her flowers
(glorious gladioli
swaying in the sweet August
breeze), picking posies
for some village nuptials,
roses and black-eyed
susans galore,
her straw hat see-
sawing as she moves from bloom
to unruptured bloom;
I watch her for hours,
awed by my next-door
neighbour, afloat
like Miranda on her sea-spawned
bower.

CAREER

Oscar and I boxing
in the home-built ring
rigged up in Saunders'
basement – I bob
and weave like Billy Conn
eluding the Brown Bomber,
when suddenly my chin
obtrudes a hair
too close to the gist
of Oscar's toxic fist,
and down I go, sprawled
on the cellar floor, knocked
here and everywhere
at once, and contemplating
the demise of my illustrious
career.

THE RIGHT

Tommy and I playing
cowboys and Indians
among the sand dunes
of Canatara, poised
like pyramids along the
wind-whispered shore-
line; for all of a long
summer's afternoon
we were something other
than ourselves, our war-
whoops and sallies
proclaiming our right
to be whatever we dreamed
while the dunes looked on
with their thousand-year smile.

HEATHEN

"Don't worry," Butch
says as he dispatches
the adder with a hectic blow,
"Snakes always come
back to life again
at midnight." "The little
heathen," my Grandma says,
"What a concoction!"
When we hurry back
next day, the creature
lies in the grass, unalive.
"It's okay," Butch says,
"I don't believe in the
Resurrection either."

SUNDAYS

On Sundays we sang of Jesus
and his glory and the precious blood
of the Lamb, our voices high,
as if we knew what it was
to be affixed to a cross
and have your highway
to Paradise paved,
or be strong enough to roll
that stone away and live
again – leaving us
to sing your story, and wonder.

HOPE

When the noon-bell rang
we vied to be the first
in the schoolyard to mimic
the heroics of our Dads and brothers,
swooping and dive-bombing:
spitfires and kamikaze
kudos to the courageous
as we scoped the zeitgeist
of the Zero, living with pride
on the cliff's edge, and not
unaware of the gazing girls
under the stiff pine:
harvesting hope.

FALSE ALARM

When the station-whistle blew
with all the enthusiasm of an air-
raid siren over London,
the whole village shuddered
awake, and soon the bright
red engine was being pursued
by every boy worth his salt:
our heads full of flamboyant
flame and damsels demanding
rescue as the blaze inched
higher than the steepest steeple;
but, alas, the chuddering machine
came to a half-hearted
halt in front of a smouldering
dune, and we no longer
dreamt of a full-fledged
five-alarm fire.

MOMENT

My Dad was no ordinary
fisherman, he cast
the spinner with all the allure
of a slow curveball,
and when the lunker struck
he played the fish like a
picker strumming the fickle
strings of his guitar, while I
watched in envious awe
and wondered how much of
the artful ease
he had bequeathed to me
and just how long
such a moment of pure
convergence would last.

NIGHTFALL

When night came down
upon the village verge,
we gathered around
the intergalactic glow
of the streetlight like
marauding moths, and it
was hide-and-go-seek,
as, in our pulsing panic,
we combed every ell
and alley to burrow in;
then ululating ally-
ally-in-free, we
rocketed out of
our hiding holes, triumphant,
until something
darker than night called
us ineluctably
home.

THE STRAP

The slap of the strap echoed
as far as our second-floor
room, and a shudder of shame
ran through every grade-
four, as if we were all
somehow responsible
for the sins of the one now
wincing under the sting/
the assault of that instrument
we feared as no other,
and the principal pounced
with relentless impunity,
whose tyranny kept us
in thrall, reminding us
that we were still children
in a world of unconsenting
adults.

BELOW

Flying our home-made
kites on the River flats,
racing into the March breeze,
our prize held high,
until an oomph of wind
sends it fluttering sky-
ward, where, with a swish
of its raggedy tail, it swoops
and swivels, poised upon
an edge of atmosphere:
we feel its every torque
and tug through the taut tether,
satisfied that it's sailing
on the sea it belongs to,
leaving us languished
on the land below.

ADVENTURE

Curled on Grandpa's lap,
while he spins the tale
on the Three Bears, I
succumb to the thrall
of the story, spun a dozen
times or more, drawn
to the ancient tug
of its three-pronged plot,
riding tall on the velvet
voice I adore,
and we both guffaw
at the inept antics
of Goldilocks and her
ursine adventure.

CHRISTMAS NIGHT

I lay awake, feigning
sleep under a full moon,
fallow in the wintry sky,
straining to hear the
tintinnabulation of
sleigh-bells, but all
I heard was the lowing
of Mr. Leckie's cows
wide-eyed in their mangers,
as if something hallowed
had stirred them in their stalls.

DEVIL'S NIGHT

The night before Halloween
we delved deep for the devil
inside us, ringing
doorbells and dashing away,
our hearts hitting high-C,
and soaping every way-
ward window within sight
(while our country cousins
tilted outhouses,
left the odd gate
unlatched, and spooked
the cattle in their spirited spree)
as if we were all purging
the pent-up strain
of a whole year's-worth
of Sunday school civility
and Old Nick himself
had sanctioned our Satanic
urges.

HOME GROUND

My first bicycle:
a Firestone special
and I went loco-
motoring across the
suddenly shrunken
village, the wind's
wilful whisper
on my bent brow, I
pummelled every path
I could find, wafted
a careless hand to the girls
struck dumb by the swift
sweep of my passage,
until I hit the utter edge
where the world ended
and I might take flight
at any moment to nowhere
I knew, and I stuttered
to a stop: both feet
on the home ground.

BEYOND WORDS

My Dad was addicted to the booze;
he preferred his whiskey watered
to make it last a little
longer, but he never failed
to smile through his blurred haze
with everything but his eyes,
where all the disappointment
of a lifetime oozed
out at me, and bereft
of the pride he hadn't had
for a dozen years, I heard
him say, "I can lick this,
lad," and I longed for those
rare moments when he snoozed
through the afternoons: all
the hurt finally drained
from a face I loved
beyond words.

BEE-DEEP

Mrs. Bray: bee-deep
among her flowers, aflame
in the simmering sunlight:
autumnal roses still
bright in the local loam
and glittering gladioli —
not a home in the village
ungraced by her tactful
touch: nosegays
boutonieres, sprays
of crisp chrysanthemums;
she stood among them all
and let them ease the pain
of her widowhood.

STORIES

Sunday school was the room
where God from His throne
gazed down on all
of us as we sang sweetly
of Jesus and the Trinity,
and, going home, prized
the proselytising pamphlets
with those amazing images:
of Samson shouldering Doom,
of Zacharias in his tree,
of the Magdalene cast out:
these were our first stories,
deep-boned and made
to last.

BUTCHER

John McCord was a butcher
all his life, halving
hams and jousting joints,
with a cordial wink for the regulars
on Saturday morning,
an artful manipulator of meats
fit for the village table,
but when his shop was shuttered,
he found himself in an abattoir
disembowelling fresh-
killed carcasses,
and no-one friendly enough
to wink at, and when the drink
failed to ease the pain,
his heart ruptured
like a venomous vein.

A MEMORY: DECEMBER 1943

A memory, sudden, un-
muted – I'm tucked
into the comfortable crook
of Uncle Ivan's arm,
my six-year-old
head heavy with heat
from the motor's steady
pulse, the dome-light
more lulling than a lullaby,
the engine's drone hypnotic;
dreaming within this cosy
cocoon of metal and chrome,
that I could do whatever
I endeavoured in a world
construed mainly for me,
and that Uncle Ivan
would live forever.

CLARITY

How many hours we'd spend
at Canatara: Indian
hunting among the treacherous
trees, Comanche-proud,
we mimicked the best
of our Saturday matinées;
then it was a dash to the dunes,
sifted from the sands of a
thousand forgotten seas,
where we pressed our taut bodies
against the foetal warmth,
then rinsed ourselves in the
blue clarity of the lustrous
Lake, certain that days
like these would have no
end.

HYMN

In Sunday school
we sang aloud of Jesus
and His unending love
as if the song unbending
inside us was more than
singing itself,
and we were somehow
blessed beyond
our avid innocence,
and felt ourselves
a heartened part
of that Heaven-sent
hymn.

THE CHAIR

"The War is over!" we chanted
in the schoolyard, a cheer
flung for miles around,
and I headed straight home,
ululating all the way,
but when I came into our kitchen,
a perfect stranger was seated
in my grandfather's chair,
puffing on a cigarette
and beaming me a smile.
"Say hello to your father,"
my mother said: and I turned
from the sound, and fled.

THE SNOWS OF MY BOYHOOD

The snows of my boyhood
were always bigger and better,
enlarged by my ardent
imagination: I recall
the muffled implosion
that huddled our house, bent
its angular eaves
into curves as curt as a
Turk's scimitar,
that whetted its colossal
weightlessness upon
chimney-pot and post
as we scurried to be the first
to taste it coy on our tongues
and feel ourselves
turned inside out with joy.

A CRYING MATTER

When Peter Rabbit almost
got caught in the clutches
of Mister MacGregor,
I did my best not
to cry at his impossible
plight, but when one
morning I found my pet
cottontail dead
in his hutch, one pink
accusing eye staring
straight up at me,
I knew that Death was more
than a crying matter.

UNBLADED

Unbladed on Foster's
Pond, we skidded a-skew
after the bobbing puck
with hand-me-down
sticks, the wind brewing
over the Marsh, cherubic
on our cheeks, and who cared
that we couldn't afford skates:
we were alive and free to dream
of Rocket Richard and other
glorious gladiators,
beamed to us effortless
through the air every
Saturday night.

OLD WARRIORS
Juno Beach, June 6, 2014

Unable to stride with the
practised ease of their youth
(embers of age aglow
in the eyes of these old
old warriors), they
nonetheless shuffle
with proper pride on the arm
of a grateful niece
or elderly son, recalling
that plunge through the waves
and bold rush up the
shell-shattered beach,
comrades falling all
around them: they carried
on because courage is more
than just a word, and here
on this hallowed ground
they gather together, some
seventy years on,
to remember those
who cannot speak
their bravery from the grave.

RENDEZVOUS

In the midst of our mid-day
play, my brother would pause
and, like a bloodhound
tasting the wind, would turn
an ear northward
and cry, "It's the one-ten!"
and sure enough the big
sixty-three-hundred
would churn into view with all
its pistoning power
and bellicose steam,
pulling a dozen coaches
jammed with go-getters
on their merry way to some
roseate rendezvous
we would never know.

DRAWING BREATH
For Anne

I wake at the edge of dawn
and, drawing breath, I think
of you and all the years
we've travelled on in tight
tandem, and shared
that secret part of the self
pledged only to the one
we love: take heart,
my dearest, each dawn
is both beginning
and renewal.

A STORY
For my Grandson, Tom

Even as a youngster
you loved horses, the un-
dulant trot of a pony
tucked under you, and further
on: astride the thundering
gallop of a gelding
you gripped with glee and rode
for glory; no wonder
then you bequeathed
your life to animals,
tendering them your concern
and supple skill: a fitting
end to your half-told story.

AGLOW
For Grace Leckie

I worshipped Grace on her
high-stepping stallion,
the summering breeze
alive in her hair, her face
aglow, triumphant,
as she galloped right past
without a glance to either
side and certainly not
in the direction of the one
who knew at last what
love was, and despair.

INCORRUPTIBLE

I dream my way into
scenes long gone,
that interrupt my sleep,
as fleeting as a feather
winnowing on the wind
but nonetheless whelming
upon that seasoned eye
where images untether
themselves and reprise
the serendipitous days
of my brief boyhood,
the jubilance of its joys
and purging pain, and I
wake, unable
to reclaim that lost
incorruptible innocence.

FANCIES
For Katie and Rebecca

My granddaughters are dancing
to a tune heard only
in the head – doubling
the delight as their bodies
manufacture moves
that might have amused
Margot Fontaine
or a novice Nureyev;
they beam me a smile,
untroubled by anything
as guileless as stage-fright,
knowing they have made me
complicit in their furious
fancies.

CAMERON LAKE

I was just sixteen
when I first saw
Cameron Lake, a perfect
oval ground out of
Precambrian granite,
as blue as a heron's wing
under a summer sun
that settled in the wavelets
and lingered there lovingly,
and when the night-wind died,
it cast a moonlit sheen,
a leavening light all
the way up to my uncle's
cottage, where I was welcomed
as a second son and taught
how to tease black bass
onto the lure and jig for pickerel,
and where, among forests
more ancient than Heaven
itself, I became part
of something bigger
than my own being
and more profound.

HELEN

My heart still stirs
when I hear that numinous
name: Helen Stahura,
there wasn't a boy for miles
around who wouldn't do
his mating dance for the girl
whose smile was as silken
as the sultry siren of Troy:
I worshipped her from afar,
entranced by a beauty
I could neither explain
nor claim.

TRUE

With trepidation I ease
through the terrain of my childhood
in search of what I might
recognize as having been known
and prized: the jocular tilt
of a neighbour's gable,
the errant angle of an eave
next door on a home
built brick by loving brick
and lived in till they resembled
those who resided there,
who plied me with playmates
and pals, and the aroma of tar
on the pebbled streets where my
grandfather's house
stood tall with its double
verandahs – but all
is altered; I shudder
at the shock of the new, for only
that which is familiar
strikes the heart as true.

YOUNG

I still see you young,
limned in that lemon-
yellow dress, your hair
swept up like a burst
rose, your eyes a-light
with the lilt of living, me
tongue-tied on the curb
as your slim coupé idles
down and off we go
to tinsel town, where together
we sing all the songs
still unsung.

CHRISTMAS SNOW

It settles upon rooves
and gabled gutters as soft
as the hay in the Babe's manger,
if it were a word it would be
an adverb uttered
eloquently, and on this
Day of Days it speaks
of Bethlehem, a star-
lit stable and those
eternal truths we seek
to live by.

THE GIFT

How well we remember
as we ease into our age
those moments when we
embraced as softly
as a sea-swell against
a far horizon, believing
ourselves to be immortal
and the gift of bliss our prize,
and we have been sea-riding
the memory of that wondrous
wave ever since: it
lingers in the tendrils
of our touch each diminishing
day and leaves us
loving.

FLOWERING
For Katie-Ann and Rebecca

My granddaughters are lovely
as a rose is lovely in morning's
light, and they move as lithe
as lilies on a polished pond,
and the love they harbour
for me and mine glows
like gladioli brightening
under the moon's breath:
may we waltz hand-in-glove
towards Time and Eternity.

DUSK

Dusklight over Huron:
the faltering sun dreams
its way into the patient lake,
its last rays erupting
in a blaze of haunted hues
that leave me, safely
ashore, in a dappled daze,
recalling a time decades
ago when I stood boldly
here in the unbrightening
dusk and dreamt of what
it was to be old.

THRIVING
For Tom, Tim, James and Kevin

My grandsons are as sturdy
as oaks on a wind-surged
afternoon, their loving
as loyal as it is unspoken
or when they gazed at me
out of innocents' eyes,
their minds as bright as new
pennies on an upturned
palm: may you thrive,
live long, and each
in your time surprise
the world.

ENNUI

I spend the afternoon
squinting at squirrels
as they leap through the trees
like acrobats on a flying
trapeze; at ease
with themselves they have no
need to wonder who is eyeing
them or worry about
a step too quick or soon,
they are what they are,
without a care for precious
poets or empty afternoons.

HERE AM I

Here am I surrounded
by these family photos,
fading but still true
to the lives lived in them;
I'm instantly grounded:
my twin grandfathers
smiling out at me
with English or Irish eyes
and I can feel the tug
of those faraway isles
in every vivid vein,
and somehow I know
they're watching
with a wink and shrug
to see themselves
reintroduced to the world.

THE GLOW

In the long years of our loving
we grow stronger, despite
the slow erosion of age,
knowing our passion, subdued,
has delved deeper like roots
rationed of light and rain
stretch downward against
the doubting of drought.
and strengthened too by the bright
glow of love's legacy.

ALL IS STILL

All is still and quiet
on the groundswell of my lawn
but underneath the root-
bleached loam it's Spring
with all its rising desire
and fiery fulminations
driving the tender tip
of each green shoot
up through the Earth's crisp
carapace and into the
singing, solemnizing
sun.

LIGHT

I love the brightness of the moon
on a soft September night,
silver streams on the lake's
face: lozenges of light.

BEING

We come into this world
unbidden; there is
no-one to applaud
our irreverent arrival,
so we irrigate the air
with our prodigal cries,
succumb to the need
to breathe, somehow
inhabit the broad
acreage of that space
Nature grants us –
and celebrate the birth
of our being.

POSTERITY

My death will not consume me,
there is little room
for grief or grievance,
for I will live in the lively
eyes of my grandchildren
in those moments when they are
startled by a memory too
deep to be unremembered
or prize on a particular day
the embers of my voice in the
lilt and timbre of a poem
I wrote just for me
and posterity.

GOOD DAY

If I were unalive
the world would cease to be
in all its lingering loveliness
and I would no longer
embrace these jolts
of joy and their surprise,
but holding still my breath
I will myself to prize
the singular hours that abide,
and when the time arrives
bid 'good day' to Death.

RUTHLESS

And me composing poems:
inklings I tease
towards some sense
in words whetted upon
the wheel of memory
and swerving askance
upon the page where they lean
upright, enlinked,
ready to be swallowed whole,
raw and ruthless
in rhythmic pursuit
of the truth.

HALO

There is a stillness
about old houses,
as if those long gone
are lingering there, willing
the eaves and gables to stay
just as they were when lives
were offered there, and every
room, subdued by silence,
refuses to forgo
its lushest memories,
though all that is left now
is an elderly house held
in a hushed halo.

MANDALA

Twenty-seven years
in prison could not hollow
out your humanity,
like Christ you came down
from the cross they'd nailed you on
and taught your fellow men
that violence is neither
sacrosanct nor justified,
that black and white could find
the common ground on which
to found a nation, free
from discord and fear:
you disarmed your enemies
with wit and ceremonious charm,
a man of supreme reason
seasoned by hope and harmony.

PERFECTION

Eve was Adam's muse
as he poured out poem
after perfect poem
unblemished by sin
or Old Nick's eye,
and suffused with Eve's
innocent image her lover
adored with missionary
zeal, and together
they tended the flawless
flowers of God's garden,
while something sly
and elegiac slithered
through the garlanded grass.

AGAINST ALL ODDS

For three years and more
against all odds
my grandfather fought
to survive the malignant
muttering of mortars,
the stunned thrum of a machine
gun's stutter, the very
air toxic to the taste,
when courage was a daunting
dash into a land laid waste,
where whole cities
whose syllables twisted
the tongue lay desolate,
and where men prayed to any
gods alive who would pity
them and their own, and bring
them safely back to the
loving hum of home.

DYING STALLION
For Tom

Once you rode the winds
of some far savannah,
as galvanized as Pegasus,
your feathered mane out-
flung like simulated silk,
nostrils flared against
every weather, every
threat to your stallion's
pride: and here, now,
in this stifling stall,
you stand on the withered
sticks of your legs, and pray
you're too far gone
for any vet to fix.

SENSE

There are no ordinary words
in verse; in poems they are dense,
derelict, and obedient
to no law but the laconic
logic of rhythm and rhyme,
the strictures of the unreasonable
made cogent by the flow
of iambic and the tight flight
of almost-but-not-quite
sense.

THE URGE

When Cain slew Abel
in his jealous rage,
the bereft brother brooded
over Canaan, and God
drew on his brow a mark
as burning as a ranch hand's
brand, and Cain cursed
the fields he no longer
tilled with Abel's blood,
and roamed the barren land
until he grew into his sin
and willed it upon
a murderous world:
the urge to kill.

VIRGINIA

All your brief life
you wrestled wittingly
with words, wove them
till they gleamed like a bright
tapestry of truth, but the weight
of such travail bore
down upon you
and you let the sea and all
its tender serenity
take you to a world
without words.

Tidings

Black Moss Press
2015

THE WAY HOME

The way home is thru
the heart, every blood-
beat hums with remembrance,
the village at the nub
of our being runs deep,
keeps our aloneness
at bay wherever
it finds us: estranged
as we are and listening
hard for that
emphatic thrum.

TIME WAS

Time was when Time
itself meant little:
the summer sun rose,
shone for a whole season
and settled in the welcoming
West, and all the while
we plied the ritual games
no rhyme or reason
could spy the end of,
or needed to, and swam
dolphin-eyed in the Great
Lake till evening
sank softly into it
with the promise of dawn
and another run with no
thought that Time was whittling
down the days one
                by one.

URGES

Who can ever forget
that sun-softened day
when we metamorphosed
into Fox and the Hounds,
across fields wild
with wheat and the unplumbed
depths of Leckie's Bush?
Intoxicated we were
by the chase, and like Hansel
and Gretel, grateful
for the paper spoor we tracked
like Comanches on a righteous
raid, and when the Fox
succumbed, we roused him
for fresh rounds of piracy
and the Cisco Kid:
forever reconciled
to the child-wise urges
in all of us.

MOVE UP

How many daylight
hours did we spend
on that vacant lot
playing our favourite
ungendered game?
Where the boy-girl divide
was rendered moot,
and anyone who could catch
a ball or cling to a
bat was free to move
up, was cheered and jeered
with equal ease, until
at last we deigned surrender
to the twilight shrouding
inexorably down
upon us whether
we willed it or not.

BITE

What I remember
most about those summer
days slung between June
and September is the feeling
of freedom at being
abruptly sprung from the
schoolyard in a daze
of jubilant release:
Tommy and I together
forever on the soothing dunes
of Canatara's beach,
where our sun-slaked
bodies lay length-
wise in their delight
and let the wavelets
of our imperturbable Lake
wash lovingly over us,
while Time itself paused
just long enough
to have us believe
it had no universal
                bite.

MAGIC

Me just turned ten
and still believing
that Santa somehow
squeezed down our soot-
steeped chimney and landed
foot-first and noiseless
on the living room rug,
a sack of goodies bulging
on his back; no matter that
they looked suspiciously
like the ones we'd spied
in the five-and-dime the day
before: magic is a
wonder hard to give up,
and toys are toys.

GRIEF

The night I first heard
my father cry: a single
anguished utterance,
the Earth tilted on its axis
half an inch or more,
and I thought of the oak
sturdy in our yard bent to
breaking in a tormenting wind,
and everything I'd known
and trusted was suddenly
as fragile as the life
of my dying grandfather,
and grief was a live being
with little time for childish
tears.

HOME-GROWN

My village made me
what I came to be:
the curve of Canatara's
bountiful beach,
the infinite surge
of Huron Lake, the marshes
below the angular Bridge
spanning the blue
cadence of our River,
while meadows bounced
with bobolinks near a park
where we played until
the evening evaporated –
these were all of God's
geography I would need
to track the terrain of a story
or the swerve of a poem
with my cartographer's eye,
or people them with characters
even Dickens would die for:
home-grown and in-
advertently comic,
they acted out the minor
flaws of their little lives
as if I were the only one
watching, and beguiling
the village air with my
grateful applause.

GALILEE

For a hundred Sundays
and more, I became
acquainted with God, His Son
and the blood of the Lamb (of which
we were all washed clean),
with lurid tales of Adam
and Eve rambunctious in Eden,
with Zacharias trembling
in a tree, with luckless saints
who beat the odds and the
occasional flood, with David
whose pious pebble bested
Goliath, with Samson's
plucky locks in Delilah's
severing scissors,
and of course with Jesus
pinned horrific on
Golgotha: images that
fired my fancy and drew
me, dazzled, out of my way-
ward village ten
thousand miles from
                Galilee.

BELONGING

When I think of the place
where I was born and ushered
into the world without ceremony,
I remember snow
falling as softly
as the Babe's breath in a
manger ten thousand
miles away, and no
breeze to blemish such
perfection, and I let
it drift upon my face
(uplifted to the Heavens)
like a benediction on
                belonging.

HUNTING

Dad fits me up
with a sixteen-gauge
("Easier on the shoulder," he says)
and cracks his twelve-gauge
with a military snap.
Dutifully I follow him
into our neighbour's winter
woods, trying not to step
into those huge footprints,
and looking out for unwary
rabbits cowering
in every hedge and brush-
pile, out of which a foolish
cottontail springs
in time to take a blast
from my father's steady gun.
I watch its life ease
out of it, one cold eye
staring straight up
as if the sky had an answer,
and then there's its mate
rabbiting into the open.
"Shoot!" my father says,
and I pull the trigger,
knowing even then
that I would raise the sight
an inch too high.
"You missed," Dad says,
trying his best to believe
I have really tried.

SOME THINGS

At precisely ten after six
every Saturday evening,
just past closing
time at the Balmoral,
Bob McCord staggered
past our house, singing
off-key and entertaining
the street all along his way-
ward route; we'd watch
him enter his front door
and stumble into silence,
after which came the slap
heard round the village.
And sometime later
Mrs. McCord would appear
on her front porch as if
nothing had happened,
smiling grimly at those
unashamed enough
to pass by, and young
though I was, I thought:
this is the way things are
in our town, and then:
there are some things
that shouldn't be.

DESIRES

Whenever the good
reverend mentioned
Heaven, I pictured
Elijah's fiery rise
or Jacob's leavening
ladder, while Cherubim
chuckled like oversize
babies and angels
provoked applause
at the Pearly Gates, and no-
one dare allow
that Satan stood just
beyond the hallowed
walls, stoking
            our desires.

BRAVERY

I was afraid of bees
before they were born
each spring out of their
cozy combs, the hum
of a drone reconnoitring
a daffodil would send
my heart drumming with the
thrill of a fear so
primal I found
no words to give it
a name, and that time
in First Bush when my handle-
bar brushed a hive
and a hundred barb-
tipped dive-bombers
spun free, I
staggered home, sobbing,
stung from stem to stern,
but Gran called me brave,
and in my endless innocence
I believed her.

THE DAY I ALMOST DROWNED

The day I almost drowned
was an ordinary summer's
afternoon, the sun
soothing the rough waters
around the village pier,
when for a dime or a dare
I offered to circum-
navigate the jetty,
and set about the challenge
with a will and a reckless
paddling, and almost
made it to the cheers
from the shoreline, when
out of nowhere I felt
a chuck under my chin
and a strong arm guiding
me, against my better
judgement, un-
ceremoniously to safety,
where I sat dazed
and thinking only that
I would remember this
as the day I almost
              drowned.

EASTER SUNDAY

When I think of Easter
I think not of Christ
stretched upon His cross
nor of that stubborn stone
miraculously rolled
away, but rather recall
a long-ago Sunday
when morning bloomed with
sunshine and church bells
tolled the faithful home,
and a ten-year-old boy
skipped the cracks in his grand-
mother's sidewalk
and hummed some Sunday
school ditty learned
by heart and singing
now within as if Jesus
and all His world were real.

THE LAKE OF MY CHILDHOOD

When I was eleven
I learned for good
I wasn't a dolphin,
thru the svelte waves of Huron
I burrowed and flailed
like a walrus without a tail,
there was no daring
in the dives I mistook
once the rollers had slowed,
I felt only fear
as I stood and shook
on the pier's edge while my
buddies cannon-balled
and belly-flopped as if
they'd been born with fins
and a rudder; even today
I cannot pass the Great
Lake of my childhood
without a nod and modicum
of shudder.

PLEASURE
For Kenny Waters

Kenny and I diving
for bottlecaps in the shallows
of the sea-deep Lake:
Pepsi, Coke, Orange
Crush – a treasure trove
of logos we dove after
in dolphin-eyed tandem
under a simmering sun,
while Huron held us in its
wombed vise, twinned
in mutual pleasure.

WORKSHOP

Fifty-five years
since you left us, and still
I see you in your Saturday
morning workshop, bent
over the lathe like a lover
his beloved, curling square
steel for the whirligigs
you peopled our village with;
I remember it all as fresh
as yesterday with a tremulous
eye and a hurt heart.

THE SWEET BYE AND BYE

Bob and I: alone
in our room, he carolling
"The Sweet Bye and Bye"
with its promise of mansions
so fair, and I: enthralled
in its singsong innocence.

Bob and I: apart now
for half a lifetime,
yet sometimes I hear
him singing still:
Won't it be glorious
when we get there.

STORY
For Katie-Ann

My granddaughter watching
Dora the Explorer, absorbed
by story, her body tuned
to every twist and turn
of the tale, the prototypal
three-act drama
complete with villain
and treasure map,
and a plot as old and deep
as her dreams.

FRIENDSHIP
For Alvin Gehl

You were always too old
for your age, ever the little
man even when you were just
a lad under your mother's
imperious thumb;
you let me be myself
at a time when I wasn't sure
what that was, quick to forgive
and loyal to a fault; I think
of you often and regret
the years I allowed to ease
between us; I wish
you well wherever you are.

FOR MY GRANDMOTHER

When grandfather died
your world was abruptly halved,
all those little rituals
that bound you one to one
now ended, you could not bear
ever again to sleep
in the bed you shared for more
than fifty years, your dreams
entangled through the long night
until morning woke you
with a new day; I remember
you best in the evenings,
you knitting in the kitchen,
Gramps snoozing through the news
a room away, but both of you
linked by love.

GLORY
On Watching James Play Football

These bantam paladins
clash in a brutal ballet
of choreographed violence
played out on an innocent
checkerboard stage:
in their daring and dash, these
fourteen-year-old
bodies harbour the heroic
and grapple for glory.

REBECCA READS

Rebecca pretends to read,
the book open on her lap:
the lips move as if animated
by the plight of the Three Bears
and she utters a headlong
singsong chant
as if propelled by the lustrous
letters on the page, as if
some rudimentary story
has already lodged pell-
mell in her bright, child-
lit mind.

HESITATION

Moon over Bethlehem:
a lonely stranger,
its ghostly glow on loft
and manger where the Babe lies
open to the air and to the star-
lit skies where angels
breathe their benediction
and all the world below
hesitates …

INSIDE

Outside the blizzard's
descent is relentless,
its pent fury smothers
eave and edge, etches
the trees' stark filigree,
diminishes any horizon
in a blind obliteration,
in a whirligig of white,
and somewhere at the storm's
nub is a dark deeper
than dark, while inside,
cocooned by snow, the heart
grows inward, dreams
of Easter's sun willing
the world green.

ALWAYS

When I'll no longer be,
the world will while away
the hours with someone
other than me, and what
I've left behind – a few
scattered words worth
repeating and a handful
of loved ones I touched
here and there over
the long years of my life –
these things will soon
matter no more than
my foolish desire
to dwell among the living.
Now and always.

HOW OFTEN

How often as I edge
into my age do I think
of that long-ago night
when shepherds, anchored
to the Earth, sat bolt
upright on their snow-
brushed hillside
and hearkened to the Good News,
while in the distant desert
Magi rolled west-
ward, stunned by a star
drawing them to a faraway
manger where a Bethlehem
Babe is born to tempt
the world out of its wilderness.

ALLIES

Nothing abides like love:
for fifty-odd years
side by side we have
weathered the world and not
grown weary, two
souls allied as one
since that moment so
long ago when we eyed
one another and satisfied
something wistful
inside; and here, now,
riding out our last days,
we smile and, knowingly,
                    nod.

HOPEFUL

More and more I think
about those long-ago
Sundays when we sang
our salvation
and Heaven rested
just above the steeple's
infinite reach,
O how we rang the rafters
with the Blood of the Lamb
and Jesus Loves Me,
praying in our hopeful
hearts that God does
see the sparrow fall,
that somewhere beyond
our sequestered selves
another life lies
                    waiting.

TUNDRA SWANS AT GRAND BEND

Out of the blue they swoop
like a squadron of B-52s,
defying gravity, and cruise
to a stealthy stop on the
welcoming water,
and in the late-winter air
a thousand winnowing
wings are furled: a triumph
of instinct over reason,
as every March they home in
upon this pat Canadian
pond to rest a while
before hurling themselves
Heavenward once more
on their way towards the far
Tundra that gives them
their name.

THANKFUL

I'd like to thank whoever
it is who arranges
the cosmic doings
of this Universe, for it would
have been just as convenient,
when I was seven and struck
down with rheumatic fever,
to have let my fractured heart
slip quietly into oblivion,
but it didn't, and I'd like
to think that it was I who chose
life, when it was actually
life who chose me and all
that followed.

PLOTS

I was the boy who told
himself stories, lisping
them half-aloud in the
schoolyard, risking
ridicule or worse
for the sake of some urging
I could not do without:
the need to wonder-weave
fanciful plots
and peaceable endings,
tales of callow courage
and daring-do that gave
me more joy than Heaven-
and-Earth usually allow.

TIDINGS

On that first Christmas
so long ago
shepherds contended
with their flocks on wind-weathered
and forlorn hillside,
when the skies opened up
and glowed golden
and Gabriel blew
his heraldic horn
and let such tidings
ride his music to the far
Heavens that they knew
in their hearts something
glorious had happened
to the world and all its
                urges.

DREAMING

I wake up still
dreaming of Nancy,
the girl I idolized
when I was barely
eleven, and could find no
words to sanctify my feelings
about one who fuelled
my fancy with a single
glance whenever I
dared meet those
forbidding eyes,
and I wonder yet
at the pubescent power
of such dreaming, then
and now.

ELEMENTAL

It's hard to believe
in your own demise:
something precious and
elemental inside us
resists the temptation
to un-be, to picture
that moment when nothing
comes after, when the last
syllable's expressed
and the long monologue
of our life is over;
O it's hard not to believe
our words will carry on
regardless.

INKLING

I stroll into the garden
and something in the hush
of it stirs a chill
I cannot quell
nor wish to, something
there is in the lushness
of these blooms, a teeming
of tulip and daffodil:
an alien inkling
of what is unwilling
to be anything
other than itself,
an intimation of what
cannot, quite, be known,
that brings us to the brink
and leaves us there
dreaming of what might
					have been.

CHARACTER

Lucky was I to be born
in a place where character
was more than a word: up
and down the village streets
Dickensian lookalikes
danced to the tantalizing
tunes in their head, and, shorn
of all pretension, acted out
their vivid lives for the one
watching, mesmerized,
in the wings – pen poised.

STASIS

Whenever I think of the
slow drift of my body
towards death and its final
stasis, I dream of those
days when the morning sun
seasoned everything
it touched and made it glow
for my eyes only,
when the air renewed itself
each noon so that I
might savour its subtle
sifting and feel again
the throb of being alive
in a world fashioned
just for me, when the days
passed by with the ease
of breathing, and I had
no reason to wonder
why

COURAGE

No better man
braved the battlegrounds
of Belgium, that blighted
ruin, than my grandfather:
criss-crossing for
almost four years
the maelstrom of No
Man's Land no man
could survive a minute in
when the stuttering gunneries
loosed their havoc upon
the poppy fields and ground
them to floundering muck,
three times wounded
he somehow survived,
calling on the great god
Luck and the deepest drive
within us: the courage
                to be.

ABSENCE

It's impossible to miss
what we already have,
we can't imagine absence
any more than we can wish
ourselves other than
what we are, thus
we cling to what
is already and still
within our grasp, hoping
against hope that love
            will last.

FANCY

When I was first eleven
I spun my stories
out of an elfin alphabet,
created a whole kingdom
of characters who danced
in my dreams and persuaded
my pen across the page
through the daylight hours
I fuelled with my fancy,
and did not guess, even then,
a lifelong pursuit of poems
and tales and the fabular
world we inhabit
when the gods aren't looking.

THE LINK

Alvin, my boyhood pal,
is on the phone wanting to know
if I remember Walter
who owned the beet farm
just west of Chatham,
and instantly I am back-
wards in time and wielding
a short-handled hoe
among the thistled beets,
Alvin beside me as row
upon row we move in tandem,
not knowing the link we forged
there in a farmer's field
would last a lifetime.

GRASPING AT LOVE

The heart is ever an exile,
no matter how much
we strive to render it free
of longing and loneliness:
though the mind reach out
to touch the tendrils of another,
it cannot bridge the gaping
gap between, while grasping
at love as if it might ex-
foliate and leave the heart
harmonious.

AN ODD THOUGHT

Woke up with an odd
thought buffeting my brain:
"I am now an old man"
huffing and puffing my way
to breakfast, no longer
growing old gracefully
or merely getting on
in years, and I think
such a thought could kill
me at my age.

LOSING YOU
For Uncle Potsy, in memoriam

You built your own
house, block by cinder
block, you levelled them
with an eye as keen as a
cartographer's and a mind
that could calculate angles
and eaves as precise
as a prism, you put
no stock in new-
fangled gadgets, relying
only on the heft and timbre
of your woodman's hands,
and the home-built structure
stood for fifty years until
they bulldozed it for a parking
lot. And I pass that
vacant space now
as if what you created
had never been there
for most of a lifetime,
and, like losing you,
I feel bereft.

THE GATHERING

Friends since school days,
you gather faithfully
each September to break
bread (lovingly prepared)
and remember the when
and where of lives lived
jointly and apart, keen
to re-tell the stories
you've heard a dozen times
and prize even more because
the years slip away
and there will come a moment
when there are no Septembers
left to celebrate,
with tears and laughter,
the love and communion
you have felt for one
another all these
     years.

MEMORY

There is nothing wrong
with growing old (try
as we might to capture
again those rare days
when life allowed us
a momentary triumph
or two) but memories
are no substitute
for the flesh-and-blood
aliveness of things
we long to reprise
but can't, though we seize
every chance we can
conjure to cling
to their fast-fading
hopefulness.

TALENT
-For my father, in memoriam

My Dad, dead at
fifty-seven, the whiskey
he so wilfully sipped
thru the delicate lip
of his kidney finally
stilled: this youth
who wielded a hockey stick
like a conductor's baton
and dazzled the crowd
with skating as intricate
as a jazzman's riffs;
this father who could hit
a bullseye at thirty
paces or mortar a seam
of bricks as perfect as a
surveyor's sighting,
who taught himself
taxidermy and mounted
bighorn sheep
in Alberta's foothills,
who could croon like Crosby
or dance like Astaire,
who was good at everything
except saving himself.

HOPE

The world is multiple
and no one thing
is quite like another,
the rose does not repeat
its variable bloom,
each leaf resists
concentricity
and makes room for a thousand
thousand brothers, and so
it is, we hug what we have
and harrow hope for the rest.

ARRIVAL

Like clockwork they come
each April in the morning:
orioles in the new-sprung
leafage, their song
as pleasantly piercing
as a mezzo-soprano's
soaring serenade,
their perfect punctuality
and airy arias oddly
reassuring in a world
otherwise random.

BRAVING THE ODDS

It's a long way home
wherever you happen to be,
the past is always past
whatever we happen
to remember in the long
days of our aloneness,
the memory can't outlast
the fleeting grasp we have
of it, but home is what
the heart craves, and so
in God's good time
we hearken there,
braving the odds
whenever we can.

HARMONY
For Anne and for John Barnett, in memoriam

Some days before he died
Anne fetched her father
from the tedium of his nursing home,
put him in a taxi
(wheelchair and all)
and together they motored
back through the village
John had known for more
than half his life, each
house precisely familiar,
jogging memories as they flashed
by, and as soon as the Lake
came into view, they paused,
and easefully Anne manoeuvred
the chair down to the beach
and side by side they sat
and stared out at the
calming waters, father
and daughter locked
in mutual harmony,
sharing all that had passed
and what was left of their
                future.

TEACHER
For Geoffrey Millburn, in memoriam

How many teachers
do you know who could call
their students "miserable wretches"
and have them smile as if
some benediction
had floated down upon
them? But that was the man,
quick of wit, sharp-
tongued whenever a gerund
or comma got misplaced,
editor extraordinaire,
a professional curmudgeon
who played that game, and many
others, well, and if there's
somewhere a God of Grammar,
Geoff will smile and say,
"All's right with the world!"

THE GARDEN

Adam was the first gardener,
they say, gouging the gaunt
earth with his home-made
plough and cursing the God
who tossed him headlong
out of Eden, where the groves
grew lush in the lustrous
light of the savouring sun
and the corn sprung of its own
accord, and Eve waxed
lovely, unadorned
and unavid for apples
or fornicating asps.

But the fruit got bitten
and here they are:
coupled and care-worn,
pitted against an un-
bending world, and tending
the garden of their own making.

GONE

If I were gone and worlds
away, would anyone
weep or say he was a
fine fellow who whittled
words and gloried in stories,
whose worth was a little more
than little; would my grandchildren
in their age still keep
me in their heart of hearts,
or will the memory of who
I was or sought to be
lie, like all the others,
fallow and unfurled.

ARTICULATE

As I ease into my age,
content with those gifts
the Gods have graced to me,
I hearken back to beginnings:
that lucid lunge for air,
my lungs bursting with their
first word: a howl
that would be the prolonged
poem of my life, by which
I would voice a thousand
thoughts – rhymed and ready
to make the unwilling
world
    articulate.

I THINK OF YOU
For my brother Bob, in memoriam

I think of you trussed
up in that hospital
with all the indignities
of modern medicine
thrust upon you,
keeping you a hair's
breadth from death,
and I wonder if you dreamt
of those days of our shared
boyhood and how
I admired what those
talented hands could do
and how your ears echoed
with the sea-sound of
symphonies and how
your fingers coaxed
each brushstroke
across the reluctant canvas,
and I pray you passed
peacefully into a place
where there is no pain.

SAID AND DONE

There will be time, when all
is said and done, for the rictus
of regret, and time, when wishes
are all that we pictured,
to realize we never reached
those skies high enough
to risk a fall or compro-
mise our pet convictions,
and time to find the rhyme
or reason for what has fled
our envying grasp,
when all is done and said.

Peripheries
First Choice Books
2016

PERIPHERIES

Freed by the recess bell
we tumble into the pristine
schoolyard drifts
and tramp out a perfect
snow-pie, a Ferris
Wheel flopped on its side,
then its Fox and the Geese,
that ancient game of tag,
we speed along the spokes
to the safety of the hub, or fly
to the pale peripheries,
the realm of all daring
at the far edge of things,
only a white absence
between us and eternity
till the school bell tolls
us happily home.

LETTERS
Point Edward: 1937

It's a long way home
to the place where the heart lies:
the village that superintended
my birth, that gave me space
in its eyes to grow under
its lavish light, that befriended
a boy in his aloneness,
that stirred the hand holding
the pen poised above
the ten-cent scribbler,
a town stippled with stories
and the inklings of poems
with their bright-ringing rhymes,
a place where the heart lives,
etched in perpetual Spring,
unravished by Time.

THERE WAS A TIME

There was a time when I believed
that God inhabited the white
clapboard church
on Michigan Ave, seated
in the back pew, I could feel
His breath floating from the
sanctuary as light and healing
as a June breeze on my grand-
father's lilacs, I could hear
His unvoiced words and knew
that somewhere near
angels amplified the chancel
air, I said my rhyming
prayer each night before
I entered the slough of sleep,
begging the Lord to take
my soul if I should die
before waking, but oh
how relieved I was to see
the sun pouring through
my bedroom window
like a giddy doubter's dance:
yes, there was a time
when I believed, I really
did.

HAVING BEEN

On lazy summer days
we lay our lean bodies
on Canatara's sand
(our blood humming in the
heat-haze, our eyes
shut tight against
the leavening light, our ears
alive with the soft tossing
of the waves) and deposit
fossilized signatures
of our having been.

UNISON

At twelve I was reluctant
to be washed in the Blood
of the Lamb, nor did I think
Jesus, pinioned on a cross,
would save me from my sins
(apparently even heathens
need something to believe in)
but never one to take
a chance, I kept an eye
out for God's slanted
glance.

ACCUSED

One summer's day
when my bat inadvertently
collided with the ball, I was so
excited I flung the weapon
aside and it struck Moochie
on his nose, and seeing this,
my father accused me
of unserendipitously hitting
the dog I loved, at that
particular moment, more
than my father.

NOTICE

Oh how we'd stare
at the budding bulges on the
chests of the bare-legged girls:
the Summer sang to us
and the hungering thrum
of our hearts,
and the girls pretended
they didn't care that our eyes
came to rest where they shouldn't,
and gave us no lip
before forgiving
our nippled notice.

JOIE DE VIVRE

We heard the Tin Lizzie
three blocks away, the ooga-
ooga horn blaring
abroad, as we rushed to the curb
to catch Herbie boogying
on by at full
throttle, with a grin on his face
that would have impressed the Wizard
of Oz, fedora flapping
and a wave and a wink at his fans
and our raucous applause,
before he wheeled homeward,
erased in a cloud of dizzying
dust: we loved the show
so much we wanted to bottle
it.

CHAMPION

Our friend Marilyn astride
her champion pony, galloping
past us as dapper as
Dale Evans in our Saturday
matineé: one hand
on the pommel, the other
teasing the reins with a tight-
fisted squeeze, riding
rhythmically into the setting
sun, the thrum of hoof-beats
tickling her ear, eyes
wide open: ecstatic.

FEAR OF FALLING: 1995
For Tom

Hiking the ledgeless
cliff of Georgian Bay,
I keep one eye
on Tom ahead, teetering,
tempting the edge, and the other
on my own uncertain
grip, and I think that if
Tom were to fall, I would,
whether I wished to or not,
have to dive in after him,
and we would both drown;
then another thought
strikes: we will go together.

BELONGING

It doesn't seem that long
ago that my uncle was a teen-
ager playing rugby
in our back forty, the ball
tucked tenderly under
his arm as he bounded and weaved
like a galvanized gazelle,
leaving me wrong-footed
yet pleased because I knew
we shared his father's blood:
the badge of our belonging.

REMORSE

Tommy and I mining
for moles in Farmer Mark's
fallow field, hacking
at the crusted clay with our
warrior's hoes until
we expose the burrows below
and a tiny universe of furred
rodents, amazed at the sky
sudden and blind above their
runnelled homes, scurry
in a frenzy of fright, and giving
way to some force
deep within us
we slew them one by one,
followed by a brief lurch
of triumph and then
irreversible remorse.

FRIENDS

I was terrified of heights
but Butch negotiated
the rigid girders of Blue-
water Bridge with all
the aplomb of a high-wire
wizard, arms out-flung
and tilting with tiny just-
in-time manoeuvres
as he inched tip-toe
over tip-toe along
the unbending steel,
and never once giving
the "Look at me!" sign,
letting me know we were
best friends.

FUSS

"Bob Guthrie has drowned!"
a cry that swept through the village
like the ripe rumour of plague,
and my mother, fearing the worst,
sent me running to the
Slip, where the pulmotor
was still chugging above
the unresuscitated boy,
and I didn't know until later
that at that very moment
my brother Bob glided
into the kitchen and said,
while being joyfully hugged,
"What's all the fuss about?"

APPLES

Eve may have bitten the apple
and welcomed woe into the world,
but we were smitten with the
cherub-cheeked Snows
we sank into teeth-
deep or the striated Spies
my grandmother tucked
tenderly into her Sunday pies,
or the Tolman sweets
we pilfered from the neighbour's
tree – these were apples
worth losing Eden for.

GLOAMING

On soft autumn evenings
we would play move-up
in the field behind Wiz's
with a half-strung ball
that sizzled when struck
by the cracked bat and floated
like a drunken dolphin till
someone, lad or lass,
interrupted its flight
and it fizzled in the dew-limn'd
grass a long way
from home-plate, as the dark
deftly descended and the moon
lurked aloft, a-glimmer
in the gloaming.

CLAYTON

In Sunday School we sang
"Jesus loves me,"
and other stirring hymns,
but Clayton would add
a flourish or two, loud
enough to make the minister
wince: perhaps the lad
thought God might be watching,
or it was the Old Nick
in full-voiced revolt,
or Clayton assumed Jesus
no longer loved him.

KNACK

We wave to Mrs. Bray
floating among her flowers
and she waves back,
content to spend her widow's
hours tending a plot
where stirred loam flourishes
(each rose or dahlia,
doted on, a moment's
remembrance for a man too
soon in his grave) and around
her head bees buzz
like numbed thumbs and navigate
for nectar to nourish
their honeycombed homes:
we wave again to be
sure, delighted she has
the nurturing knack.

ETERNITY

My Lake was bigger than the
salten seas with no
horizon but a blue blur
where the sun would sequester
each evening, with a
kaleidoscopic squeeze,
and when we dipped a toe
into its chilled solemnity
and felt its heavenly breeze
upon our chastened cheeks,
it was is if we were touching
Eternity.

CURIOUS

We watched with eager eyes
two dogs 'humping'
on Mara's sidewalk,
and thought of thighs we only
imagined until Summer
and swimsuits revealed
their lengthening legginess,
but something in the furious
frenzy of the canine coupling
left us puzzled,
hearts thumping and more
than a little curious
about the girls whose loveliness
we worshipped and the fires
of desire.

LINKED
For Isabelle Macdonald
In memoriam

In nineteen seventy-nine
I travelled the byroads
of Lambton County, armed
with a film and an audiotape:
attempting to prompt poems
out of budding Purdys,
and then at one school,
there at the back of the class-
room, squeezed into an under-
sized desk, sat
Miss Macdonald, my Grade
Three teacher, come
to see if I had fulfilled
the promise she'd drawn from me
with her partisan praise
of my ink-squibbed scribbles –
we smiled at each other
across a forty-year
divide, linked by a love
of words.

BUBBLE

Gerry's Dad was one of the
seven alcoholics who seasoned
our village Summer
and Winter, the violence
of the War could not be washed
down with vials of whiskey,
especially for a tail-gunner
hanging in the slow solitude
of his vulnerable bubble,
his weapon
jammed, bullets like berserk
bees at every angle,
and then one day, cold
sober, his heart splintered
like machine-gun glass.

PROMETHEAN

My grandfather mowing
the back forty, his torso
bare to the scorching sun,
sweat rippling his muscles,
powerful and Promethean,
his grip steady on the mower,
clipping the grass with a
rasping clatter, grass
that would surely be growing
again as if it mattered,
and I thought then that not
everything is everlasting.

SUMMER
After John B Lee

What I remember most
are the sun-softened days
when we set out for the beach
like charlatan Champlains,
unhobbled by the heat,
our towels draped over
our fair-skinned shoulders
like cavalier's capes,
until we found the path
as familiar as our crease-streaked
palms and waved at the lighthouse
that stood alabaster and beckoning
at the edge of the wind-whetted
water, then welcomed the sands
of Canatara once again,
and let the waves flutter
over our unfettered feet
like tiny tongues licking
us lean, while we stood
stark in the free-flung
breeze, daring to be
the first to dive into the
cobalt, chilled undertow
and levitate like dolphins
flippered and flying through the
breakers, abetted by a north-
nudging wind, before exhaustion
claimed us and we flopped
like limp mops upon
the stinging, sun-stroked
sand, and wondered even then
how much of these doldrum,
summer-drifting days
we would always remember.

GAZE

Somersaulting we go
on my grandfather's lawn:
lithe, log-legged
Shirley and I, tousled
and abreast as we tumble
in blithe flight, Shirley
landing with two-footed
ease, me dazed
and askew, but our eyes entwine
and something more than
a boy-girl gaze
passes between us
and the nippled ripple
of her baby-blue blouse.

ACT ONE

I was a playwright
in grade eight, penning
a witty skit for the
Christmas concert
(starring Mister and Missus
Claus), performed in the
township hall
before parents and peers
(and one or two amplified
uncles), but when the curtain
came down on my maiden
endeavour, the applause
was polite, my career
short-lived.

TILT

"It's as big as an ocean,"
my mother says, holding
my hand tight, and me
just three, gazing
out at the burnished blue
stretching to the far edge
of the Earth, where sunlight
greets the dark, and a dozen
breakers unfurl
at my feet as I dig
my heels in the silted sand
and, motionless, feel
the world's tantalizing
tilt.

MY GRANDMOTHER MAKING TEA

My grandmother hots
the pot before the leaves
drift through the same fingers
that soothed my brow whenever
my heart heaved heavy,
jot by jot until
the steaming liquid splashes
placidly over the Pekoe,
fresh from the tea-fields
of Ceylon, and when our cups are full,
we sip in ceremonial civility,
her hand next to mine:
at times like these I'm sure
she could turn water into wine.

MAYPOLE

The schoolyard pump
was the Maypole we circled,
boys and girls hand
in hand singing, "Here
we go round the mulberry
bush ("Husha, husha")",
a-whirl on a carousel of air,
we chanted our jump-rope/
hopscotching genderless
joy – till Ronnie Young
detonated the girls'
giggles with lush gushes
from the palpitating pump
and broke the boy-
girl circle.

TIDY

On Sundays we wore
our store-bought clothes,
shoes shined and hair
parted – ready for Church,
as if God Himself
were a connoisseur of clothes
and good grooming, and pleased
to see the effects of a sin-
riddled week tidied
up.

POP
For My Grandfather

We called him "Pop"
because all the real
Dads were away at war,
we trailed behind his corporal's
stride, hopping from foot
to foot to keep pace,
as if he were the Pied Piper
and we his willing worshippers,
until we reached the work-
shop where he wrought wonders
with wood and delicately shorn
steel (we watched it peel
away from the oiled lathe
in tiny girlish curls),
thence to be rendered into whirl-y-
gigs the whole town prized,
and while he stood there
with his wide, patient smile,
we peppered him with our child's
questions about the world
and its doings, like Socrates
interrogating the Wise,
and wished
the war would never end.

HIDDEN

There was one house in town
that was strictly forbidden,
which seemed odd to us
because its gaudy gables
and cheerful chimneys
stood out in a village
where Presbyterian plain
was the order of the day, so
we made sure to pass
it by whenever we could,
slipping past its shuttered
windows in a hushed
hurry, delighted to know
at last there were some things
going on between adults
that had to be hidden.

STEADFAST

When my Dad decided to dig
a well in the blue Lambton
mud beside our kitchen,
he pooh-poohed the local
water witcher and jammed
his shovel straight into the
unending earth, and inch
by grudging inch the ground
gave way, while we watched
the summer's sweat sweeten
on his back, and knew then
that we would have running water
and a father's steadfast
love.

SEVEN

When I lay in my sick
bed in the aftermath
of rheumatic fever,
my Uncle Bill dropped
by to entertain me:
we played a game of Parchesi
and I forgot to tell him
how to get his tokens "Home,"
and as he circled the board
aimlessly, I tucked
my tokens safely in:
even at seven, I
wanted to win.

ADULT

My mother: sundering
a banana for our supper,
we sit transfixed by the slick
flick of the bare blade,
its edge never quite
touching her humming thumb;
a dozen perfect slices
peel away, and we eye
her deft dexterity,
abrupt with wonder
and unadult love.

NIMBLE
For Rebecca and Katie

My granddaughters knitting,
sitting still as statues,
each stitch the itch
of a thought in the mind before
the fingers nimble it into
place: there is such serenity
in their faces as they re-imagine
this ages-old art
of women everywhere,
and carry it out
with loose-limbed grace.

VERSE

I was never averse to writing
verse, poems popped
up in my grade-six
scribbler like mushrooms
after an April rain,
I rhapsodized in rhyme,
tried in vain to assume
a sonnet or two, trotted
out iambics and anapests
galore (not for me
enjambement or tripping
trochees), I was a budding
balladeer in search of
literary glory, flush
with the wit of words and savouring
every bit of it.

TANDEM

We grow old together
in tandem with time, like a
fine wine lovingly
casked with Amontillado,
we are a pair of slow roses
easing into autumn,
our crimson fading
in the year's last light,
but our vines are tethered in good
ground, our days pass
peacefully by, and love
lingers without a wherefore
or a why.

SIDE BY SIDE
For Potsy: In Memoriam

My uncle and I striding
side by side along
the fairway, our tee-
shots looming ahead
like miniature moons,
and I watch my uncle strike
his wedge with an arc as precise
as a surgeon's deft cut,
and it lands no more
than a foot from the pin,
while my nine-iron, listing
to the left, finds a bunker
as big as a lunar crater,
but I make no fuss,
for we are walking side
by side towards a green
glistening just for us.

CAPED CRUSADER
For James

You stare out of this photo,
your three-year-old
body like a caped crusader
ready to pounce: you un-
furl a smile as wide
as the Sargasso Sea, and the
gleam in your eye announces,
in passing "I am here to stay,
I am me – look out
World!"

69

LILY'S STORY

I always wanted to write
the story of a pioneer woman
born in the deepest bush
south of the village (not yet
on any map) where I
was eventually spawned,
and to follow her through the decades
of her long life, with all
the travail and sorrows, never
more than a heartbeat
away, and see her
in her old age in a town
that no longer remembered
who she was, and celebrate
those minor triumphs
that made her a heroine
worthy of her own novel.

WHERE LOVE GROWS
For Tom

When first I held you
in my arms, you were as light
as a feather's shadow,
your smile lit up
every room you ever
graced with your presence
and charmed the most committed
of cynics, you brightened our lives
and left us all
in the place where love grows.

STITCHES

My granddaughters learning
how to crochet under
Grandma's guiding hand,
stitch by stitch, they sculpt
what might be taken for
a scarf or tea-cozy,
each stitch a figment
unravelling in the mind
before the fingers niche
it perfectly into place,
and above all, in the rich
and rosy afternoon,
these are labours of love.

OAK
For John

If you were a tree, you'd be
an oak, tall and stalwart,
your grain running tender
and true to the root, your leaves
breathing easy in the affectionate
air, the generosity of your
shade rendering hope
and, above all, your love
is as resolute as it is
unspoken.

ARIGHT
*For Tom, Tim, James
and Kevin*

 I love to hear the laughter
of my grandsons, an out
loud, deep-belled
braying of delight, a rib-
tickling roar of formidable
mirth, which soothes
my soul as I edge into age,
and it goes without saying
that the world is now aright:
three generations strong
whatever comes after.

SUCH A LONGING

I have such a longing
for the days that are no more,
when the sun rose over
my boyhood town each
misted morning, hefting
light for my eyes only
as I circumnavigate the streets
(like LaSalle on the prowl
for gold and glory), looking
for the point poised between
the Lake and the River, greeting
each friend and rival
with equal ease, knowing
we shared this cozy
desmene, that ours was our own
story to tell, and that
we would never be bereft
of belonging.

ARIA
For Katie

"Somewhere...somehow":
the aria lifts and lilts
from some reservoir deep
inside you, the words
leap from your lips and the melody
flows sturdy and strong
as an oboe's soprano
air, and you soar to a final
note so high
and sweet it would make Orpheus
weep.

SONG AND DANCE
For Katie and Rebecca

My girls are doing their song-
and-dance routine: oh
how lovely is their long-legged
grace, arms afloat
on the regular pacing of the
music and eyes a-light
within faces that glow
like their grandfather's
pride in seeing them thus:
galvanized by my appraising
glance.

TAUT
For Rebecca

You take to soccer like a
lamb to the ewe, you have
your father's footwork,
taming the bewildered ball
with one taut, tender
toe and, untackled
at the far end, you get
free and, with a knowing jerk
of the jaw, you bend the back
of the net.

BEING

Whenever I think on death,
particularly my own,
seeing too clearly
the end of it all, I try
to treasure those things
I wished for and won,
then grit my teeth and relish
the unbreathlessness of being.

COLM
For Colm O'Sullivan In Memoriam

All the willows in Gibbons
Park are weeping at your leaving
us; you who were black Irish
to the bone, who plumbed
the pun-numb prose
of Finnegans Wake, who taught
a generation to love the alliterative
lisp of a well-penned poem,
who never saw a small
slam he couldn't liberate,
who wore his wit and wisdom
with a Gaelic grin and just
the briefest of winks – who
has left us alone with our
sorrow and our grief.

TOM, SWIMMING: 1998

Perched in the side seats,
I watch you bound
from the diving board like a
porpoise with a purpose,
your taut body incising
the water with the precision
of a surgeon's cut,
after which you stroke the surface
like Johnny Weissmuller's
Tarzan stalking a croc,
your legs torqueing your form
forward till you touch
the far edge of the pool,
and my heart swells in its socket
with a grandfather's foolish
pride.

FULL FLIGHT

When I was younger than I
deserved, I could run
like an antelope in full
flight: my legs in sync
with the thought that teemed
in my brain: speed in its essence:
I ran only to feel my body
in its own unreserved
delight, no end
or destination in sight,
no inkling of seized
knees and little hope
for celerity.

PARADE
For Tom

On a warm summer's day
at Circle-R, you strut
your stuff in a far field,
galloping your mounts
as if their tails were afire,
with your cowboy hats
and six-gun glamour –
all eyes now
on the peripatetic parade,
we hold our breath, but you
lead your pack with elementary
ease in their headlong
flight as you defy the laws
of gravity on your amiable
Appaloosa, head erect,
chin out, enamoured
with your own delight and our
polite applause.

BLOOMS
For the Gardeners in my Life

Whenever you grace a room
with your presence, all the plants
you fostered with the tenderest of
touches tip their leaves in mute
gratitude, your fingers
have the deft caress of Demeter
herself, coaxing root
and shoot alive into the
admiring air where they flower
and thrive: you make your abodes
bountiful bowers where love
blooms like the rose you resurrect
each joyful June.

NUMINOUS

I shall not rage at the
dying of the light: I've lived
too long under a luminous
sun to be at odds
with death; my days have been deft
with delight with just enough
pain to keep me ept
and witting; I've filled a thousand
pages with my word-scattered
scrawl, but I have left
my legacy in the brightening
eyes of my children's children,
and when the time arrives,
I will go gentle into that
numinous night.

FOREORDAINED

I scribbled my first poem
when I was barely twelve:
about the epic clash
of French and English on those
celebrated plains, penned
in flawless ballad form
(with thump-a-thump rhythm),
and though now lost
to my mother's housekeeping,
I still see those heroic
deaths and the stir of martial
pride as I strive to be
faithful to both sides
(with just a slight tilt
towards the Union Jack)
and paid my homage
to all the glories gained;
I like to think now
that starting my career at the
epic end and ending
here with this squeezed lyric
was somehow
foreordained.

THE BEASTS OF THE FIELD
For Tom

You were raised among animals:
rambunctious dogs, a lizard
or two, a pair of lovebirds
twittering their joy, and so
when the horse reared its maned
head, your life's work
was sealed: your hands upon
their flanks as soothing as the music
of Orpheus, your voice a willing
whisper to calm the most
skittish of colts, your warmth
working an equine wizardry;
we loved you for the love
that poured out of you
and settled on the beasts of the field.

SPECTACLE

I wake and it's Spring,
when crocuses Christen the grass
along the hedgerows
with purple and golden bliss,
amid bud-burst
and furious leafing, where the rain
falls like a grateful grace
upon the erupting earth:
this must be the garden
at the edge of the world God
grew and then cursed,
banishing Adam for wondering
why, who, to the surprise
of his Maker, began
a garden of his own devise
and wakened one morning
to the spectacle of Spring.

NIGHT FEVERS

The dark comes down
as sudden as thunder ripping
breeches in the sky,
while I wait for sleep to anaesthetize
and condole, but the under-
tow of the day's dealings
ebbs and flows at the rim
of a dream, impeding reason,
unenhancing hope,
while I quest for breath, feeling
the brush on my brow: the delicate
dance of death.

THE GAME

Three hundred yards
away, sits a gouge
in the ground no bigger
than a mole's abode, while
a man (or woman), hopes
high, stands on a green
tee, threatening a miniature
dimpled globe with a
slab of persimmon
and waggling the club
without a trace of fore-
boding, despite the odds
that even God couldn't plan
this Faustian game.

LUCK

The Garden was so perfect
that Adam spent his days
plucking plums and pomegranates
(from trees rinsed
with rain and dried by sun)
and ogled the plump-thighed
creature he'd rib-delivered
(wondering what beauty was for),
while Eve eyed the apple
and prayed for something
lucky to happen.

JUST SO

The words in a poem must
be just so, there is no
room for maybe this
one or that: the order
is preordained by the home-
thrust of meaning; the way-
ward metaphor or the
coincidence of consonance
must be made anew;
with poetry it is boom or bust,
no other sleight-
of-hand will do.

BOY ON A BEACH
For Aylan Kurdi: In Memoriam

Boy on a beach, curled
upon the tidal sands
as if he were merely sleeping:
no sign in his peaceful repose
of the murderous mayhem
that drove him from his homeland
and onto the sea's treachery,
nor all the weeping in the world
will unblemish the blood
that stains the hands of our
humanity.

WILD HORSES

They are harbingers of freedom,
these marauding mustangs
wheeling among the hills
of Dakota, the stallion
stalwart in the lead
(the mares flying behind
like gulls on the soaring sea)
galloping Pegasuses
annihilating every
horizon with their break-
neck speed and the heft
and heart of an American Pharoah:
no bit or bronco-
busting cowpoke
will ever gentle them
or compromise their un-
bridable spirit.

DYING SUMAC

For a dozen seasons or more
you breathed, breathless,
into the air for acres around,
your roots like larcenous lungs
delved deep into the ground
and energized each leaf,
stem and seed-cone
that fed wheeling flocks
of sparrows and their cousins,
but now you droop like an old
man withering in his age,
no wintering robin
far from home will seek
you out, and the scarlet blaze
you brighten us with
each autumn will fade
like a vintage painting,
unlasered by light.

NOD

It is said it takes a God
to manufacture a rose
with its rapturous red whorls
as bright as Christ's blood,
but then who knows who sent
the frost to devour the flower,
and are we all Darwinian
simians who must remain
forever fuddled and never
ask the World why?
But roses got made
somehow, and if I
had my say, I'd give
the nod to God.

AMERICAN PHAROAH

He springs out of the gate
like a new colt feeling
his first field, the stride
elongated and ringingly
regal, his breeding there
in every step he uses
to assume the lead with his
nostril-flaring speed,
a wild stallion at heart,
leaving all pretenders
like moon-faced mares
in his wake: as the stretch looms,
he puts the pedal down
and cruises to the Triple Crown.

AXIS

The first snow descends,
tip-toeing on feathered
feet over branch
and bowed limb, seasoning
eaves, curling into window
wells, soft as a breath
on glass, it smothers the greenness
of the grass with surreptitious
stealth, and somewhere
in the high Heavens beyond
the weather, something
as ancient as Mother Earth
can be heard turning
on its inevitable axis.

AFTER

Eve never saw
an apple she didn't like,
they hung like bright baubles
from the Tree of Good and Evil,
and Adam, no lover
of the luscious beyond
his helpmeet's carnivorous
curves, and quite surprised
when she took a bite with her
alabaster teeth (eyes lit
with laughter) and he,
not to be outdone
followed soon after;
and when God cried foul,
Adam led Eve
out of Eden in the unleavening
light, his howl heard
as high as Heaven.

UNSAYABLE

I've spent a lifetime
seeking the reason for rhyme
in pursuit of the perfect poem
where dactyls dance until
they make indelible sense
in the midst of metrical meaning,
where I find my heart stirred
by the motive for metaphor
in the ept uttering of the un-
word, the saying of what is,
alas, unsayable.

SURGE

It begins with an urge,
an inkling of an inkling
and then, insurgent, a word
or possibly, in a blink,
a phrase, brimming with
syllables not yet uttered
but tantalizing on the tongue,
waiting for a rhythm or a rhyme
to bring them home to the
surprised page: my pen,
surging now, pregnant
with a poem.

AFTERTHOUGHT

When God set out
on his seven-day binge,
there was no Adam or Eve
or leaf-fringed Eden,
so the Great Poetaster
hurled the Word into the
Void and a thousand poems
popped up, peopled
with unhoused creatures
of every ilk and a dappled
garden with seas enough
to keep it intact,
where, as an afterthought,
He manufactured Man
and his apple-dazzled spouse.

PRIVILEGED

The past is a privileged place
where we can turn inward
to face those pieces
of ourselves we never
quite left behind,
and live again in the shadow
of their yearning to be, and what
has been lost can be redeemed
in the fulcrum of remembrance,
guiding us towards acceptance
and a future encumbered
by grace.

TRACES

The dead pile up
in front of those who linger
among the living, their faces
pass before us in the depths
of our dreaming: a remembered
smile, a glint of eye
or the timbre of a word the only
traces of their having been
and mattered enough to be
the pinpoint of a poem
or two I write in spite of
the end that waits to abrupt
us all.

MISS STEVENS

Miss Stevens taught
English as if it were
a military exercise:
she shook the pages of Macbeth
till every syllable fell out
and stood up straight,
she made us stand
to give a one-line
answer, lost in the clatter
of our desks, she wore
a thimble on the middle finger
on her right hand to thwack
the ear of anyone whose love
of the Bard was not perfect,
and we laughed when she raced
her new Ford over curbs
and potholes, and we mourned
her death, speeding on a mountain
road in Yugoslavia,
a thousand miles from the Globe
and the pitter-patter of
iambic pentameter.

Inundations

Hidden Brook Press
2016

INUNDATIONS

My Lake had the girth
of the Seventh Sea and was
as blue as cobalt
in white light, and fathoms
below fish rippled
in their millions and clams
colluded with the salt-free
silt, and when the breeze
tilted wayward,
the wind-wild waves
indicted the grain-dense
shore and gave birth
to inundations of dunes
in their sun-sifted silence.

THE VILLAGE WITHIN

We all have a village within,
a place where we go
when the world fails us,
the home-ground where every
face is familiar and child-
size, where the streets welcome
our walking and each house
is a variation of our own,
its idiosyncrasies known
and loved just for being
there from the beginning
when our eyes were as wide
as any horizon, when all
was new and unrehearsed:
O the tug of the town
that gave us birth is one
of the sweetest joys we know.

THE POINT

Dickens would have loved
the Point, the streets bristled
with characters who would've been
at home in Pickwick
or Oliver Twist: there was
Bob McCord who haunted
the beverage room, closed
the joint every day
at six on the dot and whistled
his way down the main
drag, or Ruby Carr
who rescued rags, combing
the alleys and by-roads
on her barnacled bike
and talking to every tree
she managed to miss,
or Butch McCord who battled
bullies on my behalf
and taught me the meaning of boy-
hood friendship,
or Cap Harness who never
saw a sea-going ship
or the sea but cut the hair
of a whole village between
salty anecdotes,
or Harry Fisher whose yard
overflowed with elderly
stoves and assorted pots
like the maelstrom of his mind
and the memories of gunfire
and bomb-blasts on the Somme,
or Herbie Gilbert
in his tin-pot Lizzie,
honking his ooga-ooga
horn at every second
passer-by just
to say he was alive and thriving,
and there was Pussy Carr,
Rip Kemslie, Long
Tom Shaw and a dozen
other nicknamed
denizens who made
my town a place to grow
up in and have your fancy
tickled and fed.

ASCENSION

When I was always young
I skated over Leckie's
ice-slick fallow
under a mellowing moon
as if my blades were wings
etching the quickened air
with crazed scrolls and singing
filigrees, till a billowing breeze,
stung to my cheeks, lifted
me up like Elijah to Heaven's
edge, and I sailed
up the dunes of the dark
to the beckoning stars.

GLINT

Shirley McCord dancing
the can-can as if it were France
on grandfather's lawn:
she lifts her legs as high
as the glint in my eye and swings
a deft toe chinward
until a tingle of thigh
peeps free, and praise
the Lord: I am too
far gone to think of
sin and gay Paree.

ABSENCE

When my grandfather died
I wondered how I would live
out the rest of my days
and find him gone from the
workshop or the Saturday
supper table where he listened
to me recount the gun–
slinging shenanigans
from the afternoon's thriller,
as if each word mattered
and I became for a few moments
the story-teller I would soon
choose to become despite
the absence of that loving
ear and my desire
not to be.

ETERNITY

O what a village
I was born to, where the
sun over First Bush
rises reinvented each
morning, layering its
lacquered light upon
streets fresh from a
hushed night's dreaming,
and I sally forth like a
sea-going Argonaut
for the ells and alleys where roses
grow umbilical on
barn-board fences,
ablaze in rhyming red,
and stiff-trunked trees
are surprised by breezes
breathing serenity, and I am
now Earth's original
cartographer, nosing
amongst the by-ways
and fractured shadow:
foraging for a future
unhorizoned by time
or eternity.

HOME FIRES

After the Christmas turkey
we gathered in the front room,
cousins and all, and someone
started singing "Keep
the Home Fires Burning"
with dark clouds and silver
linings, the swell of the voice
was loud enough to bring
the boys back home, and joined
soon by booming baritones
and tinsel-tongued sopranos,
and then my grandfather rose
after a pair of cordials
and sang "Sweet Adeline",
solo and so soaringly
his throat throbbed and his Adam's
Apple bobbed like an angler's
cork, but under the melodious
tremoring of his tenor, there lay
something deep
and torqued about to be
released: a yearning no
home fires could put out.

CRY

Our village was as quiet
as the proverbial mouse,
but one summer evening
the spell was broken by a
piercing, uncurbed
cry from Mrs. Bradley's
house, like the yelp of a small
animal trapped and trembling,
it rattled windows all
along Monck Street:
"She must be mad, poor
dear," was the local buzz,
but come next morning
the Missus sat on her front
porch and peered out
at the world, wondering
where she was.

AIRBORNE

Our village had only one
hill but it was Olympian tall
and when the snows came
as they did at the sun's
slouching southward
each Fall, we flung our sleds
headlong down
the hard-packed slope,
gaining just enough
momentum to send us
airborne, riding
high on a sliver of sky,
and slung like galleons gliding
on eddies of air, we were
cantilevered cargo
in frantic flight – until
the Earth steadied herself
and we skidded to a stalwart
halt on the bottomland
below, where we limped back
up the arduous steep,
dragging our sleds behind
us like winded Argonauts.

GARY

Gary was gay when the street
word for him was "queer"
or something more
toxic, like "faggot" or "fairy":
a dear boy with no harm
in him, but one day
his drunken father, sensing
something odd
about his only son,
took the strap to him
and shaved his head bald,
but Gary, fearless,
said nothing to that
and walked about the village
without a hat.

PLEASURE

My grandfather at ease
in his Saturday morning
workshop: me
on the floor gazing up
at those humming thumbs
guiding the walnut wedge
through the side-winding blade,
as precise and as loving
as a husband's hands
upon his bright new
bride, and I longed
to see the checkerboard
maze he would fashion
out of these wayward
pieces – for the sheer pleasure
of seeing something
beautiful, made
and offered to me and the
world.

LEILA

Leila couldn't count
the kids she had on a good
day and there weren't many
of those, what with her husband
who sobered up just
enough to get drunk
again, and a ramshackle
house she scrubbed board
by blistering board because,
though she gave the whole
village something
to feel superior to,
she defied them all
and carried herself
like the dark, Arabic beauty
whose name she bore
with a preternatural pride.

DELIGHT

My Uncle Bob prized
his hand-crafted bird
feeder, but the squirrels prized
it more, purloining
the robin's morning meal,
and every trick or devious
device he dreamed up
in his loneliness failed
to surprise or out-think
the fund of rodent wit,
until the day my Uncle
wrapped a coiled Slinky
around the greased pole
and watched the little beasts
swing and sway in every
direction but up:
so now robins could sit
and feed in the morning sun
that shone brightly on an
elderly man's delight.

GRACE

Down the toboggan-run
we raced, propelled
by the gratuitous gravity
of Doidge Park hill,
aching to be airborne,
the wind-chill on our faces,
we clung to one another
as if it were Christmas Eve
every day of the season
and the world, for the time it took
us to careen to the bottom,
gave us a whee-taste
of its grace.

EVENSONG

Bob and I tuck
ourselves in,
hoping that slumber will
overwhelm us,
while a thousand miles
away another child
lies awake in a manger,
where cattle are struck dumb
in His presence and shepherds
are wild with surprise
and three kings have come
through desert dangers
to bow down with hope
and frankincense before
the Babe who does not cry,
while I remain with eyes
unopen and my brother hums
"In the Sweet By and By."

EXIT

When I was only six
my mother packed me off
to Sunday School, where we
sang of Jesus and the bountiful
breadth of His love, after which
we were chivvied to the big-
arched church above us
to be silenced by the cleric's
sermon that spoke of Hell
and its ferocious flames
roasting small boys
who had misbehaved, so
I ran as fast as my heathen
legs could carry me
all the way home,
trailing God, Jesus
and the Holy Ghost.

RITUAL

In the Autumn we played out
the yearly ritual:
burning the leaves along
the Monck Street curb,
but first there was the frolicking
in the sweet, bottomless
bed of Manitoba maple
and then the frantic raking
onto the road where flames
took hold and smoke
stood boldly up,
alabaster white and pitched
skyward, until only
the embers remained to remind
us that Autumns pass
away and we all need
something fiery
to remember.

SHELL

My Dad was as proud as a panjandrum,
performing for the home-town
crowds with a skirr of skate
and an intricacy of dekes, glidings
and whirlwind bursts
of speed that left them all
breathless with applause
and cheers so loud
the Bridge above them shivered
in its rivets: he was living
his dream, an Icarus at the summit
and prince among his fellows,
and who then could have imagined
what war and whiskey could do
to a man, his self-esteem,
and the shrivelled shell
of his pride.

SHINNY

In the Winter on Saturdays
we played shinny on Foster's
Pond, with hand-me-
down sticks and a borrowed
puck, battered and burred,
and a goalie brandishing a broom,
like Turk Broda in his prime
(not even the catalogue-pads
so tenderly stitched
could undo his pluck)
as we skidded and slewed on the slick
surface in our galumphing
galashes, but we were young
and in the air above us
we could hear the skinny,
high-pitched voice
of Foster Hewitt urging
us on, while the crowd cheered
like Romans for the lions.

TAG: 1948

When we were just kids
we played squat-tag
on the ledges of the village
war memorial, and gave
no thought, as we skidded
and dodged, to the cryptic names
of battles fought in far-
away places: what was Ypres
or Courcelette to those
too young to have regrets
or the knowledge of war
with its maelstrom of mud
and blood-lust and the crippled
cries of those dying
without lament so that
three boys could play tag
on the town's monument.

THRILL

Whenever we wanted a thrill
our parents didn't approve
we would head for Barr's
Billiards, where lingering over
a Pepsi we would edge as close
as possible to the shrouded sanctum
and shiver as we listened to the
sinful click of the cue
ball and the subdued hum
of the profane commentary
from the no-good-nicks
who defied God and the populace
for a game of snooker and the kick
it gave them, and us.

MYSTERY

They called it a girl's game
but every Saturday
after football Tommy
and I joined the sisters
Laur for hopscotch,
chalked on the sidewalk:
we kept an avid eye
on the bare-legged one-
footed antics of Bonnie
and Sharon as they nimbled
from square to square with envious
ease, their skirts a-swirl
around their lissome limbs
and the mystery between them.

ARBOUR DAY

One sunny day
each Spring we were freed
from the clench of the classroom
and set loose to groom
the school's grounds: we felt
like those first gardeners
in Eden, purifying God's
pastures: hoeing
and raking for the Lord's sake,
who tended the tulips
and roses of Paradise;
we took a perfectionist's pride
in the perseverance of our labour,
and when the day was done
we sang our thanks as one.

BLUE

In the swelter of a July day
we dove into the cold
elemental grip of the
Huron lake and swam
as sleek as salmon silvering
a stream, and let our bodies
be emboldened by the
giving up of gravity
as we urged the high waves
to break above us as they did
when the Attawandaron dipped
their faces into the teeming surf,
older than Gitchimanitou
Himself and as blue as a
sweltering July sky.

STONE'S THROW

There were seven alcoholics
within a stone's throw
of my house: the wastage
of war or the daily drudgery
of the six-day week
took its toll on the men
we spotted on the streets
teetering home from the Balmoral
or sipping silently in forlorn
kitchens, bereft
of any hope or pride;
we viewed them as something
other than ourselves,
alien adults to be mocked
or pitied but never
encountered, by chance or design,
without the shock of recognition,
the sideways glance
that made them human.

FUSS

"Bob Guthrie has drowned!"
a cry that swept through the village
like the ripe rumour of plague,
and my mother, fearing the worst,
sent me running to the
Slip, where the pulmotor
was still chugging above
the unresuscitated boy,
and I didn't know until later
that at that very moment
my brother Bob glided
into the kitchen and said,
while being joyfully hugged,
"What's all the fuss about?"

FRIENDS

I was terrified of heights
but Butch negotiated
the rigid girders of Blue-
water Bridge with all
the aplomb of a high-wire
wizard, arms out-flung
and tilting with tiny just-
in-time manoeuvres
as he inched tip-toe
over tip-toe along
the unbending steel,
and never once giving
the "Look at me!" sign,
letting me know we were
best friends.

BEYOND WORDS

My Dad was addicted to the booze;
he preferred his whiskey watered
to make it last a little
longer, but he never failed
to smile through his blurred haze
with everything but his eyes,
where all the disappointment
of a lifetime oozed
out at me, and bereft
of the pride he hadn't had
for a dozen years, I heard
him say, "I can lick this,
lad," and I longed for those
rare moments when he snoozed
through the afternoons: all
the hurt finally drained
from a face I loved
beyond words.

MAIN STREET

The map of Michigan Ave
is embossed on my brain
seventy years on:
entering the main drag
I see Kopp's Meat
Market where sausages hung
like twisted intestines
and Butcher John wielded
the cleaver with particular
panache and smiled
while he did it, then on to
Burgess Market with its bursting
bins of sugar and flour,
paper bags that snapped
like tiny thunderclaps
and ice-cream cones
as big as balloons,
then it's the Post Office
where gossips gathered
and reputations died,
then came Harry's Confectionery
where we sipped Pepsis
through softening straws
and gazed at the barber pole
across the road, where Cap
Harness snipped and lied
lavishly about his sea-
going days, and at the end
of the street stood the pool
room, the sanctuary of sharks
and no-good-nicks,
forbidden terrain
we shuddered to contemplate:
I remember them all
with a fondness that seems
to grow stronger with each
year I add to my allotted
number.

ENVY

And me at twelve, unable
to swim a stroke, watching
Nancy and Jerry make
elongated leaps with
acrobatic ease from their
improvised diving board
above the village Slip,
fathoms deep and forbidden
terrain, and come up
swimming as deft as dolphins,
Nancy breast-stroking
without a hint of ripple,
Jerry orchestrating the crawl
as if he were Aussie-born
while I was left ashore:
alone and knowing now
what envy was.

MISSIVES

If Butch had another name
I never knew what it was,
even his mother used
that moniker to interrupt
our war-time play,
while his Dad purveyed
chops and joints to a hungry
village who called him just
John, and so on a Sunday-
school morning with the shop
shuttered and closed
Butch and I would sip
Pepsis in our backroom
bunker and glue ration
stamps onto brown booklets,
wondering when the War
would be over and what
the Government would do
with our million glue-licked
missives.

GENDER

In the little patch of road
that marked our territory
there was a dearth of both
genders, so the girls
passed the football
(with surprising ease) or helped
us mimic the western
we viewed together on a
Saturday afternoon:
(Hoppy and the Durango Kid
with damsels in distress
waiting for a six-gun
salute), and we boys
teetered and wobbled at
hopscotch or dithered
at double-dutch, amazed
at how the tender sex
could do the fandango with the
whistling ropes, a bare-
legged, hair-raising
blur we watched with very
much a gendered gaze.

HOLLYHOCKS

Along the village lane
not a stone's throw
from the surging St. Claire
red, pink and purple
hollyhocks hung
low over the barn-board
fences as soft and glowing
as a new bride's tresses
or Goldilock's curls:
so we whiled away
the afternoon hours
fashioning hollyhock
dresses out of upside-
down belled blooms,
and dreaming of nuptials
and pied gowns in some
distant ballroom,
far from any ordinary
village lane.

EASTON

When Easton Burgess
had one sip too
many, the size of our rosy
cones would grow more
rotund and our grocer's
smile would widen to include
even the good burghers
who disapproved of drinking
and other peccadilloes,
but we loved him
anyway, smiling back
with double-dips in hand
and pretending not to notice
the ache in his eyes.

NIGHT

When the evening grew numinous
we gathered with the alacrity
of bats sheering the near-
darkness with their swerve-and-glide
antic, while underneath
we fanned out from the solitary
lamp along the length
of Monck Street, playing
hide-and-go-seek
below a manic moon,
waiting for the all-free
to summon us back
to that luminous globe
like suicidal moths,
where we huddled before the
slow, slithering onset
of Night.

ENDEARING

My grandmother never
said, "It's five-thirty";
it was always "Half past
five" or "Quarter to six":
time measured by the quadrants
on the kitchen clock and called
out with such cheering
aplomb; I regret
her passing but even more
the loss of those words
that made her both treasured
and endearing.

FLOPSY AND MOPSY

At the first nip of autumnal
air, Dad would say
with a wishful wink of the eye,
"Time to go hunting,
lad," and I would abandon
my boyish games and tuck
the twelve-gauge in the crook
of my arm, tight-lipped
as we reconnoitred side
by side at long last;
"Well, it'll be rabbit
stew tonight," he grinned,
but I thought of Peter
and his cottontail sisters
under a greenwood tree,
until we spooked one out of
a brush-pile and Dad
yelled, "Lead him by a foot!"
and as the terrified creature
zigzagged in front of me,
the gun exploded against
my shoulder and the rabbit
carried on, unbloodied;
Dad's gun barked
and I was staring down at a single
unseeing, accusing eye;
I looked over at my father
but did not see him:
there, holding a smoking
gun was Mr. MacGregor
in his guilt-gripped garden.

MY FATHER'S EYES

"You have your father's eyes,"
my mother says, not certain
it's a compliment, but I did not
inherit that Roman nose
nor the high handsomeness
so captivating to women,
nor can I skate like Gretzky,
or a winged Pegasus twisting
defencemen into pretzels,
and my fingers do not fancy
the fine-toothed saw
and its willing ways with wood,
nor can I whistle like Bing
or strum a ukulele's
strings until they sing
like Sinatra, but to no-one's
surprise, I have
my father's eyes.

SHY
For the first girl to notice me

I was always shy
around girls, their beauty
both enticing and alien
I could find no words
to demystify, until
the day you took my hand
with a sly intimacy
and unfurled some-
thing inside me
that lasted a lifetime.

BABY STEPS
For Katie and Rebecca

Everything you did was
miniature: your thumbs no
bigger than a dwarf's thimble,
your fingers afloat in the easy-
going air, you used them
to manipulate your playthings
with gentle gestures and tiny
nimble tossings to
and fro, nothing grand
or gaudy to interrupt
the joy you felt in such
minute possibilities,
whiling away the infant
hours: yours was everything
Lilliputian except
your mile-wide smiles.

LILAC

When my grandmother died
at the dead end of February,
they had to break the earth
apart with picks to fit
the coffin in, and I felt
I had been forsaken,
for the woman I loved like a
mother had left me with no-one
to turn to in my grief: a world
had ceased but I was still
breathing, uprooted heart
and all, and then that June
I went for a last look
at "our house" and saw there
my grandfather's lilac
bushes licking lavishly
at the Spring light.

TANDEM
Valentine's Day 2015

For such a long journey
we travelled in taut tandem,
hand-in-glove: if we
were a song we would be,
in our halcyon years, a jazz
jubilee with Louis
tantalizing the trumpet,
and even now when our music
is diminuendo, we remain
melodious: touched
by tenderness, still
surprised by love.

WILD ROSE
For Kate

If you were a flower you'd be
a wild rose, rejuvenating
June with your bountiful blooming,
and when the morning breezes
whisper through your leaves, I hear
a voice faintly warning,
"Beware the thorns."

I remember the day of your birth,
you greeted the world feet-
first, as if to say,
"I've landed, I'm me, I'm
no-one else on Earth!"

OLD MEN

Old men weep
easily: a jolt of joy
taking the heart by surprise
or the image of a boyhood
chum, now dead,
swims surreptitiously
into the mind, and sometimes
it's just a word too
kind or an abrupt hug
from a cherished friend,
but mostly we weep for
ourselves, the tug
of what once was
when we were newly alive
and our world had no end.

MOYA

She was old, blind and deaf
but some spirit, some will
to live deep within
the boldness of her breed,
lingered, as she reconnoitred
for food, sideswiping
chairs and table-legs
in her bountiful begging,
nose ever alert for the
last tidbit left
by a foolish, loving
family, and so I
imagine she had no
regrets when the needle
slipped in and her great
heart was, finally,
stilled.

MOYA

She was old, blind and deaf
but some spirit, some will
to live deep within
the boldness of her breed,
lingered, as she reconnoitred
for food, sideswiping
chairs and table-legs
in her bountiful begging,
nose ever alert for the
last tidbit left
by a foolish, loving
family, and so I
imagine she had no
regrets when the needle
slipped in and her great
heart was, finally,
stilled.

ADORED

I am staring at this old
photo of my grandsons,
Tim and James (now
emphatically grown
into a world they did not dream),
kneeling on the front seat
of my Ford Tempo: they
smile for the camera and me,
caring only for this moment
when they know they are both
beguiling and adored.

TOUCH
For Tom

You move among the animals
at Circle-R-Ranch
with the ease of a young man
at home with himself
and happy to groom and curry
these elderly horses
who have served their time
in the trenches and look now,
after a drudging day of un-
hurried labor, for a loving
hand and the lingering stroke
of fingers through matted manes:
like Orpheus you have the prized
touch to tame and harmonize.

PLUCK
For Tim

"Free spirit" does not
capture the elongated
leap you took at life:
you had a boy's reckless
curiosity (we had to plug)
the electrical outlets
to stop you from fingering
them for the sheer fun
of it), you were a terror
in the sandbox, pummelling
my castles with an impish
glee, you drove your plastic
car with all the aplomb
of a dump truck bumping
into walls, door jambs
and me, you rode your Grandma's
vacuum cleaner like a bucking
bronco, your blue eyes
bright with surprise
and perfect pluck, and when
it was time for Raffi's songs
I danced you around
the kitchen floor like a
rambunctious ballerina:
you taught us what it was
to be joyful, to love
the child still in us.

VIM
For Stewart Geddes, In Memoriam

At supper you beguiled us
with stories of the old days:
your Dad the blacksmith
hammering horseshoes
hot enough to make
a fashionable fit
for the gelding's hoof,
or the morning of your birth
when Dr. Stewart braved
a blizzard to usher you
into a waiting world and give
you his name, or your loving
anecdotes about Lorraine
and those songs she'd sung
with such vaudevillian vim –
and when you'd wrung
all the pleasure out of a tale,
you'd flash us a smile:
ninety-four years
young.

EONS

We called it "our Lake,"
not knowing it was eons
old, when Attawandarons
roamed the dune-strewn
shores and braved the brunt
of its fury in birch-bark,
hand-hewn canoes,
nor did we know that Ojibwa,
sallying seawards,
gazed by chance across
its elliptical expanse, stunned
by its beauty, and here we are
centuries on frolicking
in its relentless rollers,
infinite in our ignorance.

HOPING

When I leave this world
the Earth will continue
to circumnavigate the sun
and I will be remembered
if at all, by those
few who loved me,
and when they too are dead
and gone, I'll no longer
be anybody's memory,
merely a name on the cover
of a book discovered by chance
on the far shelf of some
library: encumbered by dust
and hoping to be read.

GONE
For My Brother Bob, in Loving Memory

Now that you are gone
I think of all the questions
I meant to ask and never
did, and I stare at these
old photographs
of our shared boyhood
immortalizing the memories
I must muster alone:
the way you hung upon
the words of my stories and brought
them alive in your eyes
that will not brighten again
at my preposterous plots
and characters carrying on –
now that you are gone.

GIFTS
For Katie-Ann and Rebecca

The Lake must seem as wide
as Methuselah's lifespan,
and yet they glide like svelte
sylphs from some newly
minted urn into its blue
glaze: I hold my breath
as they hold theirs
and vanish for a suspended
second before they rise
more radiant than Venus
herself adrift on her sea-
spawned shell – amazed
at the lightness of their being
afloat, and smiling at the old
man on the shore: enthused,
and grateful to the gods
for their gratuitous gifts.

A BIRTHDAY POEM
For Sandy

One summer all
those summers ago
we held hands with shy
defiance and wore out
the walks that linked our houses,
moments that still glow
like a jewelled star
among the many millions;
together we made a memory
out of a teen twosome,
lingering and warm
for the years between.

DAPPLED

When I die I want
it to be in the Spring
when the crocus erupts,
tulips tantalize
the sun, my maple's
leafage abruptly
levitates and the hedgerows
are hung with berries ripened
by light, when apple blossoms
blow blizzard-white,
and I may lie in some
dappled shade and dream
of being young.

WIT

Once more I sit
down to compose,
amazed again at the
limned linkage
between the ink-dark
word and the flush of feeling
induced – the pivot-point
in the poem's truce with truth,
where the reader embarks
on a voyage that will leave him
dazed with knowing: words
are both weapon and wit.

THE GAME

I'd like to write a poem
to take your breath away,
but words have a will of their own:
once uttered indelible
into the air they will have their say,
and when they are stilled on the page,
stiff and resolute, they may
be read in a dozen different
ways or, playing the guessing
game, remain un-
engaged or merely mute.

RHYMES

In my advancing age
let me still be the one
wrestling with words to wield
the world anew, to send
them dancing on some
distant dais, sylvan
with simile: the page
where all my rhymes ring
true.

SEPTEMBER

If September were a woman
she would be as lean and lithe
as an antelope leaping,
her voice as lilting as the
autumnal songs of robins
dreaming of the blithe South,
her hair would be as yellow
as goldenrod or the last
of the black-eyed Susans,
and her smile would mellow
the lacquer of moonlight
over an ink-tinted
lake: she would have no
regrets about Springs
unremembered or the
intimations of Winter's
coming on: content
to be the loving link
between the seasons.

BIRDSONG

Robins hobnobbing
on my lawn with a soundless
strut: then, still
as stone, one ear
cocked for the writhe of an
earthworm under
ground, before the blithe
two-syllabled note:
a burst of birdsong
thrilling the throat.

BIT

When Adam and Eve delved
in God's garden, tulips
bloomed in the dappled shade
and the grass grew as green
as emeralds under a sky
preternaturally blue,
and the lucky couple
helped themselves
to the fruits of their labor
and all was well and fit
until one of them
against all odds
nursed an appetite for apples,
and bit.

CHIME

It's all about the ringing
of rhyme and the crispness
of consonance as they predicate
the patterns of possibility
for the choosing of words and the
mindset of meaning,
and when they chime as one,
they leave us a poem
singing.

LOST LIGHT

When our world has withered away
it kindly offers to shut
down our softening sight
and leaves us loitering
in the darkness at the end
of all things, looking
back at the lost light.

PITCH

Working with words all
my life, I remain amazed
at their willfulness, the way
they engage the page
as if they did not flow
from the million syllables
of my mind but moved instead
with their own pace and provenance,
unfazed by my paltry
attempt to twist them into
meaning, they hitch a ride
on the tide of their own intelligence
until they find their way
home in the perfect pitch
of a poem.

POISED

I pause: pen poised
to execute a poem,
something stirred within
moves me to lay down
a virgin page and begin:
a metaphor unfolds
itself astutely, and I
drown in words.

SILENCE

For sixty-odd years
I've been a wielder of words,
my pen propelled across
the page, metamorphosing
into three-beat iambics
enmeshed in metaphor
and circulating into sense;
when I can no longer be
a purveyor of poems,
I shall leave it all
to God and silence.

ASPERGER

'Out there' overwhelms,
it is all speed and fractured
light, colours collide,
grow tangible, voices
veer, hands hover
threatening touch, and in the midst
of it all a chasm of calm
where thought moves at its own
pace and feeling is curled
in its own delight: wanting
so much to reach out
and hug the chaotic world.

BLOOM

The wind moves mournfully
over the fields of Flanders
and the gunnery-gutted moon-
scape, where a million men
were made immortal by a war,
their souls still clinging
to the shell-rutted craters,
the winding mud-drenched
trenches, and bayonets abandoned
under a numbed sun
in a place deboned
of foliage and the buddings
of Spring, where birds refuse
to sing in the bomb-blistered
trees – but somehow
when the wind shivers towards
warmth, a blood-red
poppy blooms,
alone.

AGE

Why is it that as we ache
into our age, the faraway
past looms large
in our daily lives and in
our night-deep dreams
where childhood dramas
play out in technicolour
vivacity and each morning
is a bountiful beginning
to a day that is its own
reason for being, and where
the village tucked between
River and Lake keeps
us from straying off
the edge of everything
and we embrace the Fates
with indestructible innocence?
What else is there
now that we can do nothing
but rage against what
awaits?

LE GROS BILL

There wasn't a rink or grand
arena big enough
to diminish the graceful
striding of Jean Beliveau,
who swooped and swerved among
the greats of his day as if
there were only space between
him and the net, where the luckless
goalie had time for a single
blink before the twine twinged –
with all the civility and verve
of a swan taking flight;
he possessed a kind of puck-
wit and stick-savvy
that carried him through
twenty seasons or more,
and a gentleman's mien
that lit up any room
he entered and put a gleam
in the eye of a million fans
mouthing, "He shoots, he scores!"

CIGAR STORE INDIAN

When I first saw him,
stiff and posed in front of
the United Cigar Store,
I thought to myself:
he doesn't look like Cochise
or Crazy Horse: this is
a caricature of those
who peopled the woods and plains
with principled pride, whose
sad legacy is to be held
hostage to a twisted history
and the ignorance of all those
who peddle cigars.

CHARM
For Anya

You give new meaning
to the word "impish,"
you entertain us
daily with a tail-wagging
delight, your rumpled sheep-
dog grin dis-
arms and your winsome
zest for life reminds
us of our own capacity
for joy and the simple pleasure
of succumbing to a canine's
charm.

NIGHT FEVERS

The dark comes down
as sudden as thunder ripping
breeches in the sky,
while I wait for sleep to anaesthetize
and condole, but the under-
tow of the days' dealings
ebbs and flows at the rim
of a dream, impeding reason,
unenhancing hope,
while I quest for breath, feeling
the brush on my brow: the delicate
dance of death.

TIMBRE

I love the lilt and timbre
of your voice, ever soft
and low, like Cordelia's
in the presence of Lear: hard
to believe we've carried on
ten thousand dialogues
and every word of them
lean and limber.

CARESS

My Uncle Tom played
golf from the sinister side
and so did I: we navigated
in tandem the undulant hills
of the Thames Valley links,
stride for stride, while I
watched in avid awe
the enviable arc of this irons
as they feathered the ball utterly
into the air and it landed on the
far green as soft
as a lover's touch, and his putts
were administered with a crisp
caress before they brushed
the bottom of the cup; we shared
a passion and much more
till the day he beat a tennis
ball as if it still mattered
and his heart shattered like a
baffled balloon and there
would be no more affable
drives to sweeten the winds
above the valley of the 'Thames'.

TOO SOON

The grandmother I never knew
stares down at me
from the framed photo above
my desk with a penetrating gaze:
I like to believe she's peering
into a future that embraces
both of us: where we two
walk in tender tandem
down a garden path
festooned with hollyhocks
and daisies, until, imbued
with love, one of us
looks up and whispers:
"Too soon...too soon."

WHY

In the summertime days
when the sun still flowered
high on the horizon, pouring
honeyed light on our lawn,
Bob and I would hurl
ourselves near-nude
through Grandpa's whirl-i-gig
and its sprightly spray, while
my grandparents sat
on the placid verandah
and showered praise on our
outsized antics,
and O how clever
we were not to ask
why such prized moments
could not last forever.

SATURDAY MORNING

Every Saturday morning
I found myself in grand-
father's workshop,
the stinging perfume of saw-
dust sweetening the air
as I watched the man at the
machine nimble
tiny lozenges of oak
and walnut through the singing
blade into dazzling filigrees
with hands that once cradled
me lovingly in his lap
while he poured intoxicating
tales into my avid ear,
and I wanted nothing more
in this world than to be and be
there every Saturday
morning.

INDELIBLE

Gerry Mara is dead
and all the willows are
weeping in Gibbon's Park,
their lingering leaves a-droop
like elongated tears in mute
remembrance of our shared
boyhood, enlinked
by that liberating bond
that keeps a friendship
strong and true: we swam
each summer away
at Canatara beach
and played gratuitous games
of shinny on Foster's pond,
slamming our sticks joyfully
on the shimmering ice, glad
to be young, alive and together,
our friendship written
in indelible ink.

SECRET BALLOT

The Tories who lived in the Point
(some few of them)
were as organized as ants
on a king-sized hill,
and on voting day a sleek
black sedan pulled
up in front of our house
on Alexandra Avenue
and ferried my grandparents
and my parents to the polling place,
where the elders duly voted
Conservative and the other two
uninhibitedly voted
Liberal.

LOU

Dad's pal Lou
loved two things:
fishing and guns. But
his wife put the kibosh
on the latter, and so when he came
calling he pinned his peepers
on my Dad's collection
of rifles safely cribbed
in their cabinet, until one
evening, fully in his cups,
Lou seized a 30.06
and at midnight in our back
yard discharged his prize
gleefully straight into the air,
interrupting the shut-eye
of an entire neighbourhood,
while his laughter could be heard
long after the echo
of the shot had faded away
and we all gave up
guessing where the bullet
had landed.

ABIDING

Each Sunday morning
my grandfather would circum-
navigate the village
that held us warm and safe
from the horrors of the war he had
suffered and from which he had
returned with an encumbered
heart and in need of this walking
with its brisk, soldierly strides,
while I skipped along
behind drumming clever
questions as if I were Socrates
interrogating the truth,
and he told me all I needed
to know about the world
except that Sunday walks
were not forever abiding.

WIZARD

My Dad was a wizard with wood,
his hands had a wisdom of their own,
going gracefully with the grain:
he fashioned a home for us
brick by loving brick
and a picket fence to make
it look lived in;
I know he was saddened
his son was all-thumbs
and merely an unbecoming
wielder of words, but
I honour his memory the only
way I know how:
with the potency of a poem.

AMBLING
Guelph: February 1961

That night the snow
fell as soft as rose
petals on a bride's veil,
and we walked through the
brightening air, hand-
in-glove, our dreams aloft,
while flakes feathered your lashes
and left your eyes aglow,
as if the world were there,
without preamble, to welcome
lovers and their slow, passionate
ambling.

The Blue Flow Below

Black Moss Press
2017

THE BLUE FLOW BELOW

The Blue Water Bridge
was hoisted above the roaring
River the year before
I was born, its span no
more than a stones' throw
from my grandfather's house,
where I marvelled at its canti-
levered leap above
the blue flow below,
and in the dark its luminous lights
glowed like a radium
rainbow, while the hum-
drum of tires wheeling
away left me wondering
what dreams lay ahead:
I see it still through the
numinous lens of memory
and give it voice in this poem.

THE POINT OF IT ALL

The point of it all
was the village I was born to,
where each morning the sun
sizzled out of First Bush
on the eastern edge of everything
and eased me into its cushioned
arms, my pencil poised
to tell its stories, where village
characters startled the streets
with their Pickwickian ploys,
and I roamed the town with my pals
Butch, Bones and Wiz
in search of adventures I would weave
into plots-to-be, and where
the incandescent waters
(under a sky pricked
with stars) of Huron would engender
poem after poem, rhyme
after rhyme, where there was time
to savour the unjudged joy
of being among the anointed,
of making my point.

RIDING DOUBLE

Butch and I riding
double on his Dad's bike,
me slung over
the cross-bar like one
of the Flying Dutchmen
trembling on his trapeze;
we raced down the pool-
room alley, flawlessly
free, with one eye
on the lookout for the
cop: courting trouble
and pleased as punch to be
breaking the law.

STIRRING

I saw it each morning
when a simmering sun awoke
me: that silver arch
bridging the blue flow
below; I waved to the
shimmering shapes of cars
as they blurred past towards
some magical kingdoms
that make my dreams seethe,
while the whirr of their wheels
was a music I gloried in,
alone in my room, parched for
something stirring,
something new.

YOUNG

"Jesus loves me!"
rang out across
the Sunday-school room:
our voices raised in praise
of He who gave His life
to redeem our sinful souls;
we sang as if the whole
of our hearts would heave
with joy – yet as soft as
and lilting as milkweed
silk on an Easter wind,
for we were very young
and still believed.

CAPTURE

Playing Red-Rover-
Come-Over under
Mara's street lamp,
while a marigold moon
navigates the night sky
tingling with stars: this
ages-old game
passed from the tongues
of the young
to the young, their names
called out one by one,
summoned to run, if they can,
the ancient gauntlet:
cocksure, but thrilled
nonetheless at their
rapturous capture.

HI-JINKS

My Dad, the hunter, shot
and killed the mother for her fur,
then, in a moment of un-
characteristic compassion,
rescued her offspring,
bringing home a pair
of infant coons, who soon
entertained us with their
impish impulses and acrobatic
antics, not once
casting an unblinking
eye on the skilled and stretched
cadaver, hanging not
a foot or two beyond
their hi-jinks.

THERE IS A LANE

There is a lane in my village
where hollyhocks lean
into the light over fences
unembraced by paint,
where lovers stroll on the edge
of evening and children
go hide-and-seeking in the sun-
softened afternoons,
where poems teem in the brains
of local rhymsters, un-
aware that in the tall-stalked
grasses on the lane-side,
an adder seesaws
silkily, like Lucifer eyeing
the garden of delight.

GAMES

Every soft Autumn
evening, it was hide-
and-go-seek under
Mara's streetlamp,
that winked like a startled star
and cast its amber glow
into the fluttering shadows,
where every boy-girl from the
neighbourhood sought
anonymity until
"It" and the countdown
were done (in its chanting fives),
and then began the ritual
calling of names – one-
two-three, and those
who dared sprang for the
oh-li-oh all-free
pole, drenched with the delight
of being young and un-
impeded, whose blood
sang salvos of serenity
until Night, unnourished
by the moon, descended
and ended utterly all
our games.

BRIDGED

My grade-three teacher,
Miss Isabelle McDonald,
prompted my maiden story
and praised it even
though my final flourish
was purloined from the
class Primer: she saw
in me something
I had not yet seen
in myself, and I owe
her more than this poem
can say: even now
I look back at the
years between her gentle
gesture and my lifelong
appreciation with a whirl-
i-gig of wonder:
all those years,
bridged with words.

GRACEFUL
For Katie and Rebecca

My girls are as graceful as a
brace of swans soothing
a pond with feather-breasting
strokes, and when they dance,
long-limbed and smooth
as dimpled waves cresting
a sea-side shore, I prance
with pride and bless
the gods who fashioned for me
such bonds of love
and consanguinity.

THE WARS

I was almost eight
when I first met my Dad,
home from the wars, a stranger
I longed to be a father,
and so I watched him
as he built us a home
brick by loving brick;
he could whistle like a pro
and croon like Crosby, and what
did I have to offer but a few
stories scrawled in a scribbler,
and when he saw me skating
on my ankles, he laughed, recalling
those days when he flew
across the ice like a
kite in a whistling wind
and basked in the home-town
applause: no wonder
then we never really
met, the wars
notwithstanding.

ALONE

My widowed grandmother
listening to the radio: soap
after soap carrying
from the dining room all
the way to the kitchen chair
where she sits knitting:
Helen Trent's romance
gives way to Pepper
Young's family – unless
the Tigers are playing at Briggs,
only then will she drop
a stitch or two with the crack
of the bat like wood on bone
or the thud of a pitch in the mitt
as the crowd cheers and she wishes
she could be anywhere
but here – unsung
and alone.

LILLIPUTIAN

Bob perched on one
knee, me on the other,
as Grandpa spins the tale
of the three misanthropic
bruins, doing the voices:
gruff, piping and wee,
and we cry out
as Goldilocks shatters
Baby Bear's chair
with her girl-sized rump,
and hold our breath as the
blond-bobbed intruder
is caught in the tiniest bed,
and we follow after her
scooting thru the brooding woods,
then bear-hug the story-
teller, crumpled by our
Lilliputian laughter.

DREAM

On route to our one-room
country school, passing
Leckie's pasture, we noticed
the young roan stallion
with his male member un-
sheathed, blood-pumped,
dreaming of stud and ready
to ride the first fertile
filly deemed worthy
of his pedigree: the girls,
bud lovely and in shock,
blushed as pink-eyed as a
hollyhock, while we
boys, cocky as cockerels,
just dreamed.

BEACON

The lighthouse was our beacon
even though we were not ships
zeroing in on that bright beam
across a fog-laced lake,
we turned in its shadow every
time we wove our way
to Canatara beach
or sauntered back later
when the sun shrivelled, happy
to see its red and white
benign façade as we passed
by, knowing we were safe
within the reach of home.

IN

Each September we would walk
the mile and a half to our
one-room country
school, the road-side
agog with goldenrod,
the fields delirious with daisies,
the farms as familiar as our own
breathing, the sunlight
leeching from the far horizon
as we jogged up to the
unlocked gate
and welcomed ourselves
in.

SUTURES

My grandfather's surgeon
was celebrated all over
town, but he was also
addicted to the drink, and in
the O.R. he sometimes
reached for a tot and found
a scalpel in his fist, and so
it was the man I loved
the most was butchered, his blood
pouring out through the sutures
while his surgeon wondered
where his whiskey was.

PRESBYTERIAN

When the fire siren wailed
like a gored behemoth,
we poured out of our houses
and raced to the fire-hall
two steps behind the volunteers
who had jettisoned supper
and surprised wives for a higher
cause, none of us knowing
that ten minutes earlier
the Reverend Bell, stepping
into a dark vestibule, smelled
gas, lit a match
and found himself dazed
on his lawn a rod away
from splintered wood and scorched
brick, and we stood beside
the ruined manse, appalled,
ecstatic, and wondering
if God were still a Presbyterian.

JIM

Dad's crow, Jim,
was a born mimic: he'd
park himself outside
the back door and call
with split-tongued glee:
"Bill! Bill!" in the voice
of one who was a best friend
seeking an afternoon
of wayward play,
and Grandma would dash
to the summons every time,
listening to Jim chortle
with his crisp Crow's caw.

POOCH

My dog Moochie, every
weekday morning
trailed us to school
a mile and a half away,
where, thinking he was pupil,
he sat politely on the front
steps, paws folded
as if in prayer, until
lunchtime, when morsels
of half-eaten sand-
wiches fell like Manna
his way, and free of charge,
and Ronnie Young laughed
as he cried, "That's one
smart pooch!" and I
had to agree.

MAYFLIES

They rose out of the Lake's depth
like the ten plagues of Egypt
(and Moses steeped in prayer)
for one day only
each Spring: thick
clouds of "fish flies"
sticking to billboards
and lampposts and any
surface unwary
of their six-legged death-
grip: we watched their wings
shiver in the May breeze
like breath on a candle's flame,
and wondered how the Pharaoh
must have fared.

THE FLATS

A hundred years ago
these river flats,
now lushly meadowed,
were a switching yard for the
Grand Trunk Western,
when my village was a hub
of industry, and where boys
now let their kites
fly (bolstered by the big
wind off the Lake),
and flush with the joy of tilting
the sky upwards, the kite
string like silk in gravity's
grip, taut against
the suave swoop and gusting
thrusts of their winged Icarus,
they have no thought
of lusty locomotives
echoing in their ears or of overly
succulent suns.

TIMID

Nancy and I in league
at last for those few
moments we sat hidden
in the bush-lush shadow
of Foster's porch, waiting
to make our "all free"
rush to Mara's lamp-
post and its meagre glow,
two abreast we were,
brimming with prurient aplomb,
and on our way, much
to my surprise, our fingers
trembled in timid touch.

HALLOWED

My grandfather leading
his callow cadets, eyes
rigidly ahead and no
wave of the hand as I
stand on the sidewalk,
dancing with a five-year-
old's delight, watching
the man I loved more
than any other striding
with perfect precision,
in tune with his troop and carrying
his pride with envious ease:
a soldier without blemish
or blame, whose name
I hallowed.

OUTRIGHT

Every Sunday morning
at ten o'clock on the dot
my grandfather, his heart
weakened by war, would go
for his weekly walk, circum-
scribing the village, before the
summer sun got
too garish, and on my lucky
days I would tag along,
a skip and a half behind
his soldier's stride, and fire
question after question at him
about this sight or that
along the way, and he would answer
slowly and patiently, not losing
a step, when all that was required
was: Gutteridge, private,
first class, and I knew then
what it was to be cherished
outright.

WONDERS

I was barely a year old
when concrete was poured
into the first stanchion on the
Blue Water Bridge,
(my Dad, I was told, a-strut
the girders Heaven-high)
and I must have been three
when Gran and I walked
down Alexandria
and stood under an arching
span that threatened the sky,
and heard the hum of tires
above us, and I thought,
if I had any thought then,
what wonders are to come?

PRIDE
For Marilyn Matheson

Oh how we envied you
astride Buttermilk,
the Shetland pony
with the pistoning stutter-step,
who, whenever you let
us pet him, nipped
us on your behalf,
while you spurred him on
down our Fourth Line,
your Dale Evans' silks
a-flutter, your chin
just an inch too
high, but we forgave you
such pride because
as you galloped on past
in cinematic style,
your smile was winning and a
mile wide.

OUR SIDE

Saturday was matinees
at the aging Imperial,
double-feature day,
the third balcony condemned,
but who cared? We came
to be dazed and bedazzled
by Hopalong and Roy,
untroubled by six-
gun mayhem
in sagas where the villains
died bloodlessly
for our entertainment,
and the Bowery Boys kept
us in stitches till the cartoon
catapulted in colour on the screen,
and we waited breathlessly
for the Indians to arrive, war-
whooping a chill through
our collective bones, but when
the cavalry came, roaring,
scattering redskins
far and wide,, we roared
right back: our cheers
visceral, reminding us
that once again God
was on our side.

MUSIC

On Good Friday we sang
of Jesus and His Precious Blood,
dripping from His hob-nailed
hands and feet on that
grim Golgotha, and dreamt
of an Easter morning when the sun
rose and solemnized
an empty tomb with the
stone rolled wondrously
away, and we felt a new
music throb in our throats.

BEAUTY

Beauty is in the eye of the beholder,
so the saying goes,
and I gazed upon Nancy
and found her beautiful,
as a rose is beautiful
in newborn light,
and there wasn't a lovelorn
lad in all the village
who did not look upon her
with that unadulterated
delight we reserve for those
among us who come
alive in our appraising eyes.

SHUDDER

The sun always shone
on Canatara beach,
at least on those July
days when we paddled in the
Great Lake in a juddering
breeze or fantasized
among the dunes, whose sand
was as old as silicon itself,
and whenever we paused
to stare westward
at the infinite stretch
of unhorizened blue,
something inside
us shuddered.

NEVER

It was the time of lilacs:
my grandfather's house
was circumambulated
by pale purple blooms
like tiny anapests, un-
rhymed, and we, young
enough to believe in ogres
felt safe in those
confines from the shocks
looming just beyond,
while in the north yard
spiraea fountained
in alabaster showers
as if there were only a single
season, and I was certain
I knew the reason why
my grandfather would never
die.

LARK

Every schoolyard
has at least one of them
and Margaret was ours:
her bones too boisterous
for her body, she would lurch from side
to side like a hobbled heifer,
while we chanted "Moo cow!"
"Moo cow!" in a deriding
chorus, but on the eve of the
Christmas concert,
Margaret, in her turn, stood
tall and sang solo
like a lark in the lucid air,
and shamed us all.

DOLLY

When Dolly Gordon was
three sheets to the wind,
he'd stagger home via
the Balmoral, holler
"Hi, Hon" and whistle
for his supper, but the little wife
stood on a stool and tapped
him once upon the noggin
with her skillet, and laid him out
behind the stove, where he simmered
until done.

GRACE
For Grace Leckie

You were the first girl
to set my heart aflutter,
your figure just swelling
into womanhood left me
without speech, so I
pictured you as a day-lily
opening afresh each
morning in lissome light
or perhaps Dale Evans
astride the staunch stallion
you gripped with a two-legged
galloping ease, while I,
unembraced, loved you
utterly.

HEROES

Gerry's Dad was a tail-
gunner, impassive in his
glass target, my father
fixed the fighters limping
in to Goose Bay from their mid-
Atlantic heroics,
and when we mimicked
the dog-fights of the War,
Gerry's grin was always
just a shade wider
than mine.

CAUTION

One Saturday morning
Alvin and his buddies
constructed a raft
and floated it upon
the forbidden Thames
like Huckleberry Finns
on our make-believe Mississippi,
while I stood on the far
bank, luckless,
unable to swim or play
Tom Sawyer or any
other swashbuckling
kid.

GREEN
For Kate

You have the green thumb:
at your tendrill'd touch, daisies
dimple the lawn's edge,
daffodils dally
with a blaze of yellow
while peonies prosper in the simple
sunlight, roses roam
sill and ledge, and poppies
thrive in their scarlet daze
amid the hum of bees,
everything alive owes
much to Minerva's magic
you bring, O daughter
(queen of all that grows)
to this wondrous Earth.

PERFECT
For Anne

Our love is aglow as a rose
is red in the lustrous light
of an August afternoon,
as a bird is a-wing in the bright
blue-blink above,
it soothes us into age
like a June breeze gusting
slowly into the hallowed hallow
of our hearts where there is no
need for speech: only
the palliative poetry of touch
and a silence too perfect
for words.

GRACEFUL
For Katie and Rebecca

My girls are as graceful as a
brace of swans soothing
a pond with feather-breasting
strokes, and when they dance,
long-limbed and smooth
as dimpled waves cresting
a sea-side shore, I prance
with pride and bless
the gods who fashioned for me
such bonds of love
and consanguinity.

PRECIOUS

My girls are sewing again,
putting the finishing touches
on their knitted dolls, sitting
beside their grandmother,
much absorbed in learning
the lore they will remember
more and more as the years
go by and memories
become as precious as the eyes
of a long-prized possession.

BENIGN

I wake to Tom ululating
in his crib, pleased that he
has woken up the morning;
he flashes his blue eyes
my way (above his beguiling
smile), his little body saying
"Lift me, lift me" and hopping
up and down like a finely
tuned marionette,
and I know that any tribulation
or regret that may dampen
my day will be as small
and becalmed as this
unexpected gift
from a benign God.

WHENEVER I THINK

Whenever I think on my demise,
I write a poem and toss
it into the Universe, and when
Darwin comes to claim his prize
my body will yielded be,
but something shall remain
to entertain Eternity.

POSE

I stare at this photo:
cherub-cheeked Tom
framed by a slow explosion
of unsevered leaves and apples
rosier than Eve's lascivious
glow in the Garden, and I wish
he could, against the odds
and God's imperfect Will,
hold this orchard pose
forever.

KERRYMAN
For Colm O'Sullivan
In Memoriam

You were a Kerryman
through and through, you roamed
the blue-green hills
beyond your ancestral home,
with nine hundred years
of Irish cruising untroubled
in your blood, you paddled your hand-
made currach across
Dingle Bay, outwitting
foolish fish, eyes
stretched far across
the sun-lit sea,
you hopped to toe-tingling
jigs and raucous reels –
and when you landed on this
strange terrain, you faced
its alien ways and twanging
tones with aplomb and good
grace, and found a final
resting place for your incorrigible
Celtic bones.

MIRACLES

I wonder what the Babe
thought, waking up
in that miraculous manger
and seeing, beyond his mother,
a ring of shaggy shepherds
straight from the hillside
of Galilee and three
magisterial sheiks
whose smiles were as wide as
the desert they'd crossed
under a lone star
as bright as a moon-grazed
stalactite, and, peering on
amazed, a ragged cluster
of cattle, sheep and goats –
all come to welcome
Him into the world among
the lost and the forsaken,
and to let the Good News
stun the ears like a blast
from Gabriel's trumpet.

SNAPSHOT

I'm staring at this photo:
Gran and my mother on the
side verandah of the house
I hallowed above all
others, bursting bouquets
in their arms, open wide
to the lingering lens, for a moment
unfazed by the War
and the loved ones a long
ways from home, the heart-
glow of their smiles a snap-
shot I will treasure,
along with the immeasurable
memory it sings of those
near-blissful days.

BELGIAN
For Tom

He arrives at death's door,
this Belgian beauty,
once more powerful
than Heracles in his prime,
now staggering towards hope,
his life turning on a delicate
dime, but the doctors
work their small miracle
and the patient survives
to spend another day in some
fattening pasture – and here
you are, loping at his side
towards the camera, which catches
your smile and his stride.

BEREFT
For Tom Fahselt: In memoriam

Seven full years
after your death I read
your obituary: I'm glad
you had a long and fruitful
life, you left us children
and grandchildren to carry
your name into the next century,
we were friends when friends
mattered, sharing a brief
boyhood, ranging
far and wide over the
breadth of our joint terrain:
it's been a lifetime
since we parted, yet I feel,
strangely, bereft.

GRATITUDE

My lover's breasts are as soft
as a summer breeze alighting
on lofty leaves, her limbs
as silken and soothing as a
brightening breath on the elfin
air, and when she speaks,
her voice is a lilting timbrel's
tune, and I, mirroring
her mood, am seized, not
with desire, but a gust
of gratitude.

AT CAMERON LAKE

Tom and I horse-
playing in the warm waters
of Cameron Lake: me
the wallowing whale and him
porpoise-proud as he cruises
with ineffable ease
through the rippled surface
before he submarines
and tips me topsy-
turvy, glad to be alone
with me in this moment,
and when he laughs out loud
I feel a joy at the nub
of my heart and a love so
consuming it bruises the bone.

END-GAME

When my octogenarian genes
find reason to say
farewell to all I have thought
and done, my heretic heart,
(which has harvested love, sacred
and profane, willful
and wayward, but never
in the scheme of things matter-
of-fact, my head trembling
with tropes and words I cannot
undream) my heart
will shatter like a window pane.

CHARM
For Katie and Rebecca

My granddaughters are as charming
as twin doves purring
in a golden garden, their love
given with the ease of breathing
and an unhurried heart;
certain of their devotion
they bring me acres of elation,
I could swallow them whole,
they sing to my soul.

RIPE

My heart leaps high
when I think of my grandchildren
carrying my name and much
else, I trust, deep
into the century, and if
they think of me at all
(defying God's odds),
I will do a dead-man's
dance if their thoughts as such
are ripe with remembrance.

GAMBLE
For Colm O'Sullivan:
In Memoriam

My golf course,
however green, will never
again bear witness
to your full-figured
stride, your seesawing
sashay, nor the gleam
in your Irish eye when a putt
surprised the cup;
you were a man of elegant
erudition who jousted
with Joyce and prized the ambling
iambics of William Butler,
and after all's said
and done, you gambled on life
and won.

REMEMBRANCE

In the midst of my remembrance
I see the characters who fostered
the first fiction of my life:
childhood chums
like Wiz, Butch and Bones,
together we made the village
in the image of ourselves –
cruising the dunes of Canatara,
dolphin-diving in the Lake,
and then it was cowboys
and Comanches, our war-whoops
rousing the bundled burghers
awake before the sun
harrowed the horizon and we
slept in our bountiful beds:
in the midst of my remembrance
there is little left but these
evanescent embers.

JUST RIGHT
For Katie and Rebecca

Lovely is the rose that glows
in the lustrous light of the
noon-hour sun, and lovely
are my granddaughters, who flower
in the midst of my dappled delight,
and bloom like full-petalled
gladioli with the ease
of breathing, and when they smile,
bright-eyed, the word
above turns just
right.

CAW

I am walking to the raw
rhythms of my heartbeat,
savouring the summer's day,
giving nothing away,
I am seemingly content
in my solitude when I am
interrupted by a rude thought:
Time ticks onward
with each step I muster,
the blood thins and thaws
despite our quickening
resolve, and I hear the brusque
breathing of something
'out there': its cry
sharper than a crow's caw.

AFFECTION
For Katie and Rebecca

My granddaughters hug
me whenever we part,
their small bodies pressed
against my welcoming
bulk, as gentle as lambs,
and tugging at the heart-strings,
their affection freely proffered
to all within their ardent
ambit, and their love without
qualification.

WORTH IT

When Adam had eaten the apple,
did he grapple with the snake
in the grass or did he pass
out of Eden meekly holding
his woman's hand? And what
electric touch there must
have been on Earth when Eve's
breasts tingled in his fingers,
and one of them cried,
"It was worth it!"

IN TOUCH

In our Japanese maple
a pair of Northern Cardinals
take up residence,
threading twig after twig
with the ease and panache
of a Navaho basket weaver,
until they've fashioned
a birthing nest, into which,
after a discreet interval,
two tiny eggs
appear, to be brooded upon
by each doting parent,
their feathers as soft as
milkweed silk,
urging the siblings to peck
their way into the June breeze
with nods and jerks and beaks
yawning to be fed by a brace
of God's own, deeply
in touch with the way the world
works.

CIRCLE R RANCH
For Tom

You: just sixteen,
walking the horses from the corral
to the barn with the practiced patience
of a seasoned cowhand,
at the end of their long day
plodding the trails; the gentleness
of your touch transferred
to these fragile creatures
you lead one by easy-
going one to the solace
of their stalls, where you curry
and soothe, unhurried
in the least, the bond between
you sealed by silence and that
understanding which passes
from passionate man to grateful
beast.

BURIED

The eyes of my grandchildren
are mirrors of my own,
and when I have said good-
night to all I have known
and loved, they will carry
in each advancing glance
some part of me
recognizable still:
and buried in the bone.

DANCE
For Katie and Rebecca

The girls advance, pirouette,
pose, then move with a
gratuitous grace,
limbs married to the music
like sylphs to a minstrelsy,
all serene slenderness
and slim silhouette:
as willow as a wren's wing,
they freeze in the throes of an
intricate twirl, then turn
to face the applause with smiles
beaming a dancer's dream.

PHOTOGRAPH
For Tom

There you are: riding
your miniature truck,
all cheeks and cherub,
your eyes as blue as the Lake's
sheen in the noontide
sun or the sky's cerulean
shimmer – only three
but already loved beyond
loving, and now near
thirty years on
you are still adored
as if you were brand new
and guiding your cherry-red
truck across the back
porch, and our shining eyes.

MISTS

Through the mists of my memory
I can just make out
a small boy, toting
a toy Tommy gun
and a two-fisted pistol,
reliving battles lost
and won, while thousands
of miles away the malevolent
mutter of mortars
and young men dying
so a small boy could laugh
at the rat-a-tat-tat
of his Jerry-jolting gun.

WORDS

For a few short months
silence reigned in the Garden,
Eve smiled with her eyes
at Adam's abortive gestures,
there were no nouns to name
the flowers and trees and say
what the heart felt about
this dappled bower, before
God gave the guardians
of Eden words to articulate
their joy, to embody
the inanimate and, against the odds,
to argue over an apple.

SERENDIPITY

It is both odd and endearing
to stare at the two-year-
old me in this photo:
pug-nosed and with the
elephantine ears
I was born with and the
half-smile, half-
nod even then
I concocted for the camera
and posterity, sporting
the hand-knitted sweater
my grandmother so
lovingly fashioned for me
because love can't be measured
in hugs alone or the
glint of serendipity
in a toddler's eye.

DAY LILIES

They are the journeymen
of the horticultural set,
blooming once a day
as if to say: beauty
is a fleeting thing, but see
the quintessence of orange
we bring to the envious eye
in an embossed blaze
of blossoming, and what
persistence we show the world,
for as one lily shrivels
in the debilitating sun,
another is budding and tangible
in the morning's languid light
teasing it into blessed being.

STEWART

Stewart was always
the wise-cracking one,
mimicking Dizzy Dean
on the mound, the Babe at bat,
and when he pitched, his tongue
curled around his lip
as if to say, "See,
world, I'm here to stay
whether you like it or not!"
but then, halfway through
his third swing, the seizure
would strike instead,
and one of the kinder souls
amongst us would walk
Stewart slowly home,
where, the next morning,
he'd come out laughing,
keeping us in stitches
once again, unaware
he would die young, mourned
by all who knew him.

HARMONIOUS

My heart hearkens to every
quiver of birdsong:
the robin with the throb in his throat
chirrups the morning dew,
the thrush in his thicket
pipes his shy note,
the lark in his rarefied air
wafts his melodious music
to the skies above, while
the cardinal, red-robed,
whistles variations on a theme,
and the warbler high in an elm
curls his sonorities in tight
tremulos – and to my surprise
I find the wayward
world harmonious.

NAVIGABLE
For All Young Lovers

Young lovers in one
another's arms, their touch
as taut and tender as the
underbelly of a fawn;
he stares deep into the well
of her eyes and sees there
a reflection of his adoration,
her answering smile runs
radiant, star-stunned,
their love a bulwark
against a fraught world
and the temerities of time,
they live in righteous hope,
gentling each other
long into the navigable,
unwondering night.

TINGLING

A poem means what it is,
a welding of words to rhythm
and rhyme and the vicissitudes
of metaphor; a poem
is the breath of being: tingling
with truth.

KISS

On a summer's evening, warm
as honey sweet in the hive,
my first girl and I
contrive to cuddle on her
father's couch; our glances
collectively collide, and a mutual
leaning in brings
our lips into tingling touch;
we slip apart, much
amazed at the bliss of a
first kiss and the dazed
dance of a first romance.

WILD

Nothing roams as free
as a melee of wild horses,
unbranded and un-
broken mustangs,
rampant on the halcyon
hills of Arizona, their manes
aflow like flurries of flame
in the wake of the great stallion
who guides them: dreaming
of Pegasus and his wing-wafted
celerity: no breed
of man or beast can measure
the algorithm of his heroic heart.

TWINNED

When the last leaf lingers
on my backyard tree,
fearing to fall lest
it proclaim the end of autumn
and all that sprung alive
when April arrived on time
and threatened to go on
forever; so I eye
that lapsing leaf,
looking for signs that its fate
was twinned with mine.

GOOD FRIDAY

It was the darkest day of the year,
when three crosses stood
on the gaunt hills of Golgotha
and Jesus lay pinioned
upon the cruelest one,
and we too wondered
why God had forsaken Him,
whom we sang every Sunday
with our lusty young voices,
harvesting hope and good
will, but on the third day,
on the very brink of doom,
Jesus rose from the tomb
to right the wrongs of the world
and sanctify our songs.

COIN

What are the odds God
doesn't exist? Even
up, you say, but that
would assume that the Earth
and its moon were made by some
benevolent Boss in a
seven-day binge – or not.
Perhaps the Big Bang
was not God's cough
into the void but the devolution
of a million infinitesimal
particles for the sole purpose
of manufacturing Adam
and providing him with a coin
to toss.

SEPTEMBER

If September were a woman
she would be as lean and lithe
as an antelope leaping,
her voice as lilting as the
autumnal songs of robins
dreaming of the blithe south,
her hair would be as yellow
as goldenrod or the last
of the black-eyed Susans,
and her smile would mellow
the lacquer of moonlight
over an ink-tinted
lake: she would have no
regrets about Springs
unremembered or the
intimations of Winter's
coming on: content
 to be the loving link
between the seasons.

DANCE

Each autumn the leaves
on this Maple unhurl
themselves, reconnoitre
gusts and wind-whirls
to reach the ground, now
a-prance with unimpeachable
yellows and tawny reds,
as, breathless, we toss
them high and handsome
into the ardent air,
as if somehow this wasn't
an annual dance of
death.

THE URGE

When Cain slew Abel
in his jealous rage,
the bereft brother brooded
over Canaan, and God
drew on his brow a mark
as burning as a ranch hand's
brand, and Cain cursed
the fields he no longer
tilled with Abel's blood,
and roamed the barren land
until he grew into his sin
and willed it upon
a murderous world:
the urge to kill.

UKRAINE: 1935

While the wheat ripened in the
rapacious sun and the cattle
fattened in foddered fields,
the people of the land grew
back into their bones, and stared
in disbelief at the harrowed
harvest, carted off
in hopper and stock-car
to feed the fat cats
and matronly comrades
in Moscow, while the world
looked on and dithered
as a country traded
human life for the indelible
dye of the ideologue.

THE SANDS OF CANATARA

First Choice Books
2017

PRECINCTS

The pitch-dark above
Monck Street was scattered
by Mara's lamp, as bright
as a seasoned sun, under
which we played our ritual
games: there was no
rhyme or reason for our frantic
antics, but they mattered
to us as if they ran,
unfleeting, as deep
as any desire inked
on the hearkening heart or the
lonely precincts of love.

CADENCED

When Leckie's fallow froze
after January's thaw,
we took to the ice like ducks
on rudders, our blades scrolling
meridians we skimmed tenderly
under a moon hallowed
by the dark and a sky budded
with stars, boys and girls
together, hand-in-glove,
cadenced and going as the Earth
goes: we were all pluck,
ungendered, brimming
with hope and whatever
else comes before
the niceties of coupled love.

CANATARA

O the sands of Canatara
are as svelte and summering as
seven Saharas, and we buried
our bodies in sun-furrowed
warmth, while nearby the Lake
glistened, bluer than the Baltic's
salten sea, and drew
our surmising eyes towards
the storied horizon and thence
upwards to Heaven, where we glimpsed,
in their glory, the gods – listening.

GLIMMER

The girls of Canatara
cavort on the beach in their
one-piece bathing
suits: all curves
and swerves and sun-stroked
flesh, before sporting in the
blue shimmer of the Lake,
and then displaying their limp
bodies on the hot sand,
daring us to stare,
giving us a simple
glimmer of hope.

CONSOLATION

Mrs. Bray's husband
was killed in the War that shook
the world, but she took
consolation in super-
intending daffodils and daisies,
whiling away the hours
philandering among her flowers:
some said she was crazy,
but she loved all things
budded and unfurled:
they hearkened to her heart
and blossomed in her blood.

PIVOT

After the heat-seasoned
June shower comes
the rainbow-riveted sky,
and puddles proliferate
on our unpaved roads
in unpolluted ponds:
we paddle bare-footed
through them like disoriented
ducks, happy to be alive
and here, empowered
by the vim and verve of a village,
and lucky to be boys
watching ourselves
pivot towards joy.

REACH

On sultry summer afternoons
we watched the wind-wafted
waves of Huron, as blue
as morning glories stroked
by lasering light, break
upon Canatara's
fabled beach, and we also
found time to cast
an unrighteous eye
upon the girls who once
were merely our chums
as they lay now full-
frontal on the sun-infused
sand, knowing all
along with our penultimate breath
that these creatures, lazing
there, feigning boredom,
would be forever beyond
our reach.

BOYS AND GIRLS

"Boys" and "Girls" was carved
in stone over the doors
on either side of the building,
we entered two by two
in gendered columns
the ark of the schoolhouse
and sat in separate rows,
looking longingly,
but when the last bell rang
we raced home up
Michigan Ave and played
our ritual games, the girls:
hopscotch and skipping,
the boys: marbles and move-up,
then when twilight lit
the street with its grey haze,
it was boys and girls together
in hide-and-go-seek,
red rover and may-I,
our laughter commingled,
we brushed bodies in casual
contact as we sought
the strangeness in the other
and knew in our hears that all
the schooling in the world
couldn't keep us apart.

HEAT

The long-legged girls
lie leisurely upon
Canatara, hugging
heat to their sun-strummed
bodies and begging to be
ogled, but we, struck
dumb, are too shy
to say "hi" or good
gracious, and pass them
by like nice little
dogies (eyeing instead
a stray wavelet licking
the belly of the beach) and for
good measure we kick
sand in their faces.

THOUGHTS

On the ice-glazed fields
of Lecky's fallow lot
we skidded and skedadelled,
playing bump-the-body
tag and tumbling together
like cubs in a mother's den,
amazed at such cozy
contiguity, and if one part
of a forbidden bulge
accidentally bunted
another in the roly-poly
of the game, what the heck,
we were young, shamelessly
indulged, and kept our prurient
thoughts hidden.

HOME TOWN
For Gene Burdenuk

You and I trod
for the final time the streets
of my boyhood: I note
those angled gables
and friendly front doors
interrupted only by a vacant
lot bereft of the vivid
lives I still remember
there, and notice too
what's changed over the years
that intervened: the abrupt
thrust of a new-fangled
bungalow or a store-
sign with neon too
bright for the slow glow
of a village I've stashed in the
embers of my memory,
a home town that gave me
the unfleeting joy
of growing up strong
among the gods of belonging.

DEMETER

Mrs. Bray moves
among her flowers like a
denizen of God's original
garden: everything
she breathes on with a
tendrill'd touch grows:
daffodil, day-lily,
rambling rose as gay
as gemstones: she moves
like Demeter through a Grecian
bower, a gardener to the
core, fulfilled,
unlonely, widowed
by war.

FURY

How many summers did we while
away the days on Canatara
Beach, where the sun hummed
on the heat-soaked sand
and girls, new-breasted,
smile-beguiling and thigh-
shy, stretched out
before our salacious gaze
(hoping to be pursued perhaps),
but all we could do was shout
something rude
and plunge, unfazed, into Huron,
where we stroked each wave
with mammillary fury.

GLAZE

After a January rain
from plump, purpling skies,
a sudden freeze and Leckie's
pastures are a mottled maze
of wind-whipped ice,
so glassy we can see
the Globe's meridian gleaming
through, and as smooth as
obsidian, so we can measure
the curvature of the Earth
under our surging blades,
we draw fantastic
filigrees in the unflawed
glaze, and then it was Crack
the Whip, hurling the girls
whee-ing into the chilled breeze,
thrilled by their ecstatic cries.

UNINHIBITED

In the village that welcomed
an upstart scribbler
like me, I was blessed
with friends: bosom pals
like Wiz and Butch, Bones
and wee Gerry Mara,
collaborating cronies
flying our kites on the Flats
till they caressed the clouds,
with pick-up games
on Foster's Pond, where we cast
our liberating glee aloud,
or Move-Up with long-
legged girls in Withers'
field and a ball that un-
wound itself and fizzled
in the grass, or lazy days
on Canatara, where the sun-
glazed dunes gave
way to Cowboys
and Indians, and where we shared
our joys: uninhibited.

GENDER

When Winter comes with its
numbing winds and crackling
cold, the swamp below
the village freezes tight,
and we on buoyant blades
are released from the vice-grip
of gravity for the seconds it takes
us to glide from west
to east like Vikings on a
silken sea, and if we,
emboldened, happen
to tumble backwards
into someone of the other
ilk (and inadvertently
tease a tender curve),
the ice will bear the blame
as we all surrender
to the pleasing ploys of the
gender game.

CHAMP
For Marilyn

You rode Champ with the
flair of a rodeo-bucking
bronco, your hair billowed
by the breeze as you scampered
past our envying eyes,
and O how we wished
we had your pluck and ease
in the saddle, your grin un-
surprised by joy,
unhampered by luck.

HEAT-HAZE

We spent our summer days
on Canatara beach,
the heat-haze hovering
above, the Lake as blue
as Louis' tantruming trumpet,
the dunes, eons-old,
humped behind us
(where we played away
the rumpussing afternoons):
we would swim as sleek as salmon
silver in a dreaming stream,
and keep vigil until
the sun drowned in a far
horizon and we carried on
home, amazed that the world
 was meant mainly for us.

PRONE
November-May, 1944

How many nights,
prone on my sick bed,
did I stare out at a
sky, backlit
with stars and a ceremonial
moon, whose lacquered light
spilled across my counter-
pane? And wondered how soon
it would be before I could run
free through the sunshine
of the village I tried to remember,
or stroll unalone
under the flickering firmament,
heart-whole once
again.

HOPE
For Nancy Mara

I sit in the sand and watch
Nancy dive, in the air
elegant as an antelope
holding its breath, she whispers
the water with barely a ripple
stirred, her lissome limbs
vanishing, saying goodbye,
and leaving me, a non-
swimmer, crippled by shyness,
without hope.

STRANGER

When our dog Moochie
fell ill with distemper,
my father drove him into the
countryside and dropped
him off, and I've always
wondered what dog-thoughts
went whistling through his head
as, confused, dazed,
abandoned, he started up
the nearest lane, hoping
some stranger would call
out, "Here, pooch!"
and show him more love
than we did.

TUNDRA

After the blizzard's blow:
snowball fights
along the smoothened streets
and lusty boys sleigh-
racing down Custom's
hill, ululating all
the way, as a brightening breeze
dithers into drifts, and my pal
Wiz Withers and I,
bundled and wool-scarfed,
go gallivanting through the
vanquished village
like dual LaSalles traversing
the ice-blighted Tundra.

BOWER

Mrs. Bray's wide-
brimmed, floppy hat
seems to float above
the blood-red poppies
and towering gladioli,
as if she were in a dream
of flowers, her garden pied
and gay with the simple bursting
of bloom and she, like Gaia,
grooms her bower with love.

MILLENIUM

These dunes are as old
as Methuselah's sire,
washed ashore by a thousand
wavelets tonguing the beaches
of Canatara, dried
by a thousand breezes sifting
and enthusing the sun-
drenched sands into hummocked
hills that shimmered in the light
of the midsummer moon
and where, in an afternoon
of Junes, we played pirates
and thought of the Attawandaron
long ago greeting
the gods and the dream of dawn
and pressing their bent bodies
against the dune's drift
and listening to the millennial
hum of heat below.

EXUBERANCE

In Sunday school we sang
of Jesus and the blooded Lamb
as if we knew what suffering
took place on Golgotha
or what the Reverend meant
as he rambled on about
God so loving
the world or the dubious charm
of Lucifer, but somewhere
in the soul of the song we found
a voice that spoke to us
and we rubbed the vaulted rafters
with the mutinous joy of our own
exuberance.

GREEN THUMB

From our yard we can see
Mrs. Bray among
her affable daffodils,
bending down to touch
a tulip blood-red
in the lavish light, and moving
on to those blooms still
budded, a bunting breeze
airy above the garden
she'll care for till
kingdom come
(her husband's loving dower):
Mother says "She's got
the green thumb." We say,
she's the flower fairy.

SERAPHIC

Barr's Billiards (or
as, Gran would call it,
that den of iniquity)
had an anteroom where Butch
and I would go for a twelve-
ounce Pepsi so we could catch
the calligraphic click
of the cue ball or the "thwock"
of a kill-shot in the corner
pocket behind the thick
forbidding curtains
where ne'er-do-wells
gathered to spite their elders,
and we longed to breech that
inner sanctum where
life surely would be
both unsanctified
and seraphic.

MEMORY

When the church bells tolled
for one of our departed,
we watched Mrs. Bray,
shears in hand, clip
a spray of gladioli,
a bouquet to bless the bier,
then pause, as if startled
by something in the sky,
the blip of a memory perhaps:
of an unmarked cross
on an knoll in Flanders field,
bereft of such flowers
and yielding not to her tender
touch.

UNREDEEMED

Above the hushed silence
of Cameron Lake, a menstrual
moon brushes the surface
with its tidal touch, and the woods
silhouetted with alabaster-
beaming birch are bereft
of birdsong except for Owl's
harmonized hoot, and the ink
of shadow within is sucked
shoreward to shrink
in the luminous wake where
loons abruptly rhapsodize,
and all seems tranquil
and true, while I stand
alone on the edge of everything,
fretful and unredeemed.

MOVE-UP

On sultry summer evenings
we played "Move-Up"
on Withers field, the bat
bussing the ball airward
into the crotch of Nancy's
palms, and the girls cheered,
doing their best to ignore
the contending sex,
and what a wonder to see
wee Billy Saunders
botch a pop-up,
and Wiz, vexed at such
a tawdry attempt, pounded
the bases and stopped on a dime,
and Butch slid safely
into home between Marlene's
legs, and everyone
took a turn before
the gloaming settled upon
the dregs of the day like an
eiderdown and the Earth
hummed, ultimate on its axis,
one more time.

SCRUM

Apple-cheeked Tom,
as strong as an ox's grand-
daddy, gathers up
the rugby ball and surges
chin-first into a maze
of arms and legs, taking
knocks from all sides
until at last he's grappled
to the ground, grinning
at the sheer, ecstatic thrill
of it all, for this is no
humdrum scrum
with a scruffy nine, this
is a tug-of-war on the perfection
of the pitch with pride on the line.

NUMB

On some summer days
the Lake was cold enough
to numb the toughest testicles
and shrivel that privileged
part of us with its riffling
ripple, while the girls,
unruffled and wondering
what the fuss was about,
cavorted like chilled Jills
in Huron's nip, imperviously
plump.

POVERTY

When Moochie was just a pup
we couldn't afford to have
him take the shots that would've
prevented the distemper
he suffered, but instead
of letting him die among
those who loved him, my father,
to my alarm, drove him to the
countryside and dropped
him off at the nearest farm,
where I was certain he would
crawl to the barn and let
his life slip away,
alone and shivering, and I thought
how hard my father's heart
must have been, but then
by and by I had
another thought: my father
couldn't endure watching
Moochie die: even
so I still couldn't forgive
him for being poor.

ROAN
For Grace Leckie

I watched you galloping
across the fallow field
on your stalwart stallion
with a thigh-gripping ease,
and waited while you went
coursing by, your hair
bountiful in the breeze,
the roan tight-lipped,
nostrils a-flare, and I wasn't
sure whether I loved you
more, or the horse.

GLOW

My girls are like the glow
that roses make when bussed
by the summering sun under
a moonless sky and no
clouds above to brush
the bountiful breeze aside,
with eyes alight and wide
with wonder they brighten every
room they sidle into,
like poppies blushing crimson
in June: I never grow
accustomed to their levitating
love.

163

LEAVENED
For my Uncle Potsy:
In Memoriam

When I was just eleven,
you were still a big kid,
loose-limbed and romping
on the 'back forty' with my rugby
ball tucked under
one arm and me
keen to catch your zig-
zagging end-run
and the punt you propelled
half a mile, enthralled
by your Heaven-sent sense
of fun and bidding for
your adoring attention and that
smile that was more brotherly
than I could bear, tugging
at the brim of my being and, above
all, leavened by love.

PLAYROOM

Tom and I in the play-
room, he: with five-year-
old eyes as blue
as dahlias groomed in the
sun's delight; me: new
grandfather on his hands
and knees, wriggling like a
jigged worm, and watching
him dally with Duplo
or topple our "big" tent
with a chin-grinning swish,
and so pleased, his giggles
tickle my funny bone
and we laugh together, knowing
that love is our brand, ours alone
to be shared, and lavished
with light.

TRILL
For Tom

I awake each morning
to your melodious trill,
the crib shaking with your
bib-bobbing dance
and you, like a marionette
with its strings on fire, prancing
for the sheer joy of being,
and I smile at your blue-lit
alive eyes and a sweetness
so deep in you
no cynic could parry,
and the unalloyed thrill
you take in the new day's
startle, and I thank the universe
for the grandfather's role
and for offering you up
as first prize in my heart's
desire and my soul's serenity.

CYPRUS
For my Uncle Potsy,
In Memoriam

The sun teetered above
the treetops as we motored
to the far end of Cameron
to the Cyprus creek, the sky
uncluttered by cloud
as we entered the mouth
in utter silence except
for an over-size bull-
frog plopping into the water
from a lily-pad with its little
nosegay of blooms
or grasshoppers vaulting
from ferns and fronds,
and thus we poled the boat:
me on the starboard,
uncle on the lee, our rhythms
synchronized, finding just
enough room for our caressing
craft, and then, at last,
storied Cyprus: pristine,
as blue as a morning glory
in a lash of light, un-
fished by any but we two,
encircled by birch
and spruce in every direction,
and the day passed without
a word to be heard
while we jigged and cast
and reeled in the odd
perch: a smile stealing
between us every hour
or so, strong enough
to seal the bonds of
our affection.

STIPPLED

Nothing can retrieve
the aching days of my youth,
when I was unencumbered
by doubt, when the God I beseeched
to take my soul each
night before I slumbered
on safely through the night
routed my sins and follies,
and the sun unfurled
above First Bush
every morning and would do
so forever, and a
summering breeze strummed
the leaves of my grandfather's
maple with all the zest
of a jazz quartet, and I trod
the rippling streets of my village
ablaze with possibilities
of soothsaying and stories
stippled with truth, while Jesus,
pinioned and forsaken,
would rise again like Lazarus
and astonish the world.

LOVELY

My girls are as lovely as moon-
light on a lacquered lake
when midnight un-
curls the glimmering dark,
as lovely as the sun shimmering
on a bluebird's wing
arced against the breath
of a breeze, and as lovely as a
goldfinch singing
at ease above an elfin
elm: I wouldn't give
an inch in declaring them
as lovely as loveliness
itself.

RIGID

It's been more than a year
since Colm left us bereft,
and I miss him not one
millimeter less:
his death defies belief,
he was so alive in his living,
I can still hear his bidding
in bridge like a Vegas gambler
and picture him plying
his pupils with ambling pentameters
or Finnigan's pun-struck
prose, or stroking a putt
with a Kerryman's craft
and an Irishman's luck,
or spinning a tall tale
with such Celtic charm
and ingratiating grins
he disarmed us with laughter;
it's been more than a year
and I am still stunned
by his leaving and rigid with grief.

WITHIN

For Katie and Rebecca

I want my granddaughters
to be at home in their own
skin, to allow their beauty
to glow from within,
to flow with natural grace
into a room of admiring eyes,
to have a sense of pride
in all they do with no
trace of hauteur or the will's
abide, and to no-ones'
surprise they fit the bill.

AFFECTION
Valentine's Day: 2017

Our love has reached the golden
years, which means we've grown
old together, forsaking
the piqued passion that first
brought us gliding
together for the metamorphosis
of this mellowed life –
with amber afternoons
and a predilection for yellow
roses on a window ledge
savouring the winter sun:
we will not fear the future
for we have weathered
our way here without
preamble and with the kind
of affection that abides.

WARMTH
For Becky

If you were a flower you'd be
a rose without thorns,
deep-rooted with a heart
bigger than a bloom; we love
your thoughtfulness, a smile
that glows, a warmth charming
all who know you and affection
that disarms the most
cynical: kindness adorns you,
you tower, unassuming,
above the ordinary, and what
is more, you are ours.

NUGGETS

I stare at this photo
of my son and my first grand-
daughter so compellingly
I expect them both to leap
lovingly out of the frame
and surprise me with a hug:
Katie wears a smile
that would ingratiate granite
and John a grin he holds
till the sun comes in,
nor is there anything coy
about the way they liberate
the lens: they are at home
in the world, above its stinging
intricacies: I prize
such nuggets of joy.

SYLLABLES

I'd like to write the perfect
poem, where all the rhymes
have reason and all the rhythms
have the essence of iambic,
where the similes are seasoned with
sense and the tropes in their quatrains
ring with home-truths:
a goal I may attain,
given enough time
and, with hope intact, hear
my syllables sing.

WILLOW
For Tom

If you were a tree, you'd be
a red willow, hugging
the banks of clear mountain
streams; you bend but do not
break, your callow limbs
make the best bows, whose arrows
whisper the wind straight
and true, like your heart
flows; you have the soul
of a poet with a root's rugged
cling: you smile when you sing.

LOVELINESS

My girls are roses glowing
in the Garden of Innocence,
where sunshine shimmers
and the moon above casts
no shadow: they light
up my life with every
smile they bestow,
and even though I know
better, I hope they grow
slowly into their loveliness.

BREATH

My neighbour, Mister
Corbett, died yesterday:
I saw him at the corner
store just a week
before, looking hale
for an octogenarian (and me
only a year away);
death surprises us
all, and should we know
the date of our demise,
would we welcome
the days ahead, fearing
not our last amazed
breath?

RAINBOW

My girls are brown-eyed
Susans after a summer's
rain, their golden-yellow
petals aglow in the rain-
bow-rinsed air,
they are as soft as
milkweed silk
on a wafting wind: to my sight
their beauty is unbearably
bright, the mildness
of their manner a grandfather's
delight.

O

I am almost eighty
but really can't complain:
I've lived a life of plenty:
I've promulgated a thousand
poems and strung out
a string of stories, both
frivolous and weighty:
but O to be twenty again!

IT

Safe in the arms of Death's
dominion, I shall not rue
my lifelong pursuit
of the perfect poem, my childish
need to hear my rhythms
purr or know the surging
minutiae of my metaphors
are true to themselves and no
other, and I shall not
mourn the loss of my word-
wit nor the wild swings
of borrowed pentameters:
for I have led a charmed
life and feel little
sorrow in leaving it.

STUDY

I sit in this room
I call my study, but
I'm not the owner, I merely
rent the space I love
more than any other,
where poems were propagated
and home-bred stories
saddened my imagination,
but sometime soon
a stranger will install himself
in my place (who'll not forgive
my absence): even so
we cling to those things
we prize above most,
as if by letting go
we'd tempt the Fate that dooms
all those who dare
to live.

WHIRL

My girls are growing apace,
like the slow opening of a rose,
and when the blossom is struck
with the lissomeness of light,
their true beauty is gracefully
exposed; no luck
is needed to appreciate such
pulchritude: my sight
is overwhelmed and my heart
whirls.

TORCH

Rebecca, at ten, pens
a book report on Lemony
Snickett and to my surprise
and delight the prose flows,
every word clicking
into place and untortured
by the grip of grammar or the vise
of petty punctuation:
a story has been recast
with verve and artful
insight: impeccable
enough for me to aver:
a torch has been passed.

EXALTED

Loving you is an act
of remembrance, a recalling
of all those days when we were
too young to be tempered
by tactful touch or the soft
collision of lips, when being
amazed was our common fare,
when I knew such jolting
joy at a glimpse of your hair
haloed by juddering sun-
light or your eyes as blue
as crystallized cobalt
or the effortless allure
of your youthful gaze:
in truth our love was too
exalted to be nipped
in the bud.

BID

I bid you good morning
with the sun subliming
your blue gaze, and you reply
in tones like angel's breath,
and we interrupt one another
in mid-sentence, laughing
at the timing and our contiguity,
and pledging to spend our days
being stalwart and true
to our hearts' caress and a love
unharnessed from envy
or age till death do us part.

PLEA

Seven-year-old
Bana al-Abed hurls
her plea into the ozone
behind the camera, from the
embrued ruins of Aleppo,
that fabled city,
gilded by mosques and minarets,
the land of Aladdin and the
Arabian Nights, but
there is little delight
in those eyes as brown
as burnished berries, even
as her words flow like a
poet's screed, calling on
the world to banish flesh-
flaying barrel-bombs
and the crushing of infant bones
under cracked concrete,
and like all children,
here and everywhere, Bana,
in her need, just wants
to be.

SLAKED

I dip my pen into a
lake of ink, stirring
words on the brink
of utterance, slipping towards
thought that cannot quite
be expressed until some trope
offers hope and a poem
creates itself and carries
on till the thirst for
significance is slaked.

HAMELIN
For Jean McKay

You are a cross between
a pixy and the Pied Piper,
you move through the piebald world
on tingling tip-toe
the better to sense the myriad
oblong objects you trans-
mogrify with your singing
flights of fancy and dainty
dioramas; there is nothing too
small to fit your exquisite
eye, and all the while
you toss out flute
tunes, frenzied cadenzas
and a poet's prose to those
of us who love you
and are happy to follow you
all the way to Hamelin.

TALKING POEMS
For Tom

An afternoon with you.
talking poems and mining
our memories, mutual and other-
wise: the motive for metaphor
lies deep in the embracing
bone, excavating the past
that ties us together,
makes us one blood
and sanctifies the home-ground:
we share a tear inter-
laced with some laughter
at the frantic antics
of my fallible family,
and bond, like mating birds,
over the everlasting
love of unstoppable
words.

RAPTURE

Whenever I write a poem
I picture a quill dipped
in a pot of ink and flowing
out into lettered lines
that capture the essence
of some thought I hadn't the will
to think until my words
righted themselves
on the puritan page in stanzas
of unfettered rapture.

UNIQUE
For Sandy

We surprised one another:
I fancied you and you
me in that summer
of hand-holding and the single
tingle of the shy kiss
I landed obliquely, your eyes
widening for me alone,
and hit or miss we prized
our prim romance and made it
uniquely our own.

ARNIE
For Arnold Palmer
In Memoriam

Arnold is dead, and we
will miss those long
sweet drives with the flawless
draw that kept them as pure
and straight as any meridian,
and Arnie's Army marching
boldly with him down
the fairways of their fantasies,
and the King, with his regal strut,
greeting them with a tousled
grin amid the din
of their perfecting applause,
and when the last putt
has dropped into the last cup,
we will still remember the Kid
from LaTrobe who made a run
at the world, and won.

CRIES

I hear the muffled cries
of children under the rubble
of Iraq, and I think of
my grandkids safe
and untroubled in a country
that cares, and I think of
my Tom, unruffled
in his crib, blue eyes
smiling back at mine
with infinite innocence,
bibbed and bubbling and gay,
and I wish for him and all
the infants of Iraq that no
harm would ever come
to detonate their day.

TRUTHS

A poem is an odd thought
that's been rhythmed and rhymed,
and the meaning resides some-
where inside, where similes
and other tropes embody
what they ought to be,
carrying the hopes of he
who let his being loose
in syllables that sing serenely
of timely truths.

MURMURING
*For the victims of the massacre
at the Quebec City Islamic
Cultural Centre*

Two dozen men
folded in impeccable prayer,
rug-resting and murmuring
worshipping words heard
across the centuries since
the Prophet first proclaimed
the righteous route to Allah,
no other sound
to disturb the sanctity
of their fervid faith, until
an unbeliever, harassed
by a hatred so deep
it could only be appeased
by an act of savagery,
the expurgation of gun-
fire and the stilling of Muslim
men mouthing Amens
for the heart's ease.

WAND

God, that great M.C.,
waved his magic wand
and Eden popped out of
the ether: a garden where tulips
and other blooms spawned
hither and thither until
Adam arrived, conjured
out of dust, to groom
the fruits and flowers and welcome
Eve, of whom he soon
grew fond, so that
when the slithering serpent,
in cahoots with Lucifer,
offered the Apple of Knowledge,
and Eve, grappling with temptation,
took a lusty bite,
Adam, pleased to assist,
and to spite his Maker, followed
suit, and the Lord, in a huff,
blew them both out of
Eden with a paradisal puff.

EMBOSSED

In this photograph:
an old stone bridge
stretched above rapids
rushing below and wrenching
themselves into furious
whirls, then easing into
a pelucid, blue pond,
white-lillied and over-
arched by birches that brush
the unrippled surface
with shimmering shadow:
there is a stillness here
and a timeless silence,
into which I toss my rhyme-
embossed thoughts.

QUILL

I dip my quill into the
ink-pot, hoping that the
syllables singing in my head
will jot themselves down
on the pristine page,
and soon surge into words
I will towards some plot
never before thought,
then, still, I let
it age.

SUBLIME
*For Bill Exley
and the Spasm Band*

You wield the megaphone
like a carnival barker on steroids
and tremor your tin pot
like a shaman his death
rattle and your spiel is a
tone poem of negativity,
a cadenza of majestic moans,
while backing up your projectiles
of prattle, your nuggets of nonsense
is a zoo of cranky kazoos
and other instruments torturing
sound for its own sake
without pitch or poise
in chasms of spasms: this
is divine concatenation,
sublime noise.

COLT

The colt drops slick
from the mare's womb and greets
the world with a feet-first
jolt, tests his wobbling
legs on the stall's cobbles,
feels some strange
strength flowing there
from his heraldic heart, then
does a little prance
across the room, rehearsing
for the day he will do his pedigree
proud on some far
moon-struck race-
way, cheers aloud
in his ears as he thunders towards
the finishing line, where he takes
his victory dance.

ODD

Adam thought God
was omnipotent, plopping
him down in a green garden
where petals never drooped
and fruit hung heavy
on every tree, but a
serpent managed to slither
hither and draw Eve
to the lip-luscious apple:
still, and oddly enough,
God refused to stoop,
and watched Adam and his
rib-wrung mate
slip away out of Eden.

THE TRAGICALLY HIP

This band makes music
out of mountain streams
and the lay of the land, they rock
with the dreams of a million Canadians:
Paul and Rob throbbing
on guitar and Gord strumming
the bass to the drumbeat
of Johnny Fay, while Downie
is the lyrical lion, driving
home the Man Machine
Poem, doing his last
solo, saying so
long, his goodbye words
so magic on the lip
the singer is subsumed by the song:
these are the Tragically Hip.

LOVE-LIGHT

We all want a death at home,
passing alone frightens
us to the bone of our being,
we crave the comfort of the
family we've nourished above
all others and those friends
with whom we've travelled
during our brighter days,
and now as our life abrupts
with each interrupted breath,
we save the last one
for our final words and a
wistful wave of the hand,
(breathless now
and perhaps seeing what is
to come), while the mourners
stand by, waiting for the
love-light in the eyes
to die.

PREARRANGED

God must have seen the Serpent
slithering, belly down,
into Eden; after all
He made it in one of his images,
and He must have known
that Eve was not exempt
from temptation and that Adam
would be smitten with his mate's
allure, and so, stranger
still, to think that the Fall
was prearranged.

HALO

Did it snow in the hushed
hills around Bethlehem,
muting Gabriel's anthem
to shepherds stunned
by God's good news?
And were there clouds to obscure
the one-starred en-
guiding sky over the
jewelled Judean desert,
while mystified Magi
abided below? And the Babe
lay mangered on the inn's
hay, brushed by the breath
of oxen and the curiosity
of lambs – all waiting
for the stilled stable to be
haloed, and glow.

WHETHER

Snow is falling again,
feathering eave and the last
of summer's leaf, glistening
the grass – and soft as a
swan's underbelly,
and soon there are children
to taste it on their tongues,
listening for its silent descent
and wondering why the seasons
shift and whether the young
have reason to believe.

NO REGRETS
For Sandy

This late-winter snow,
prancing effortlessly on the air
outside my window,
reminds me of our summer
romance, the surprise
as we stared into the other's eyes
at the glow that refused to go
away: it was just a budding
of love, our first mutual
dance, but we had no
regrets, not for a minute:
there was no winter in it.

CYPRUS LAKE: 1951

There is no loneliness
like this lake, hedged
by cedars, birch and spruce
older than Adam's rib;
a lurch of wind induces
ripples on the silvering surface
that do not disturb the dark
deep where fish live
in soundless serenity,
and wavelets lick the stone
ledge where I stand
waiting for that first
word to propagate a poem
and set my bones aquiver.

FILAMENT

The alabaster page,
unbruised by words,
daring me to propagate
a poem: the first fragile
filament of phrase casts
its shadow, silhouettes,
engages, and begets
itself.

INKLINGS

Black Moss Press
2016

FOG
Point Edward: 1944

I lie safe in my bed
and hear the fog horn's
boom (oo-aah)
like hippopotamus in pain,
a sound so loud I think
it haunts my very room,
and I picture the deck-hands,
fog-frazzled, peering
into the shrouded night
like blinded Argonauts:
"Steady as she goes!"
and when I finally fall
asleep, I dream of hippos
and a morning bedazzled
by sunlight.

WHAT WAS

In this photo my Gran
looks pensively towards
some future, chin high,
while the Sunday Jello
cools on the verandah
behind her: she has no
thoughts of church or its
self-serving sermonizing,
nor does the past intrude:
better forgotten the child
in the grit-endued streets
of central London and the mother
who was a lady of the night;
better remembered the family
who took her in, and safe
in Canada passed her off
as one of their own, a secret
kept for more than five
dozen years, and I'm left
wondering what courage it took
to abandon your home and say
hello to a far country,
but then I see it there
in her eyes, and I weep
for what was.

GOLDENROD

In the goldenrod daze
of September, we set out
like larcenous LaSalles
for the schoolhouse a mile
and a quarter away, along
a road garnished with gravel,
where puffs of dust beguile
our footsteps and we while
away the time spooking
sparrows from the rough
underbrush and some-
times a spray of cowbirds
who take flight as the girls
cry "My wedding!",
and we pass meadows
where Holsteins graze in the
heat-haze and huge-
hoofed horses plunder
the grass and toss their mutinous
manes as we nod to barn
after barn with silos
stuffed with fodder and stare
at the leaf-fringed woods: and there
on the horizon, hefting the sun
into a high sky, is our home-
for-the-day and all the days
and this awe-tinged autumn.

MOTIVE
Point Edward: 1948

The village that spawned me
and kept me cozy
for a dozen years, was pointless
(I searched for it one
day and came home
puzzled) and long ago
was a railway town
bustling with locomotives
and a switching yard, until,
like railroads everywhere,
they pulled up the tracks
and skedadelled, leaving
a single line to rust
away (and a village shrunken,
out-of-joint with the world),
a set of tracks we trod
on our way to Canatara
where the faithful
Lake was motive enough
for a day's play (while
the sun-nuzzled dunes
warmed us, where we clambered
on amber afternoons)
and the slow walk home
along those ties
where we felt the heft of history
and realized the point of it all.

ALIVE
For my Grandfather
In memoriam

How did you survive
three-and-a-half-years
in those trenches, riddled
with rats and drenched with shells
that shuddered the earth around you,
shorn of trees and the trilling
of biddable birds? Was it fear
that bolstered your blood? Did you
blench as that bullet struck
your bone? Did you mourn
those who succumbed on that
killing ground? Or were you
too numbed by bomb-
blast and machine-gun
stutter? Was there a moment
to dream of home and your son
still unseen, of lasting
things, of the sure hope
that somehow there might be
a future where you could thrive?
You do not answer (after all
what words could you utter?)
but I know that you lived
so I could be born alive.

LIGHT
For Dave Withers

Wiz Withers was a wizard
with wood, his crowning gift
to us was a racer worthy
of the Soap-Box Derby,
confected out of two
crates and four buggy
wheels, with twin ropes
to tug it left or right:
it was my honour to pole
it hither and thither
about the town, whose amazed
souls stood by and dusted
us with their applause; I think
of those intoxicating days
so long ago
whenever I need a moment's
memory to lift me
towards light.

BOYS AND GIRLS

In the dallying darkness
over Monck Street,
under a monsoon
moon marinating side-
walk and roadway
with a mellowing light
and beneath Mara's luminous
lamp, we played out
our ritual games: Red
Rover, May-I
and most of all Hide-
and-Go-Seek, sallying
into the shimmying shadows,
waiting for the "All free!"
boys and girls alike,
where a knee might accidental
another, triggering a rush
of blood and a smile as big
as the star-brushed horizon.

NO ROOM

When you are just five
each day is a live
beginning: the sun rises
rosy over First Bush,
inundating it with light,
the streets shine, saying
"Walk on me, skip
on me!"; here, to your delight,
the wind does not gust,
it purrs; my village is as
cozy as a womb and I am
at ease being me in such
a place, where there is no
room for doom.

AWASH

We couldn't afford skates
so we skidded on our galoshes
on Foster's frozen pond
like ducks on skinned ice
(no city-slicking
posh shin-pads
for us) with much-bruised
sticks bent like
boomerangs, awash in the
lithe light of a moon
as rotund as a gilded platter,
we chased the peregrinating
puck to and fro
and, with skates or no,
we played as if it mattered.

TETHER

The mores years added
to those allotted me,
the more my dreams are haunted
by thoughts of my childhood
home: that proud, jaunty
village nudged between
Lake and River, where I grew
unjudged in its care,
where each day seemed
to begin life anew
with a simmering sunrise
and ended with a lambent moon:
the older we get the more
the past possesses us
and memories marinate
in the mind: these are the ties
that tether us true
to the world that made me
what I am.

DAZZLED

Bonnie and Sharon hot-
scotching with their skirts thigh-
high in the biddable breeze,
while Johnny and Aaron play
rugby with a sturdy hurling
of the skin-tight ball:
the duos remain un-
frazzled by the other's id,
until, by and by,
the girls being to flirt
and the boys enthrall,
each dazzled at its own
delight.

CHARLIE

Charlie was our neighbour,
a decorated vet who weathered
his nightmares with whiskey,
and, when that wouldn't do,
in beer binges at the Balmoral,
but nothing could unhinge
his image-riddled mind,
not even his three beautiful
daughters who doted on him
and us, and pretended not
to see that smile with the ache
in the middle.

BEYOND MEASURE

We got much pleasure
watching the girls do
Double Dutch, the ropes
whispering the sidewalk
with rhythmic strokes as gentle
as a jazz trombone,
bare limbs frantically
exposed as one girl
glides in and another
out with pinpoint
precision, skirts flung
thighward, leaving us
dazzled, hopes high,
and envious beyond measure.

HOLY
For Gran: In Memoriam

In Sunday School we sang
as if God Himself
were keeping tabs, while
back home my Grandma
baked her weekly raisin
pies and watched her Jello
cool in its bowl on the side
verandah: I found it odd
that the Divine seldom visited
our abode, but there was affection
in those prized pies and more
love abiding there
than the Lord needed to keep
His Sabbath Holy.

UNWILLING

When my Dad uprooted
us, moving me
from the only home I'd ever
known, my best friend
Butch, fulfilling a promise
he swore to, cycled
behind the moving van
all four miles to our
new abode, defying
the gravel-strewn county
road, unwilling
to say goodbye.

ME

My grandfather endured
three-and-a-half years
in the lurid fields of Flanders,
burrowed in slit trenches
unfit for humans,
like some subterranean
beast, while the air rang
with the nickering whiz of bullets,
and shells flattened the furrows
of farms and cratered meadow-
lands whose trees were stripped
to sticks, and there was not
a bird who sang his breeding
song, and all those
horrific hours he would not
yield to death because
there was something
in every breath he took
that imagined home, imagined
family, imagined me.

DAZE

On sizzling summer nights
boys budding and girls
sudden with breasts play
hide-and-go-seek
in the juddering shadows
under the lascivious light
of a June moon: too
soon to be blessed by
some tremulous touch, they wait
for the "all free" call
and come running in side-
ways tandem towards
Mara's lamp and what
is just beginning to daze
and delight.

HEALED

When the fever finally broke,
the valves in my heart opened
like petals seized by the sun,
and I lay in my lonely bed
for seven long months
until they closed again
like lilies at the end of day,
and despite my mother's fears
my healed heart has kept
on beating for more than
seventy years.

BLAZE
For the Point Edward
volunteer firefighters

When the fire siren
assaulted the air over the
village, a dozen boys
vaulted onto their bikes
and trailed the roaring red
engine with big-muscled
men clinging on
like bos'uns on the rigging,
hoping for a blaze like the one
that levelled Burgess Market
or the gas-blast that blew
the Reverend Bell onto
his front lawn, but when
the spanking new truck
drew to a thankless halt
before a field no longer
smouldering in the heat-haze,
our hearts sank.

WHATEVER GROWS
For Anne

You were born with a green
thumb, and ever since
everything you've touched
has sprouted, budded or blossomed:
roses that tumble on their trellises,
petunia pots showering
our porch with a blaze of petals,
forget-me-nots
fringing the lawn with the
sprightliness of Spring:
you are a daughter of Demeter,
a dean of whatever
grows, and you are un-
amazed at your own delight.

DUNES

The dunes of Canatara
are older than the Attawandaron
who wandered here in search
of freshwater clams
under a night sky
trembling with stars and a
miraculous moon,
and as dawn assembled itself
on a prism-rich horizon,
they lay themselves
down on the sun-drenched
hillocks and dreamt of
Gichimanitou and sturgeon
stalwart enough to feed
a village.

SUNDAY WALK

Grandpa and I
on our Sunday walk,
circumnavigating our village,
me firing question
after question and he
answering them as if I were
some sort of Socrates;
we skirt the marsh, its grasses
stalk-dry, the cattails
shredding in the June breeze,
the air lavish with light;
his corporal's stride is shortened
for my stutter-step as we reach
First Bush, busy
with bees and birdsong,
and we find a kind of furtive
joy in taking the long
route home, and I try
not to hear some terminal
clock ticking time
away from the love neither
of us needs to utter.

SMILE
For Lilly Hall McWatters
In Memoriam

All I have left of my maternal
grandmother is this
framed photo, out of which,
bereft of breath and stiffened
with a pinch of pride she pins
me with a Presbyterian
eye, as if measuring the mettle
of the grandson she would never
know, and how I wish
she had lived another three
years so we could have met
face to face, in fine
fettle, my chubby guile-
less presence widening
her smile.

BADGE

And me the goalkeeper
in my prized shin-pads
(last year's Eatons),
sweeping pucks aside
until one of them surprises
my left eye, and to ease
the pain I imagine I am
Turk Broda taking
six stitches and playing
on: so I hitch up
my pads and wear my blackened
eye like a badge.

IRISH

My mother's father built
the bloated mansions along
the London Road with hammer,
saw and chisel, his eye
as true as a cartographer's
sighting his sextant on a distant
star, and when the job
was done, he'd dance a jig
at the next bar, until
the day he was murdered (before
I was two) at a bootlegger's
"ginger ale" party,
so I don't remember him
dandling me on his knee
or doting on the firstborn,
for I hadn't yet grown into
the boy who would laugh at his tall
tales or his Gaelic wit;
instead, with his untimely
demise, I pen this poem,
and dedicate it to his Irish
eyes.

FANCY
For Ivy

You do a song-and-dance
for us, prancing about
like a pixie with foot-
bobbing ease, and all
the time telling us
a tale of two bunnies
hopping into the morning
sunshine: one eye
fixed on the story that grips
you deep down where
fancy and the imagination
lie.

NINE YEARS
For Potsy: In Memoriam

It's been nine long years
since you left us,
nine years bereft of your rough
love or those amber
afternoons we spent
on fairways and greens
(where the arc of your swing
hummed like a Turk's scimitar)
or the summers at Cameron Lake,
the two of us passionate
about perch or the odd black
bass you landed with ample
aplomb: nine years
without those luncheons
where I sat surprised
and aglow at the stories you spun
about your prized days
in the War, nine long
years, and I still haven't
forgiven God for your passing.

FIRST STEPS
For Tom

It must have taken the courage
of a lion in his pride for you
to step into the terrifying emptiness
of air, that vacancy
of space, without ballast
or handhold, one
tentative toe at a time,
bracing against some
notion of balance
upright in your mind;
you smile at me, arms
outstretched, as you hit
your stride and fall
delighted into my embrace:
these are moments that last,
lingering in the manifold
layers of memory.

CONNOISEUR
For Amanda

You are a connoisseur
of fruit pies and raisin-
puffed muffins, and you
bring this lufting touch
to the clinic, where cats purr
at your approach and dogs
lick your face with doggy
delight, but most of all
you are yourself, comfortable
in your own skin and self-
effacing to a fault: may the world
light up your life.

IRIS
For Becky

If you were a flower you'd be
a water iris, deep-
rooted, its slender blue
beauty above the silken
surface of a pond: O
daughter, we love your fiery
spirit, your tender heart,
your acts of kindness,
your selfless service,
of which at every passing
hour we grow more fond.

ALLURE
Guelph 1960: For Anne

What I remember most
is the Volkswagon with the
sun-roof eased
open, and you in your lemon-
yellow dress, red
hair a-flair in the autumnal
breeze, your eyes as blue
as the underbelly of the sky:
you coasted up to the curb
where I was waiting, trying
not to look surprised,
and so mesmerized was I
by your allure, I must confess
I wasn't sure whether I loved
you, the car or the dress.

MAPLE
For Kevin

If you were a tree you'd be
a maple with leaves as soft
as flags flying aloft
of Parliament and a grain
as gritty as the sap is supple:
we love your wit and gentle
way with all who come
within your compass,
you are as impish as you are
disarming: may the gods
of graciousness be with you
every golden day.

PUCK
For Jeff

If you were a flower, you'd be
a jack-in-the-pulpit,
your imp's grin tucked
into respectably purple
whorls, you are Shakespeare's
Puck on his lucky day,
your Falstaffian laugh
would make a cat purr:
we love your free spirit,
your Harry Potter panache,
and that you had the good
sense to marry my daughter:
you swallow the world in one
gulp.

LABYRINTHS

My girls gather about
their grandmother like chicks
hedging a hen, creating
crafts she demonstrates
with fingers affixed to arts
learned long ago and now,
hand-in-glove, passed
down during these
amiable afternoons,
when something rather
deeper is dredged up
from the labyrinths of love.

MAGIC

Cameron Lake is a pellucid
blue, and Tom and I
cavort in its chill welcome
like tantalizing tortoises:
now lolling on our plastic
mattresses, now diving
like deft dolphins or orphaned
Orcas, and when we've had
our fill, we lie upon
the sun-saturated sand
and let the wind dry
us benign, certain
that this magical moment
will be everlasting.

COUPLED

Our love is now autumnal
and so it is we summon
up those days
when our love blossomed
like a bride's rose under
a supple sun and we looked
lovingly into the other's eye
for certitude and consolation
(our serendipity Heaven-sent),
and such thoughts, dazed
with delight, keep on
idling us into our age:
coupled and content.

WITHIN

For years too numerous
to mention, we've been a duo,
unsingled when we were young
enough to love without qualm
or question, when our lips
tingled with anticipation,
and now we glide into our age,
becalmed and pleased
at having been, and if
perchance some blip
should startle our luminous love,
we say to one another:
"Open the ears of your heart
and listen to the music within."

PINE
For James

If you were a tree you'd be
a northern pine, stout
and stalwart, steady
in the stiffest breeze:
you put the gentle into gentlemen,
you fly your flags un-
furled, strictly yourself,
and doubtless ready
to ease the pain of others
or be the one to help:
may the gods be with you
as you sally forth into an
unpredictable world.

WHEN I WAKE UP

When I wake up
after my demise, I'll be
surprised to find the world
and its will have moved on
without my approval,
though perhaps a story,
even a poem or two,
will linger in the minds of those
who care enough to plunge
into my plots or un-intricate
a metaphor before Time
expunges them all:
O it's not glory I'm after
in any guise, just a nod
or so from a merciful God
to justify my having been.

HOME
Point Edward: June 2016
For Gene Burdenuk

We navigate the streets
and lanes I trod all
those years ago,
the houses, whose every eave
and ell I know by heart,
leap out at me
whole, as if Time were a temporary
intrusion, and at every corner
a memory stirs, prodded
by the radium of recognition,
the River flats, where I cavorted
with kites, still greet
the world with their gratuitous green,
my grandfather's place,
remains, then as now,
a wide-verandahed
abode, where love abided,
and Mara's lamp, sadly
departed, glows still
in my childhood mind,
and in its honour I write
this poem of home.

WHEN I GO

When I go, do not
grieve me, for I shall leave
this world alive in the eyes
of those who've prized me
and helped me thrive so
long in a place where regret
can cripple without affection
and unfettered love;
I have done everything
I longed to: fathered
children and grandchildren,
found my life's love early
and ever, composed
poems and stories to keep
my patient peers amused,
and practised pedagogical
pentameters on unwitting
high-schoolers, and so
I ask you not to mourn,
for I will not have died:
I'll simply have run out
of words.

INKLING

An inkling is a tingle
in the brain, a sprout abruptly
unbudded, the beginning
of a word or more precisely
its first singing syllable,
enticed towards a phrase,
and then by some urge
to say the unsayable,
the nub of poem just
begun, and compelled
with a single-minded surge
to completion.

THE OTHER

A life unleavened
by love is not worth
living, we spend our days
reaching for reciprocity,
the singular pair of eyes,
lustrous with light,
into which we pour our trust
and all we have to give,
no Heaven can proffer
us more, no
deity teach us
more about our dazed
delight in the other.

WORTHWHILE
For James and Tim

My grandsons long ago
in this photo tease
the front seat of my Ford
Tempo, and their bountiful
smiles at the camera's eye
are at ease in a way only
the young and infinitely innocent
can be, and I regret
all the years that have passed
between then and a miraculous
moment that made my life
worthwhile.

WRITTEN

My words peregrinate
from my pen to the unscathed
page, wringing words
out of the whiteness there,
I let them purr or rage,
give them full rein,
let them sing whatever
song they are smitten with,
for I do not write:
I am written.

GOOD

Adam and Mistress Eve
have taken the fall for tasting
the fruit forbidden and un-
dappling the Garden; Eve
in particular is on the hook
for letting Evil into the world
to tarnish hearth and neighbourhood,
forgetting that half of Eve's
apple was garnished with Good.

BEAVER MEADOW

It comes upon you sudden,
unintimidated by the bush
that hems it in, a sweet
sway of sun-seething
grasses that welcomes you
after a long, fevered trudge
through the splay of branches
and tipped trunks, the place
where peace is more than a
word – bequeathed to us
by the unwitting labour
of the dam-derelict beaver.

CRIES

I hear the muffled cries
of children under the rubble
of Iraq, and I think of
my grandkids safe
and untroubled in a country
that cares, and I think of
my Tom, unruffled
in his crib, blue eyes
smiling back at mine
with infinite innocence,
bibbed and bubbling and gay,
and I wish for him and all
the infants of Iraq that no
harm would ever come
to detonate their day.

FILAMENT

The alabaster page,
unbruised by words,
daring me to propagate
a poem: the first fragile
filament of phrase casts
its shadow, silhouettes,
engages, and begets
itself.

VERACITY

A poem is not a thought,
it is, at first, the inkling
of some meaning in search
of words, still unwrought,
at odds with the world, until
some will distils
the lot and fashions a home
for rhythm and rhyme to peregrinate
into the veracity of verse.

COLT

The colt drops slick
from the mare's womb and greets
the world with a feet-first
jolt, tests his wobbling
legs on the stall's cobbles,
feels some strange
strength flowing there
from his heraldic heart, then
does a little prance
across the room, rehearsing
for the day he will do his pedigree
proud on some far
moon-struck race-
way, cheers aloud
in his ears as he thunders towards
the finishing line, where he takes
his victory dance.

BLUSH

It was just a crush to soften
the summer between seasons,
but desire knows no reason
when a rush of blood hums
near the heart: we circled
our block as often as the world
allows, hands enfolded,
our thoughts lofty, afire
with love's first blush.

SWEET SWING
For Ken Cooper

For twenty-odd years
I watched your sweet swing
with its air-arrowing arc
and frantic follow-through,
and observed with awe the way
you caressed a putt into the
cup, and then the shy
gentleman's grin as our cheers
greeted you: in your heyday
you could make a drive behave
as if it were struck by God
Himself, you could make a golf
ball sing.

AFFIRMED
*After a reading at Mykanos
Restaurant in London, Ontario*

There is a murmuring in the crowd
at Mykonos, all eyes
upon the ageing poet
as he grasps the lectern
and steadies himself under
the bright stage-light,
and, as those in their seats wait
to be wowed, words
drip off the bard's lips
in the sheer shape of poems,
rhymed or not, he reads
with surprising alliterative
ease, then nods at the sudden
outbursts of applause,
at the oohs and ahs in just
the right places, he smiles
a septuagenarian smile
in gratitude at something
significant having been affirmed.

PURVEYOR
For Ian Underhill

You spent a lifetime
purveying poems and stories
to generations of students,
reading aloud with alliterative
ease in your sturdy baritone
until the rhymes chimed
and the consonants collaborated,
until the metaphors stood
up and mentioned their meaning:
you gave them Munro and Purdy,
Atwood and Lawrence,
and all you asked for in return
was their passionate attention
and some small acknowledgement
that teachers, ungloried
as they are, really matter.

SLAKED

I dip my pen into a
lake of ink, stirring
words on the brink
of utterance, slipping towards
thought that cannot quite
be expressed until some trope
offers hope and a poem
creates itself and carries
on till the thirst for
significance is slaked.

WILL
For Colm O'Sullivan
In Memoriam

You die surrounded by your family,
those who loved you best,
you summon up your penultimate
breath to utter the word
goodbye in flawless
Erse, your home-tongue,
as sweet upon the lips
as the haunted hills of Erin,
and I wonder which of the million
thoughts you saved for last,
perhaps some gem culled
from your joust with Joyce, or one
of those that linger long
in the minds of those who still
mourn your passionate passing,
and let it be said of such
a man, present or past,
he went with a will.

HALF

If I could grasp but half
a lifetime, it would be
the years when poetry flowed
with iambic ease and stories
pleased their way onto the page,
their words, like aspens, quivering
with impious import
 upon the immaculate page,
and those I loved surrounded
me with effortless affection
and made the days glow:
no thoughts then
that I was not ageless
and that the poems would never
cease their daffidilian daze.

CAMERON LAKE:
A SUITE OF POEMS

First Choice Books
2018

BEFORE

Cameron was here before
the fish furrowed freely
in its pristine waters,
before the dinosaurs dipped
their three-toed feet
in its shallows, and long before
Adam unsanctified Eden
some crustaceans bid
adieu to their shore and wished
their way lakeward,
grew fins and gulping
gills, and surprised them-
selves by gadding about
as if they had been born
to roam these cobalt dells,
lidless in their element,
happy to be home.

CAMERON LAKE

I was just sixteen
when I first saw
Cameron Lake, a perfect
oval ground out of
Precambrian granite,
as blue as a heron's wing
under a summer sun
that settled in the wavelets
and lingered there lovingly,
and when the night-wind died,
it cast a moonlit sheen,
a leavening light all
the way to my uncle's
cottage, where I was welcomed
as a second son and taught
how to tease black bass
onto the lure and jig
for pickerel, and where among
forests more ancient
than Heaven itself, I became
part of something bigger
than my own being
and more profound.

HEARTS

Our favourite Lake was stocked
with rainbow trout,
so Tom and I hit
the waves like artful
Argonauts as we did a slow
troll from North to South
and then came about
for another pass, our Dare
Devils spinning red
and white in the silt-sifted
belfry below while the
afternoon sun
lay down its languorous
light, unblocked
by the circumnavigating birch
and fir, upon two
tars and all the lunkers
who never bit, but then
nothing mattered except
the meeting of our minds
and the indwelling lilt
of our hearts.

LOOK
Cameron Lake: 1995

Our Lake is as blue as the
underbelly of a right
whale and Tom and I
set out for a little
fishing, a brace of sailors
rowing into the sensuous
sun harmonizing light
on the far horizon, and soon
we get a nibble or two
from below and bring aboard
a tiny trout I quibble
about the size of, wishing
the magic of the morning would last
forever and that look
of love's wonder welling
in Tom's eyes.

HELLO

How many times
have we gone fishing
in the dolphin-blue depths
of Cameron Lake, where the sun
licks lavishly at the algae
blooms below and we peri-
grinate for perch in the weed-
beds where minnows manoeuvre
out of their reach and I watch
the glow in your eyes as your line
jerks and, behold, a big-
mouth bass accelerates
up out of his habitat,
arched like a bent bow,
and you adjust your rig like a pro
and, hauling him in, you smile
and say, "Hello, that's
that!"

DIP

Tom and I dip
our toes into Cameron
Lake, feel its chastening
chill, sense the eons
it took the glacial drag
to scoop out its cratered
canyons, its underwater
hillocks, hastily catch
our breath and plunge in,
lips aquiver but loving
the emphatic cold embrace
of our bodies; pared
down to the nub of our being,
we are part halibut
and part dolphin: we sing
like the Sirens and go the way
the ocean goes.

CYPRUS
For my Uncle Potsy,
In Memoriam

The sun teetered above
the treetops as we motored
to the far end of Cameron
to the familiar creek, the sky
uncluttered by cloud
as we entered the mouth
in utter silence except
for an over-size bull-
frog plopping into the water
from a lily-pad with its little
nosegay of blooms
or grasshoppers vaulting
from ferns and fronds,
and thus we poled the boat:
me on the starboard,
uncle on the lee, our rhythms
synchronized, finding just
enough room for our caressing
craft, and then, at last,
storied Cyprus: pristine,
as blue as a morning glory
in a lash of light, un-
fished by any but we two,
encircled by birch
and spruce in every direction,
and the day passed without
a word to be heard
while we jigged and cast
and reeled in the odd
perch: a smile stealing
between us every hour
or so, strong enough
to seal the bonds of our affection.

BROKEN

I feel safe in the
blue embrace of Cameron,
there is no thrill
like buoyancy: the body riding
the current cruising below,
where gilled fish thrive
in their own element, but I am
at least half piscatory,
my palms fin the self-
erasing waves, my legs
scissor, risking all,
and I sheer stroke for stroke
towards some shore
I cannot see, some
place more abiding,
where I can be broken
alive.

GLIMPSE

After a five-hour
trip we reach the Bruce
and its roller-coaster road,
birch and spruce hovering,
swallowing us alive,
and then we are on the route
inland, a bush-trail
hacked out of these woods
by some mad arborist,
and so we snake our way
through Precambrian shale
and moss-entwined limbs
until at last: Cameron
Lake, glimpsed through a screen
of trees: an adamantine
sheen, a boastful blue
glistening in the afternoon
sun, combed cursive
by a wimpling wind, and there
 is something so
elementally beautiful
about its lucid loneliness
that I feel serene in my bones
that this is home.

AT CAMERON LAKE

Tom and I horse-
playing in the warm waters
of Cameron Lake: me
the wallowing whale and him
porpoise-proud as he cruises
with ineffable ease
through the rippled surface
before he submarines
and tips me topsy-
turvy, glad to be alone
with me in this moment,
and when he laughs out loud
I feel a joy at the nub
of my heart and a love so
consuming it bruises the bone.

POISED

In the Lake's welcoming waters
Tom is as poised as a porpoise;
from the safety of the shore I watch
in awe as he dives delicately
under the shimmering surface
without the whisper of a splash,
and swims with the furious fins
of his out-turned palms
and comes up grinning,
shaking his hair like a
saturated Lab out of
its habitat, and unaware
as he passes me by
of the upwelling affection
in a grandfather's eye.

MARIGOLD
For Anne

Cameron Lake was our magical
place, where the sun bloomed
like a magnified marigold fully
ablaze, where the breeze off
the dimpled water feathered
our cheeks as we lazed on the
porch my uncle built
with his simple carpenter's craft,
and where the rooms were warmed
by woodstove and the aroma
of weathered elm, in which
we tidied away the effortless
afternoons, perusing tomes
comic and tragic, and certain
that this was a home where love
abided.

RED-LETTER

You and I go
fishing for the first time
in Cameron: I row us
to the nearest weed-bed,
and you, without rehearsal
guide the anchor overboard
like a seasoned sailor,
and we drop our lines into the
cobalt blue billows
of our lake, rigged with worms
to tempt the perch wiggling
willowy below and looking
for feed from above, until
your line gives a lurch
and you reel in your prize,
netted like a pro, your grin
as wide as any horizon
and the reason I love our slow
glide through this
red-letter day.

FELICITY

When I was young and curiously
callow, I first laid
eyes upon Cameron,
my uncle's cottage and the birch-
bordered shoreline
hugging the water, bleached
blue by the sun's wilting
wattage, under which
black bass fed
furiously on paralyzed perch
and minnows undulated
in the shallows out of reach,
and we drifted in Cameron's
westering waves like dolphins
in a dream of felicity, and prayed
that this paradisal place
would always be.

MINISCULE

Cameron is a miniscule lake
no longer than a mile
or two, but to a six-
year-old it seems
as horizoning as three Atlantics,
and you swim in its numbing
depths, dreaming of whales
and the sweep of peregrinating
porpoises, while I wait
ashore, my breath inheld
as you deep-dive and vanish
from my vexed view, then
come up grinning
above the Baltic blue
surface: your summoning smile
galvanized by grace,
fuelled by love.

GRINS

Tom and I fishing
once again in Cameron,
trolling for bass through the
sun's lassitude and a breeze
teasing my grandson's
hair: we are linked by our
fellow-feeling for this
lake and its blue solitude,
where finned fish swim
unblinking below
(cumuli cruising above),
and love is snagging a lunker,
reeling it in and trading
grins.

STONE'S THROW

The creek that links Cameron
and Cyprus meanders along
like an adder sodden with sun
slinking through the reeds
and water-lilies floating
flamboyant on the mirrored
surface, and from whose pads
bullfrogs leap
on their tantalizing trapezes
and land with a punctuated plop
in shallows no deeper
than an elf's ankle, and so
it is that we have to pole
ourselves from bend
to bowing bend, soaking
in the morning's saffron glow
and savouring the soul of this
perfected place a stone's
throw from Eden.

DITHYRAM

How would the Greeks have seen
Cameron? A miniature sea
perhaps with Poseidon poised
at ease on the widening waves,
or Apollo making an appearance
with his golden bow and glancing
at his face in the glacial glow,
or Minerva leaning over
the lily pond to bless
the alabaster blooms,
or Zeus himself hurling
his thunder-bolts to stun
the sturgeon, stiffen the minnows,
doom the passive perch
and lift the biggest black
bass out of his element:
before Circe waves her dithyrambic
wand and leaves our lake
intact to us and our own
mythology.

GRACE

Thirty thousand years ago
(while Eve was grappling with the apple)
a great glacier sculpted
this Lake and its countless
cousins, and God sent rain
enough to slake their granite
thirst and they mirrored the sky
with their blossoming blue surface
and deep dells where newborns
finned in colossal numbers,
and I feel privileged
to stand here on Cameron's
shore, Adam's fellow,
exultant, knowing that
for an unlamentable moment
I am in a state of grace.

CERULEAN

This Lake where we swim
like finned ferrules and troll
for bass in the summer's serene
light was gouged out of granite
older than Methusaleh's mother,
carving just for us
this graceful oval
of cerulean blue, rimmed
by birch whiter than a nun's
wimple, spritely spruce
rimpling the shallows of the curved
shoreline, and the odd
stunted pine, lucid
in its loneliness, and I have a
passion for this hallowed
place and all its denizens,
gilled and otherwise,
and shall continue to do so
as long as the gods will it.

PRIDE

What would it be like
to be a lunker? Hunkering
in the blue vestibules of Cameron
Lake? No thirst
to slake, whose lidless
eyes, unblinking
in the slanting light from above,
seek out their prey,
some undersized
perch paralyzed by the sight
of your vise-wise jaws,
or a sunfish for lunch,
and you cruise like a taut
torpedo, ungoverned
by gravity, unloved
in your lonely kingdom,
until the day you essay
to gobble a Williams Wobbler,
and find yourself linked
to my Uncle's rod, then
thrashing and boneless,
bereft of pride, in the bottom
of a boat no god
of the water would abide.

PATIENT
For Anne

Tom and I spend
half a day fishing
on Cameron, baffled
by bass, spurned by even
the lowly perch, and so
it is a day of lassitude,
savouring the sun, and when
we putt up to Potsy's
dock, you are waiting,
as patient as Penelope,
your eyes alight with love
and hopefulness, your smile
as wide as any horizon.

ELEMENT

Tom and I fishing
in Cameron: me wishing
something marine
would tease our squirming worms,
when a lurch on Tom's line
is no perch, and seconds
later a mammoth bass
arches out of its element
into an echelon of air,
bent like a rarefied rainbow,
tail thrashing and slack-
jawed on the bait, its eyes,
as lidless as a singed arsonist,
espying the boat and its tormentors,
before plunging back
into its blue desmene
and, as spent as a parson's purse,
lets us ease him aboard,
his great heart unhinged.

UNIVERSE

I wake and the world widens,
and just beyond the morning
dews the Lake swims
into view like a slow fuse,
so blue it would blind Zeus
or make Oedipus blink,
and a breeze quickens to wimple
the waves swallowing each
other and licking the silence
of the shore, and I reach the water's
edge and immerse one
simple toe in Cameron's
granite chill, feel
the immanent will of the Universe,
inked and abiding.

SERENDIPITOUS

Trolling for bass on Cameron,
but the lake is no shakes as a
fishing ground: perch
and sunfish abound
(while the lunkers keep to themselves)
bringing joy to a neophyte
angler: my worm-squirming
line cast into the deep-
delved, utter below,
praying for a nibble or an unctuous
bite, happy to be here
with the uncle I love under a
serendipitous sun
and nary a mutter or a querying
quibble.

CATCH

After a full day
angling for perch in Cameron
and then cleaning our catch,
Potsy and I fall
asleep in the sofa chairs
of the cottage and dream of bass
bourgeoning in their thousands,
hungry for hooks, surprised
by our beguiling lures,
and surging so urgently
that the surface above
is furrowed pure under
a gleaming sun, and when
at last we wake into the evening
redeemed, both of us
ar smiling: love in our eyes.

CYPRUS LAKE: 1951

There is no loneliness
like this lake, hedged
by cedars, birch and spruce
older than Adam's rib;
a lurch of wind induces
ripples on the silvering surface
that do not disturb the dark
deep where fish live
in soundless serenity,
and wavelets lick the stone
ledge where I stand
waiting for that first
word to propagate a poem
and set my bones aquiver.

ELEMENT

I remember your first dip
into Cameron's shallows,
a tentative toe followed
by a slow progression until
your body was bottled in the Lake's
blue grip, and chest-deep,
without a by your leave,
you dive like a delighted dolphin
into the morning's supple light
and I breathe out again,
recalling with a sentimental
nod my own baptismal
plunge, and happy to see you
coupled by something
elemental, something
the Earth gave birth to
before it was born.

SOLACE

Everyone has a place
they go to, seeking
the solace of solitude:
it may be as simple as a
rocker on the side verandah,
but for me it was Cameron
Lake, whose waters were the
hue of a bluebird's
breeze-brushed wing,
with a cottage mirrored in its
undimpled surface,
and ringed by birches leaking
sunshine into a sky
as high and wide and deep
as the hushed horizon
my analogical eye perceived
just before the easing
of sleep.

CARNIVORE

The odd time I've netted
a black bass in Cameron
I've wondered what it would be
like being a lunker, embodied
by water, unhorizoned
with eyes that do not
blink, even in sleep,
massively jawed to seize
each passing prey,
with no voice to converse
or utter pain or pleasure,
finned and gilled, perfectly
settled in this translucent
universe (no bigger
than a tarn), in which you are
both carnivore and god.

LUNKER

My Dad called a big fish
a "lunker," not knowing
that no decent dictionary
would touch the term, but don't
tell that to the massive black
bass thrashing on the end
of my line and lifting out of
Cameron like Lazarus on
"uppers,' hanging on a razor's
edge of air for one
momentous second before
plunging gamely back
into the undulant swell,
caring not that its name
might be nothing more
than anglers' slang my Dad
used and passed on
to his firstborn son.

BIG ENOUGH

Tom and I play
a home-made game
I called "Lunker," as we
roll the dice and try
for the winning prize, but out
on Cameron Lake there is
nothing tame about our quest
for something worth
trolling for, a bass with teeth
like a vise and jaws a shark
would die for, hunkering
down in the weeds and big
enough to make Tom's
eyes horizon.

RAINBOW

One summer the Government
stocked Cameron with rain-
bow trout and the black
bass said "Thank you,"
as did the odd oversize
perch, but a few managed
to cruise to adulthood,
and, with luck, stood
up for us out of the water,
doing their hula-dance
before our surprised eyes
in a paradise of hues,
and delighting us as much
as being strummed by the sun
or struck by starlight.

FISHER

Only once did we find
ourselves in a feeding
frenzy on Cameron:
after an hour without
a nibble, rain began
to stipple the surface
and the fish started to bite
like barracuda on our worm-
curled bait, and soon
the bottom of our boat was paved
with squirming perch, their bellies
whiter than gouda, and suddenly
the sky turned blue
again, as insurgent breezes
played cadenzas on the rippled
waves, and oddly I thought
of Poseidon, god of the sea
and that other fisher, of men,
who combed the shores of Galilee.

BOREDOM

There is nothing as laborious
as jigging for pickerel on Cameron,
our gear rigged out with one
earthworm and a jazzy
spinner, and we drift north
to south and do it again
across the woven weeds
below, relished by our slow-
paced prey, resigned
to the unpunctuated pull
of a hooked specimen, no
bigger than a humble "sunnie,"
when we yearned for the thrusting
thrash of a black bass,
but not even the fishing gods
could grant that wish or other-
wise embellish our boredom.

ANGLER

I still recall the afternoon
when Potsy and I were fishing
in Cameron's southern cove,
braving a soft rain
that obscured the daytime
moon, and hauling in
droves of perch, so
many in fact that we ran
out of worms and had to dangle
pieces of our catch for bait,
and so massed were they
in their dense domain that our sinkers
barely touched the bottom
of their immensity as we wished our way
towards thirty-odd
specimens, and we knew then
that somewhere in his lofty
church God loved
an angler.

HOLY

Tom and I dip our toes
into Cameron's shallows
precisely where the Attawandaron
scoured these shores
for clams and craw-fish
and savoured the morning sun
hefted a world or so
above the eastern horizon,
and when we dive in,
breaking an unflawed
seam of the surface, we can feel
the ghostly ripples of those
below who hallowed this
holy ground before
God dreamed Adam.

TROLLING

Trolling for trout on Cameron,
the desultory drone of the out-
board, the rod jigging
with every wriggle of the lure
fathoms below where the rain-
bow swerve pure in their
docile domain, while over-
head the sun sits
above the bone-white
birch like a dazzled doubloon,
shadows shimmering like
moonlight on a lake's
face, as we wait for the lurch
on our line and come about
to claim our prize, with a nod
to the benevolent gods
who consecrated this place
with their cosmic caroling.

HOME GROUND

Hidden Brook Press
2018

BLACK LAKE
After a painting by Gerald Parker

One alabaster moon
was not enough lustrous
light to lavish on Black
Lake's unruffled,
silvered surface, so you
added a ravishing red
dot above the very
spot where a pair of loons
ululated on the cusp of lust
and the little stream feeding
filigree never slackened
its pace, and just to subvert
the scene you drew a sunny
butterfly fluttering
on monogrammed wings
over the outcrop
where we stopped to wonder
if this was all a dream.

BALLAST

I was born in Sarnia (alas)
but was soon rooted fast
in the groomed ground of the Point,
safe in the grasp of Grand-
father's lawn, as green
as grass rinsed by rain,
I knew every eave and ell,
every sill and gable,
and I roamed the alleys and by-
ways in search of the me
I ought to be, seeing
with my enviable eye: the River
Flats where our kites flew
like swift-swooping swallows,
the River throbbing like a
struck vein, the Lake
as blue as blue-jay's
bobbing wing, Canatara
where the sand sang in the sun
and thunder rang over
its dune-dense immensity,
the elm-shade as big as a
behemoth's bellyful of umbrellas
and the pine-cones we flung
like gratuitous grenades in our joy
at being here, at knowing
this place lay deep
in the ballast of our bones.

COCHISE

Whenever my fourth line
friends and I played
cowboys and Indians,
I fought to be the Comanche
with my willowed bow and arrow
and rooster's feather clipped
to my cap (the wild child
inside me aching
to get out), and if
the script demanded it,
I would fake a cinematic
demise, break a territorial
treaty or ululate
against all things
east, and I wonder now
whether those poems
I prized about our home-
grown aboriginals (boosting
them into public view)
had their beginning in those
days when I first essayed
Geronimo or Cochise.

MOON OVER MONK

The moon over Monk Street
sits above the horizon
like a serene replica
of Mara's lamp, each
mellowing its light along
the sacred place where we play
our gently gendered games
in embossed luminosity,
like miller-moths thrilled
to be illumed and shadow-
free: we think of Artemis
and her Grecian bow, bent
wise and unneutered
by the night.

MATCH

The Reverend Bell came home
one afternoon, flung
his cellar door wide
and, though less than wise,
lit a match: we found him
sitting in a singed patch
of his grass: surprised,
a touch unhinged,
and wondering how such
things come to pass
and whether God was on
his side.

WIZ
For Dave Withers
In Memoriam

If the good die young,
you were its poster-child,
mowed down in your prime,
and you, my boyhood
chum whom we dubbed "Wiz",
were our guide and idol, whose
hands badgered, out of thin
air, gadgets and gizmos
of every ilk, and wood
worked as soothing as silk:
you kept us amused,
and we boasted of just
knowing you, and I wished
you a long and beguiling life,
humming with joy and the fruits
of your wide and wild imagination.

APOSTASY

My grandmother baked
pies on Sunday mornings
(cherry and rhubarb
in season, raisin for my
Grandpa's bucket), an echo
away from the Anglican nave
and apse she had no
reason to give the nod
of approval to nor taste
its soothing pieties, for she put
all of her love and out-
sized ardor into the gentle
kneading of her dough and braving
the wrath of a hairy-jawed
God, while we feasted
on her pastries and praised the Lord

OUR SIDE

My uncle's best and abiding
friend was Ernie Rosenbloom,
and we spent many an early
evening together on Cameron
Lake with a new moon
looming, angling for perch
and the odd large-mouth,
but no one told me
that Ernie had been super-
intendent of the Foundry,
where, at his urging, a gang
of goons with massive bats
broke up a sit-down
strike with soundless fury
and not a twinge of regret,
and sent the Polacks surging
towards their ramshackle
homes, burned to the ground:
instead, I watched Ernie
unhinge the hooks from a doomed
bass's jaw as tenderly
as a grandpa dangling
a tot, and I thought then
that God was always on our
side.

RARE

On rare occasions my grand-
father would march us
to Canatara beach, and while
he squatted alone on the sand
in his Sunday suit, Bob
and I paddled apace in the
fluted shallows, and feeling
perfectly safe in his hands,
we ventured up to our waists
and even dove under
like daring dolphins, while Grandpa
smiled at us and we smiled
back at him: it was only
later we learned that he couldn't
swim.

HELM

I might have been five
when I first wandered into
my grandfather's work-
shop, and watched the hands
I loved guide a lozenge
of elm or oak through the burr
and bite of the band-saw,
a particle of the puzzle he was perfecting
piece by filigreed piece,
and I nuzzled in closer,
waiting, in my need, for the pause
that preceded the unspoken
tousling of my cowlick,
and knowing I would be cherished
and thrive here with this
man at the helm.

CHUMS

Nancy and I were chums,
playing our garrulous games,
gender-free, in Withers
field, festooned with sun-
light in the long summer
afternoons or under
Mara's lamp in the usurping
dark of Monck Street,
superintended by a marinating
moon—until the day
I took a fancy to her burgeoning
beauty and felt my heart
hum and a voice inside
singing Olly, Olly
en-fray.

ABIDE

My Uncle Potsy and I
go hunting cottontail
in a sun-stunned meadow,
and, if we are lucky, spot
a jackrabbit anteloping
speed in an open field,
but there is this day
no game to be got,
but all I need is striding
side by side with my uncle,
our guns as silent as the thoughts
we share, with a love that abides

BULLY

Six-year-old
Susan Coote liked
to ride her trike around
our block, passing my house
en route, and one day
I simply stood my ground,
grasped the handle-bars
and pulled the baffled girl
aside, and I still remember
that infantile incident
and wonder why I became
something I was not:
a bully.

NUMB

Coop and I at Canatara,
nude in the change-room,
our young sprouts at attention
as we spot a spy-hole
(hopes a-bloom despite
our doubts) and press ourselves
numb to catch someone
gendered other than us
easing off her one-
piece and showing her un-
mentionable to our prying
eyes, when suddenly
the prize is blotted out
by a well-placed thumb,
without so much
as an if you please.

DARK

When Leckie's field iced
over after a thaw
and quick freeze, we skated
on glazed meadows
where once clover bloomed,
wild mustard throve
and larks buffeted the air –
as if the globe had hewn
one raw rink
where we left in our wake
filigreed meridians,
mittened our hands in gendered
pairs, and unmuffled
our carnal cries – two
abreast lest we fall
off the world: amazing
the moon as we moved through
the lustrous rendering
of its light towards the star-
flecked obsidian dark.

TYPICAL

On a typical July day
with cumulus clouds caressing
the high sky over
Canatara, an unplugged
sun, and a southerly breeze
dusting the dunes dulcet,
we cast an eye towards
the languid-lipped beauties
sanctifying the sand,
and in the lull between waves
we defy the Lord and his blessings
by turning our thoughts to the
luxuries of lust.

TOWARDS THE LIGHT

Nightfall along Monk
Street, Mara's lamp
tossing its amber glow
against the dread of darkness
beyond, we hover
round its blossoming beam
like moths fanning a flame,
and only when the game begins
do we test the inked shadow
where we hide like prey
pursued until the oley
oley en free
releases us, knowing
full well that, like
every living thing,
we all grow towards
the light.

RIBSY

We called him Ribsy in gentle
mockery of his mange-ridden
coat and skeletal stare,
this stranger stray
who arrived each day
at noon on the dot to win
dibs on our crusts or the odd
scrap of bologna as we basked
in the autumnal sun on the
school steps, and once
in a while one of the girls
would essay a wary pat
and the grateful dog would wag
a tail or two or give out
a rheumy-eyed grin,
but when the snows came in,
lock, stock and barrel,
Ribsy passed us by,
and we wondered if even
God had taken pity on him
or whether he found a warm
spot to die.

PLEASURE

I loved the way the girls
of Canatara lay
their beautiful bodies
belly-down on the hot
sand in long-legged
leisure, and let the sun's
fire play bare-backed
wherever it would,
and I liked to think they
were begging to be perused
by those of us too shy
to stare (our bravado soon
jellied), who welcomed
the Lake's chill upon
our thigh-high desires,
infused still with prurient
pleasure.

VAIN

In a vain attempt to bond
my Dad took me
and his thirty-ought-six
to a nearby farm where the gun's
elephantine report
would not disturb the neighbours,
and instructed me on how to be
a rifleman: I pressed
the butt against my shoulder,
aimed at the next tree,
pulled the trigger and found
myself on my own butt,
stunned and flat on my fanny,
the tree unharmed,
and it dawned on me then
that bonding was no trifling
matter.

BIRTHDAY

When, as a boy, I lay
in Sarnia General with a temperature
of a hundred and four
and the nurses poured sulfa
drugs into the midst of my fever,
I thought only of the pain
engulfing me, and when
I awoke next morning
sweatless, I wondered if I had
a date with the future or any
say in its slow unfolding,
but the story told itself,
the tale of a life lived
with little regret, way-
laid by joy and surprised
to be turning eighty.

TWO FOR GRACE LECKIE

WRAITH

You were a face in my dreams,
a blue-eyed wraith
apostrophized by a pair of
pigtails, with a smile
that would have set the sun's
beaming afire, and when
I am wakened, abrupt as a blink,
you are as far away
as an archipelago of stars,
and I must do with
two rows over
in a callow country school
bereft of your budding grace:
faithful as ever to the march
of my blood's desire.

AFAR

Romeo had a balcony between
him and juvenile Juliet
and I too loved
from afar: two rows
over where I could see
you luminous in the lickerish light
of the school windows, your perfect
profile leaving me to fret
while you dallied and beguiled
or squeezed a glancing eye
in my direction, your smile
a gift I would remember
romancing all the way
home.

TWO FOR MRS. BRAY

MAGICAL

Mrs. Bray's magical
house floated on flowers,
doused to the sills with bloom,
and we watched her dote on her
groomed garden, arrayed
in roses and poppies and rimmed
by hollyhocks with only
the brim of her floppy hat
showing, and we thought of the
shock of widowhood,
which she bore like a badge.

PHALANX

When Granny Reeve died,
I remember the golden
gladioli from Mrs. Bray's
groomed garden and a casket
buried in bloom from her pied
bower, which seemed to ease
our grieving, and I thought
of Granny being carried
to Heaven on a phalanx
of flowers.

PRAYER

"If I should die before
I wake, I pray the Lord
my soul to take" was my nightly
prayer when I still believed,
when Heaven still had heft
and God did not deceive
in one of his many disguises,
but when I am gone,
I'll be remembered in the loving
eyes of my children and grand-
children, and when they too
have passed and what is left
of the measure of their memory,
perhaps I'll still have a word
or two to say in the pith
of a poem or the startle of a story,
as long as there are ravenous
readers to treasure them:
perhaps the world will not
forsake me after all,
if I should die before
I wake.

SOME WORDS

I remember my grandmother
whispering, "He died of a stroke,
poor man," and instantly
I conjured hammer blows
cracking a skull as the victim
gasped his last breath,
his loved ones keening,
but then I had another
thought: perhaps it was a tender
thumb caressing the flesh
to death: some words
say more than their meaning

URGE

When I began to scribble
poems and stories at the age
of twelve, I had to delve
into my daylight dreams,
where the point of all plots
and the insurgencies of rhythms
lay waiting to be beamed
abroad beside those
images I liberated
from my impious imagination:
the motive for metaphor runs
deep: we are steeped in the
simple home-truths
of our youth and the unstoppable
urge to write.

STILL

How many times was I
awakened by your lyrical babble
just down the hallway,
how many Sunday mornings
did we spend dabbling
in Duplo, in the playroom
we built for the two of us,
how many hours did we spend
fishing in Cameron and its blue
brilliance? How many days
did we spend on holidays
in far-off places
like quaint Quebec or Ottawa,
mottled by museums: you
were a gift from a compassionate
god, our dearest wish
come true: you were always
aloft in our thoughts, and still
are.

HELLO, DONALD

At the Point's sesquicentennial
celebration, I found
my Aunt Betty, looking
very much her age (after
an absence of three years)
in the crowd watching the town's
new fire engine
breeze by in a blaze
of scarlet: "He's over in the fire
hall looking at old
photos," she said, so I crossed
the street and entered the fire
station, where, at rows
of long tables, a crush
was peering at vintage snaps;
I squeezed in beside an elderly
gentleman, his eyes
on the memorabilia in front
of him: somewhat tall,
a little stooped but one
who had once been an athlete;
it was then that my Uncle Potsy
turned to me and said:
"Hello, Donald."

PART TWO

IN THE NOW

ENDUED
For Anne

When you pulled up
in that brand-new
Volkswagon with the sun
roof, my heartbeat
abrupted, as the girl with the
clementine curls, a smile
festooned with freckles and a
glance that rhymed with romance
stepped into the autumnal light
in her lemon-yellow dress
and I was smitten breathless,
bitten by love's bite,
and needed no proof
for my endued delight or
my sublime obsession.

STUN

In your lemon-yellow dress
you stun the sun and the
fellow gazing at you
debouching from your Volks-
mobile unfazed
and effortless in your element,
and I fell in love with those
irradiant eyes just
for the fun of it, I must
confess, knowing my heart
could feel no other
wise and hoping some
day you would return
the favour, vouchsafing
our mutual union.

WALKING THE ICE

I wonder what it's like
to come to the edge of everything,
to walk out on a ledge
of ice with only the bare
blue of the frigid lake
to greet you, a decision
to be made in the nick
of a second, voices urging
"Do it!" and all those
dark trickling days
behind, surging one
farther into the darkness that refuses
to let go? Before
some wee instinct
inside, a voice not otherwise
heard announces the fight
to be, that there is
enough light to slake
the thirst for something
final and other: a living
on, a giving in to life's
uncalamitous cycle,
a carrying on, distinct
and true

ETCHED

In this birthday drawing
by Tom (which has pride
of place in my study): the two
of us angling for "Rockies"
or any other piscatory poacher
tempted to broach our bait,
and sitting in my uncle's boat
with our lines dangling over
the side in the weeds Tom
has scrawled in bold green
strokes, and I am distinguished
by a folksy black beard,
while my grandson
guides the motor he has sketched
with admirable accuracy,
and above it all three-
storied brown clouds
and an orange sun blooming
like a Christmas chrysanthemum,
etched with love

EXUBERANCE
For Bruce Ashdown: In Memoriam

Everything you did was out-
size, you galvanized gumption,
you put the imp in impish,
you spun yarns about
the track and all its magical
mystique like a riffling raconteur,
welcomed with a nod and a wink,
you could scan a racing form
like a blind man brushing
braille, you struck a racquetball
as if it were Hitler's head,
your golf stroke was a whiff
and two slashes, you manoeuvred
your skiff with sails set
as close to the wind as audacity
allows, your hand on the tiller
as supple as a lover's touch,
you had a heart as big as a
thoroughbred's, the blood-
lines you admired more than
the life you lived with such
endued exuberance.

SYLLABLES
For John B. Lee

We started a conversation
about poems and their making,
about the inheld breath
before we say the syllables
to ourselves and dream
them onto the page,
willing some meaning
that seems beyond knowing,
some home-truth
that needs no proof
to startle the world we build
together in a friendship
welded by words.

REMEMBRANCE
For My Grandfather, In Loving Memory

Did you hear the sonorous
soaring of the Last Post
over your country's memorial,
the bugle singing as sadly
sweet as Gabriel's music
commemorating the brave in their
quiet graves, or the roaring
of the jets in salubrious salute?
Did you, my gloried grandfather,
come awake at such
concatenation, recall
your days doleful in that
far-away war?
No longer feel forsaken
by the souls you fought so
valiantly to save? Be
assured, we will remember,
though Time itself flies,
until the Earth un-
endures and the sun dies.

BITE

Being a loner himself,
it never occurred to God
that Adam might be lonely,
but seeing it so
He created woman to be
his constant companion, and made
her curves and contours
as pleasing as possible, for there
was the issue of issue, should
the need arise, for even
the flowers had bees to buzz
from pod to pistil like
helicopters on helium and each
ripened apple dropped its seed
into the dappled shade below,
and thus all was well
and the cherubim wished Him
Godspeed, until Eve,
to spite her Maker, took
one blistering bite.

MYRRH
Christmas 2017

When Gabriel's horn awakened
shepherds on the high hills
above Bethlehem, they hearkened
to the Heavenly news and followed
it under a star-stippled
sky to the stable where the Babe
lay lovingly in a manger's
hay, feeling blessed
to be born, while further
East, Magi, forsaking all,
moved mountains to bring
Him frankincense and myrrh,
while lambs purred in animal
amazement and cattle lowed,
stunned in their stanchions, and far
away the Earth lurched
an inch towards Eternity.

PINCERS

My Dad on skates: as quick
as Rocket Richard with the grace
of Gordie Howe, he skimmed
the ice with nary a pause
for the applause that rocked
against the rafters,
he stick-handled with the ease
and breakaway speed
of a whirling dervish,
and with a pride that brimmed
beyond the rink, un-
furled against the world:
I worshipped his every
magical move, but me:
my blades sagged ankleward,
and all I had to offer
as penance were my ink-stiff
stanzas and stilted stories,
but, even though
I knew my failure rankled,
I was sure that someday
since he left me bereft
I would capture that gifted glory
in the pincers of a poem.

CUPPA

Ever since whenever
Anne and Claire have met
for coffee and innocent
chatter: the forgivable
foibles of friends and neighbours,
the pettiness of politicians,
the puffery of princes,
the entitlements of the rich
and privileged few, world
events that really matter –
all wrapped up
in a cuppa or two: the kind
of ritual that keeps the conversation
going, pertinent and prime,
that makes our collaborations
civil, and seals friendship
for a lifetime.

MOTHER

My mother lacked the maternal
touch, but she made up
for it by trying harder:
she had my baby photo
tinted and formally framed
(I keep it proudly on the wall),
I remember picnics in Canatara,
the seven months she nursed
me through rheumatic fever
without a hint of complaint,
and trips to Clyde Beatty's
Circus, where she clapped
louder than the lions, she played
rap rummy like a pro,
and I can see her on hands
and knees scrubbing the kitchen
floor or hear her listening
to "I Love a Mystery"
on the radio: she's been dead
these forty-five
long years, but my memory
of her is still radiant.

BALTIMORE

In the tallest tree an oriole
trills in the morning with a
song like the low, throaty
notes of a diva aereating
her aria, and I strain to see
that black and orange blur
brush the breeze (its black
inkier than onyx and orange
that would shame a day-lily),
and when he deigns to visit
our feeder and sift our sugar
syrup, we feel the thrum
of the natural world in all
its humbling glory, and in the
hush of evening we hearken
to the Baltimores saying
goodnight to each
other with a final chee-
cheer-up.

SIZZLE
For Tom

And so here we are
once again talking
books on a June afternoon:
under your gentle questioning
and encouraging looks
I probe the private precincts
of my memory for details
about my pentameters and plots
with forays into family
stories I share for the first
time: of long lost
grandfathers and a forgotten
war and killing ground
where no birds trilled,
and we are drawn to one
another in the succinct silences
of our caring conversation
by the sizzling wizardry
of words.

SNEEZE

Penning poems can be
a bit of a tight-rope
trick: words balanced
on the brink of meaning,
import that must be
teased out syllable
by syllable before they ink
the page with their passionate
purpose: composing is a
high-wire trapeze
act (nothing to be
sneezed at.)

A BLIND MAN BUILDS A HOUSE
For Stan Burfield

Remembering the hours spent
tinkering with Leggo blocks,
the way they welded together
with a satisfying tug,
and you thumbing the tumbled
shapes they made, and then
there was your neighbour's
doll-house, feathering
your fingertips over
its ells and angles, its pitched
gables, its rain-proof
windows, and so it was
you had the basics of a
blueprint and ventured
to build a house of your devising:
bricks laid side
by side, levelled by touch,
recall and the inner eyes
of your imagination, until
your pulsing digits went numb,
with the roof still looming
above you, now alone
with your pride in a vast vacancy
you couldn't fathom even in your
monochromatic dreams –
the last challenge, whose triangular
contours you sensed like embers
in the memory-bank of your mind,
but you were merely blind
enough to find a way
to hammer out a home
you could call your own.

JOY

And me lugging a film
and audiotape from school
to school like a failed door-
to-door salesman
making his pitch, practicing
his ploy – hoping to prompt
verse out of twelve-year-
olds, peering out
at me and my equipment
with eyes lit up
with an innocence I envy,
and when the film stops,
there is a subtle moment
of silence before the pens
start scratching and I breathe
again as one boy
plugs away at his maiden
poem, hatched from something
itching inside, where words
and joy collide.

SINISTER

My Uncle Tom and I
swung from the sinister side
and patrolled the Thames Valley
fairways in tight tandem,
and while I irritated my irons
with random rambunctions,
his wedge struck his ball
aloft and we watched it
in feathered flight as it
gravitated to the green and, with a
blissful bounce, nestled
there: now golf is a
companionable game of crisp
clicks and sun-softened
putts, and all was well
until the day Tom took
up tennis and forgot he was
fifty-eight: his heart
split like a Christmas walnut.

BOOST

My mother's Dad may
have been third generation
Canadian, but he was Irish
to the bone, and no sheep
herder he, but a master
craftsman, a calligrapher
in wood and stone, who dandled
me, September's child,
on his good knee and boosted
me high in his carpenter's
arms, his wild days
long past (without,
I'm told, reneging an ounce
of Gaelic charm), until
that terrible June day
when he was thoughtlessly
murdered, alone in the
moonlight above a
bootlegger's roost,
and so it was that he
became the grandfather
I never got to know
or love.

GAY
For my Brother, in Memoriam

The signs were there from the beginning:
you favoured the girl's games
of hopscotch and Double
Dutch and the company of their
velvet voices, their tendrill'd
touch, you eschewed the rough
and tumble of rugby or shinny
on Foster's pond or innings
in Withers' field, you were fond
of Garry with his effeminate
flutter and the two of you
played dress-up
in Gran's cast-offs
with fancy bonnets and spiked
heels (I can still hear
their stiff stutter on our
neighbourhood walk),
and I can't imagine the pain
you must have felt holding
inside some truth
you only half understood
and did not date to utter –
O how you must have longed
to be the being you were meant
to be, while I stood by,
thinking only of me,
complacent in my ignorance.

TOGETHER

In this photo, my mother
and father, standing tall
on my grandfather's lawn
in the their Sunday suits,
hold me up high
between them for the camera's
loving eye, like a prized
doll for all the world
to see, their hands tethered
to steady me on my maiden
shoot, as happy as they
will ever be, and I still
regret I wasn't enough
to keep them together.

MIGRAINE

It must be like the pain
Cain felt when the brand
struck his brow, there is
something biblical
about it: our very veins
bludgeoned with blood ex-
ploding in the brain and behind
the throbbing eyes, as if the body
were gripped whole by a vise,
and it even hurts to think,
as we do about Christ rendered
mute on His anguished cross
or Samson at Gaza pulling
down with his bare hands
the pagan temple to ease
the ache no heavenly
supplication can emend.

TOGETHER

In this photo, my mother
and father, standing tall
on my grandfather's lawn
in the their Sunday suits,
hold me up high
between them for the camera's
loving eye, like a prized
doll for all the world
to see, their hands tethered
to steady me on my maiden
shoot, as happy as they
will ever be, and I still
regret I wasn't enough
to keep them together.

THE MEEK
Good Friday: 2017

Today is like any other
except for the sorrow in the
air as that image
of bleak Golgotha rises
unhallowed in the mind:
two thieves and a rebel
mystic pinioned on crosses,
seared by a galvanizing sun,
their sweat swept aside
by the galling winds, while
weeping mothers pray
for quick death, and one
of the crucified, almost
bereft of breath, gives
birth to a final cry:
"O Lord, how can it be
that the meek shall inherit
the Earth?".

DANCER
For Katie

You float across the stage
as light as a breeze breathing
on a feather, your limbs
lissoming fanciful
filigrees as graceful
as a swan silvering a silken
pond, your tapered toe
tethered to the floor, on which
you twirl and pose prettily:
I am your grandfather,
and you a girl of whom
I am particularly fond:
for me you are both
the dancer and the dance.

MARINERS
For Bruce Ashdown, In Memoriam

We set sail for Chantry,
tacking all the way
against a southerly breeze:
you at the tiller guiding
us tactfully with the ease
of a sea-going skipper,
while we, the crew, provide
the necessary ballast,
and when at last we reach
that fabled isle, you cry,
"At least we'll ride the wind
home," but when the sun
purples in the west, the wind
slackens and dies, so that
skipper, crew and the un-
buffeted boat, fore,
aft and bow, have to be
paddled and purred north-
ward to French Bay,
where the wives applaud
such paralyzing prowess,
safe on the luff-free
shore.

THURSDAY
For Ken Cooper

Every Thursday for more
years than we wish to count,
we gathered with our gang at
Hickory Ridge and scrambled
our way around its measured
meadows: I see you still
with your sawed-off swing
and a ball-flight that sang
in the buoyant breeze, while I
whittled and walloped,
happy to amble among
such cheerful companions
and to treasure the memories
that bridge the gap between
then and the seasons to come.

HEROIC

All I have left of my father
is this plaque from the
Cosy Café for some
long-forgotten feat,
but it is enough to set
me imagining my Dad
on skates with stride-strong
strokes as smooth as a
swan flows over
the perfect parabola of a pond,
or like some winged Icarus
seducing the sun, the rink
his royal residence, while
townsfolk cheer
his every dipsy-doodle
deke and dodge, his heroic
brio, and I wonder now
if he dreamed me fondly
amid all the hullabaloo,
and did he know it would take
a war and thirty years
drink to keep us apart
and leave me heart-bereft.

MUTUAL

My grandson and I
go manoeuvring down
memory lane: me
to the village that gave me
verve and volume to beam
my voice abroad, Tom
to the place he pictured
from an overdose of my poems
and stories; I point with pride
to this dream-haunted house
or that side street
where one of my creations might have
wandered through my fervid
prose, or to Mara's lamp,
where Nancy first took
my fancy or Foster's pond
where we fleeted on blades over ice
or Withers' field where our games
began and the world ended:
Tom and I cherish this
chance to bond, sharing
these defining moments
when our mutual imaginations
meet and intertwine..

MAN OF PARTS
For John Ogletree

It must be nice to be
at home in your own skin,
even when the body it suffers
occasionally betrays it:
you are a scion of science
who travelled the world just
to see what it had to say,
an aficionado of the outdoors,
of bird-breathing fields
and trunkless tundra mirroring
the sky's aqua look,
you took up golf at sixty
and struck the ball as if
it mattered, you tell a droll
tale with an twinkling eye,
you put the friend in friendly,
you are a patron of the arts,
of poetry inked in love
and pied plays: suffice
it to say you are a man
of parts no poem
can fully extol.

NEXT

I wish with all my might
there was a Heaven, a palatial
place where I might greet
all those who have allowed
Death to inconvenience
their lives, and where we would thank
the Lord for having had
the good sense to save
our breath for the right religion
and to have avoided six
of the Seven Deadly Sins
and find our grace in God's
sanctified text:
and when our smiles have faded,
we, unjaded,
will wonder what to do
next.

MY TURN

Whenever I think of death,
I take a deep breath
and congratulate myself
on being alive, ever
since that day
long ago when I wished
my way out of the womb and uttered
my first articulate cry
and wondered how many
had come before me
in humanity's slow bloom
all the way back to the
great apes and their generous
genes and the dinosaurs who groomed
the ancient foliage of the Earth
and finally the fish-churned
sea where something
grew anew, a birth
with no antecedent,
a blip in God's thought,
and here I am against
the odds still living,
waiting patiently for my turn.
a blip in God's thought,
and here I am against
the odds still living,
waiting patiently for my turn.

BENCH
For Doug McConnell, In Memoriam

When one of our own is wrenched
suddenly from us, we do
our best to memorialize
him in poem or song
or a simple dedicated
bench on the course where his out-
size drives seasoned
the air above its manicured
meadows and all his putts
dimpled the cup: whenever
we sit there now
to reflect in the unqualified
quiet on the reasons why,
a little bit of Doug
resides beside us.

VOICE
For George Martell

A voice on the phone: warm,
inspiring confidence,
urging me to begin
our friendly intellectual
chatter: the left view
your humane choice, me
slightly on the right, we feed
at the marketplace of ideas
in the comfort of companionship;
I can't believe you've agreed
to go, leaving me alone
with my scattered thoughts, grieving
for a man who's lived his life
as if it mattered.

PROUD
For Tom

We've always been proud of you:
even as a toddler you showed
us your sweet temperament,
and as a lad you gentled horses
at Circle-R and led
your charges with devotion
and esprit de corps, and we
remember the mirth you brought
us on the teen-age stage
and how you let your eyes
seek pleasure in the world
of books and the treasury
of their poems and stories, and what
a vet you've been, the embodiment
of courage and care and wise
beyond your years: let
the all-seeing Earth
entreat your belonging
and shout out loud
its joy at your being.

HUMOUR

In this dream, my sister
and I are scrapping (I have
no sister but dreams
seldom lie) hurling
insults, near blows,
our words bent with anger,
when my Dad, hearing
rumours from the next room
of our roughhousing, comes
in and pulls us apart,
and me, still enraged,
cry, "Put 'em up!"
and Dad raises his dukes,
ready to engage, before
he grins and slowly lowers
his fists, and the dream ends,
reminding me of what
I liked most about
my father: toughness
gentled   by a sense of humour.

FINESSE
For Isabel Huggan

You were a writer before
you learned to write: plots
rose up in your toddler's
mind: fables in their infancy,
nursery rhymes re-rhymed,
images bobbling for some-
thing to fertilize their fancy,
and when the first syllables
rolled unhobbled
onto the pencilled page,
the stories you'd hoarded so
long, burst onto
the world's stage, cobbled
 crisp: character caressed
by craft, scenes finessed
with ease, humanity distilled
in the fierce piercing of words

LAUREATE
For John B. Lee

You are the poet laureate
of laureates, a farm boy
harvesting hay and silaging
corn, while words rose
out of the fallow as easily
as a bard's breathing and tantalized
with the possibilities of joy
and sorrow, and, unlaurelled,
you surprised yourself
with poems, stooked with extravagant
stanzas, encharmed by rapturous
rhythms and metaphors
that would move a misanthrope,
you gazed deep into your rural
roots and the hibiscus of our
history with a soul hopeful
of humanity: you smote the Muse
and wrote.

DEFY
For Stan Burfield

For more than a dozen years
you were surrounded by blooms
in your shop, a long way
from Alberta's unlyrical
land, and when you tried
your hand at verse, were
your first poems for poppies
and their roaring red, sonnets
for sunflowers a-burst
in lavish light, haiku
for hibiscus and their passionate
purple, or pentameters
for peonies and their kissing cousins?
Did you let them speak
for you, go soaring through the
petrified petal of your fear?
For poetry is both bliss
and consolation, a way of speaking
to the world that subsumes
both shy and defy.

A BIRTHDAY POEM
For Anne

We have stopped counting
our birthdays, but the years
glide on without permission
or our say-so, but we have eased
into our age as gracefully
as Time and Earth allow
(your hand in my glove),
and whatever fears
we may have for the future
are flouted by our abiding love.

NIGHT SKATING

First Choice Books
2018

TWO FOR MRS. BRAY

WOUNDS

Bill Bray mowed
Grampa's 'back forty'
for fifty cents, half
of which he gave to his widowed
mother, whose clapboard
house was wombed with bloom,
and in there, amid
the daffodils and daisies
she grew happy, untouched
by war's wound.

CONSOLATION

Mrs. Brays' wide-
brimmed hat floats
above the flowers she dotes
on (amid the hum
of bees) and gives no
sign of the sorrow she felt
at the grim news that made
her a widow, for these
creations, daffodil
or daisy, will have to do
for comfort and consolation.

NIGHT SKATING

We go night skating
on Leckie's fallow in a static
snow, the kind that drips
from the lip of Heaven and parachutes
to Earth as soft as a lunar
landing, and the only sound
to break the serenity of the silence
is the soft heave of our breathing
and the whisper of flakes ecstatic
on the cheeks we hold aloft
like pilgrims awaiting manna,
and even though we are numbed
by the Arctic chill, we feel
as hallowed as we will ever
be in Kingdom Come.

LUNAR

The moon gazed at itself
in the glazed mirror of
Foster's pond, and we zoomed
back and forth, shredding
our shadows, boys and girls
with tugged tuques and streaming
scarves, mittens just
shy of illicit touch,
and when someone yelled
'Crack the whip!" I found
myself tossed and flying
as sleek as a seal enticing
ice, while above all
the great Bridge loomed,
bisecting the sky
and arching towards the stars,
under which we skated
skittish and dreaming of
lunar love.

WHAT WE ARE CALLED

To be given a nickname
was our town's way of saying
"Hello, you belong," and those
so honoured could be seen
whistling down Michigan
Ave and nodding to their sobriquet
as if it had been quickened
at birth, whether it was Rip
or Butch, Cap or Wiz
made no difference,
for a village is the Earth writ
small, the heart's home,
where no one is alone
and what we are called is as
deep as a knowing in the bone.

IMPECCABLE

When Leckie's fallow glistened
like the mirrored pool of the Taj
Mahal under the auspices
of Venus and Mars, we take
to our skates and convene in ones
and twos beneath the jewelled
moon, the waltz of our wheeling
humming unschooled
in our heads, and the further we burrow
into the sheer shallows of the dark
we find ourselves listening to the
impeccable music of the stars.

LASERED

Under a sky frosted
with stars and a tangerine moon
we go night-skating
on Foster's pond, stride
by gendered stride, boys
and girls hand-in-glove
over ice as keen as the glaze
of a scimitar's blade and through
a winter chill as tangible
as the taste of a snowflake
on the tongue, and soon we are lost
in our thoughts that turn tenderly
towards wind-tossed
locks and eyes bright
with amorous surprise, and we will
the world to be benign
and lasered with love.

CENTENNIAL

It wasn't the Santa Claus
Parade or even Macy's
Thanksgiving , but the brand-
new Fire Truck,
red as a raspberry,
led the way with the volunteer
crew hanging on
with both hands, followed
by the Boy Scout's
marching band, their bugles
blustering with all the zest
of a jazz ensemble,
and majorettes in their high-
stepping pace and twirling
batons glinting in the sunshine
the gods blessed us with,
and then came the vintage
autos, the Girl Guides
striding two by two,
a scuffle of ruffians from the
wrong side of the tracks,
and the Reeve in his rented limousine,
tipping his top hat
to the throng that lined Michigan
Avenue, and there was laughter
and tears amidst the merriment
and love for a town that had survived,
against the odds and with a little
luck, for a hundred years.

HOUSES

The houses of my village
were as idiosyncratic as the
characters who peopled them
and took their bows in my
fantastic imagination:

Stewart's place with its
multi-windowed porch
like a cruise ship furrowing
the dewed billows of the lawn

Mrs. Bray's clapboard
floating in a sea of bloom
and bee-hum

Withers' with its secret cellar
where Wiz made his magic
gadgets, and the double lot
promoted rounds of croquet
on summer afternoons
flush with sun

Barker's see-through
shack where the kids,
unblushing, ran naked
and shame had no name

Blake's three-storey
abode, our lone mansion,
the attic perched on top
where widows once strode
on storm-stammered nights

Bryant's perfect domicile
as tidy as a groom's suit
without a hint of uncombed
grass anywhere
(his heart splintered like a
glass prism)

and my grandfather's house,
hedged by lilac and shaded
by tall trees, and twin
verandahs where we played
our innocent boy-girl
games when the rains came,
the place where I found myself
at ease with the world, the place
I called joy my home.

DOLLY

Dolly Gordon, after
an unfulfilling day
shovelling coal, liked
to quaff a beer or two
more than he should to ease
the pain and satisfy his soul,
but his good wife disapproved
of such indulgence, and when
he bent over, as far
as he was able, to clear
the cobwebs from his hobbled
brain, she tapped him once
on the skull with an iron skillet,
and when he woke, there was a
bulge on his bean, his head
was clear, and supper was on
the table.

AURA

Tonight the moon is as bright
as a saint's halo and perched
an inch from the aura of Aries
and its spray of stars: glowing
through the charcoal dark
above Foster's pond
just enough to illume
the village kids essaying
"shinny" with home-made
sticks and a puck pinched
from the schoolyard, while the
glacial gleam of the ice
soothes the rough-and-tumble
of the game, and when the puck
skids too far,
where the dreamless dark
un-thins, only the bravest
carries on as if
there were no end to luck,
and all his companions give
a nod to the hockey gods

CHANCES

O the girls of the Point!
I see them now sifting
in the sunlight over
Canatara, their images
uplifted to my eighty-
year-old sight:
Nancy: as beautiful and un-
attainable as Guinevere
in some medieval romance
and I worshipped her from afar
like a lovelorn Lancelot,
and Shirley, just an inch
into her womanhood, stirred
in me feelings I later
learned were lust, and her sister
Betty, a big and bossy-
breasted Minerva who spun
the bottle and chortled at our
shy compliance, and Joycey
who longed to be Gaia
in her garden, but sported only
her underpants and puzzled
at the circumstances that left
her penurious and open to my
prurient glances: I see
them all again as clearly
as Huron's sky, re-anointed
by the years gone by,
and even now I'd like
to say: I like my chances.

FIZZ

When I was seven I lay
abed for seven months
waiting for the valves of my heart
to come together like a
pair of lips pursing
to kiss, and though the days
were long and beyond, I was never
bored, for I lost myself
in The Wizard of Oz and all
its equal sequels, and followed
Dorothy and the lion with cowardly
paws as they danced down the
Yellow Brick Road
into the technicolour vectors
of my imagination, and I let them
tickle the fizz of my fancy.

SPEED

When the ice on Leckie's fallow
was just thick enough
to bear the brunt of our blades,
we went flying down the centre,
eschewing the shallow edges
that broke like brittle glass,
and stroke by stroke we garnered
speed in gusts of sheer
momentum, until at last
we seemed freed from our body's
ballast and took flight
utterly into the air, as winged
as Icarus speculating on the sun.

BEAMING
For Grace Leckie

I dream of the time when Grace
and I would skate arm
in arm on the wind-glazed
fields of her father's farm,
waltzing to the music of the spheres
in the unstinting glint
of the stars above us,
our blades biting the ice
in perfect parallel,
like couplets amazed at their tight
rhyming, and me beaming
my paramour's thought, laced
with love.

ARGOES

We would wait till the moon-glow
marinated that glazed
shimmer we called Foster's
pond, hedged by cattails
and bulrushes, and, heeding
some inner instinct,
we skated like Argoes as far
as the indelible edge of the Earth's
curve, hearkening to the demon
dark beyond, before
blading it back to the home-
rink, the shadow of some-
thing akin to dread
or the why of why inkling
inside us, and we welcomed
the glimmer of the moon again
and a sky flush with stars.

AFFABLE

At the corner of Alexandra and Monk
Gran and Mrs. Bray
met most mornings
for their friendly chat and a laugh
or two, and the village being
both canvas and manuscript,
they talked about what
so-and-so said
to whom and other snippets
of this and that, tossed
out with a twinkle, until
the town grew round
and through them like a
dyslexic poem, pillaged
from the glossary of affable gossip.

STAMINA

When the ice glazed the fallow
of Leckie's fields like the
sheen of moonlight
on a mesmerized meadow,
we skated out under
the auspices of the stars, young,
callow and gendered by choice,
our scarves fleeing behind
us like the wisping tails
of Halley's comet, and we felt
in our glistened gliding the tidal
tug of the universe and something
deeper than the stamina of the stars,
something unyielding,
hugging the bone, and leaving
us dazed, cloistered
and inalienably alone.

ALLUREMENT

Under the auspices of the moon
and a chilly winter night
we purged ourselves
of the taboos that dogged our day-
light hours: skating
hand in curious hand
on Leckie's iced-over
field and tumbling with deliberate
intent into flexible lumps
where we felt the flush
of flesh through wool
and brushed a spangled cheek
or two, humbled by the depth
of our daring and the awesome
power of the sexual urge.

EVERYWHERE

On blades ablaze we delved
into the night-dark of
Leckie's glazed fallow
under a humbling umbrella
of stars and a moon startled
by its own brilliance, our arms
so enlinked you might think
we were courting couples
swinging stride for stride
to some music heard
only in the upper spheres
of the mind, delighted to be
skating on Earth's rounded
belly, to be drowned
at birth in the ink of Everywhere.

DOLPHIN

Jerry Mara swam like a dolphin
on "uppers" or Weissmuller
pursuing the blonde in the croc's
jaw, while I trailed
in his wake, dog-paddling
like a crippled crab; even
so, I admired the sleek
ease of Jerry's strokes,
and he in turn teased me
gently with Irish eyes
about my rabid flip-
flopping: our mutual love
for the Lake and the sun-soothed
sands of Canatara
bonded us best friends
who could take a dip together
and be home in time
for supper.

JUST

Coop and I, strolling
to school, notice in Leckie's
pasture a Holstein heifer
mounting one of her mates
in imitation of the conjugal
act; I blush at such
bull-bolstering lust,
but Coop, unflushed
and cool as Lash LaRue,
says, "They're just practicin'."

CAROLLING

At Sunday school we carolled
about Wenceslaus and the three
gifting Kings, lifting
our wee voices to celebrate
in song that jewelled Babe
Bethlehemed in a manger,
whom angels with their heraldic
horns harked in the star-
dark of a Christmas morn,
and we sang for ourselves
in our infant innocence,
jubilant with joy
unparalleled

OTHER

Shirley spun the bottle
with a wristed twist and stood
above our boy-girl
circle with lips at the ready
and bug-eyed with anticipation,
while I watched the jug spin
like Cupid's arrow, dread
in my heart as it whirled
through my neighbourhood
and stopped stark beside
me, and the girls whooped
as their gendered mate gripped
me by the waist and planted
one smothering, unchaste,
tongue-tender kiss
on my startled gaze, and I sensed
something other,
some joy grazing
astride, unthrottled
and three miles wide.

SKIMMING
for Grace Leckie

Grace and I skating
on her father's iced-over
field in a numinous night
undarkened by stars
and a mellowing moon, not
holding hands for we
are just male and female
fellows, here on the glazed
remains of last autumn's
clover, sensing the Winter's
wind between us like the hum
of a hymn, for we are enlaced
by the rhythm of our blades, by the
arched arms of the voluminous
stars under the feel of the firmament,
skimming the moon's face.

SPEED

When the ice on Leckie's fallow
was just thick enough
to bear the brunt of our blades,
we went flying down the centre,
eschewing the shallow edges
that broke like brittle glass,
and stroke by stroke we garnered
speed in gusts of sheer
momentum, until at last
we seemed freed from our body's
ballast and took flight
utterly into the air, as winged
as Icarus speculating on the sun.

ARGOES

We would wait till the moon-glow
marinated that glazed
shimmer we called Foster's
pond, hedged by cattails
and bulrushes, and, heeding
some inner instinct,
we skated like Argoes as far
as the indelible edge of the Earth's
curve, hearkening to the demon
dark beyond, before
blading it back to the home-
rink, the shadow of some-
thing akin to dread
or the why of why inkling
inside us, and we welcomed
the glimmer of the moon again
and a sky flush with stars.

AFFABLE

At the corner of Alexandra and Monk
Gran and Mrs. Bray
met most mornings
for their friendly chat and a laugh
or two, and the village being
both canvas and manuscript,
they talked about what
so-and-so said
to whom and other snippets
of this and that, tossed
out with a twinkle, until
the town grew round
and through them like a
dyslexic poem, pillaged
from the glossary of affable gossip.

ALLUREMENT

Under the auspices of the moon
and a chilly winter night
we purged ourselves
of the taboos that dogged our day-
light hours: skating
hand in curious hand
on Leckie's iced-over
field and tumbling with deliberate
intent into flexible lumps
where we felt the flush
of flesh through wool
and brushed a spangled cheek
or two, humbled by the depth
of our daring and the awesome
power of the sexual urge.

DOLPHIN

Jerry Mara swam like a dolphin
on "uppers" or Weissmuller
pursuing the blonde in the croc's
jaw, while I trailed
in his wake, dog-paddling
like a crippled crab; even
so, I admired the sleek
ease of Jerry's strokes,
and he in turn teased me
gently with Irish eyes
about my rabid flip-
flopping: our mutual love
for the Lake and the sun-soothed
sands of Canatara
bonded us best friends
who could take a dip together
and be home in time
for supper.

OTHER

Shirley spun the bottle
with a wristed twist and stood
above our boy-girl
circle with lips at the ready
and bug-eyed with anticipation,
while I watched the jug spin
like Cupid's arrow, dread
in my heart as it whirled
through my neighbourhood
and stopped stark beside
me, and the girls whooped
as their gendered mate gripped
me by the waist and planted
one smothering, unchaste,
tongue-tender kiss
on my startled gaze, and I sensed
something other,
some joy grazing
astride, unthrottled
and three miles wide.

FOSTER'S POND

The stars may have been startled
and the moon mystified by the
night figures zig-
zagging below over the
grackle-black ice of Foster's
pond, as burnished as beryl,
and there the sexes commingled,
brother and sister, beauty
and beau, their breath ballooning
behind them like signatures
of their joy at being in measured
motion, with the blood on the boil
and hearts lightened by the
tinfoil air and the skimming
of tight-laced skates
at their peril over the Earth's face.

CAROLLING

At Sunday school we carolled
about Wenceslaus and the three
gifting Kings, lifting
our wee voices to celebrate
in song that jewelled Babe
Bethlehemed in a manger,
whom angels with their heraldic
horns harked in the star-
dark of a Christmas morn,
and we sang for ourselves
in our infant innocence,
jubilant with joy
unparalleled

LOST

Butch's Dad lost
his lifetime job
when Kopp's Meat Market
closed for good, and rather
than spending his days greeting
the town's denizens with a grin
and an extra chop for madam's
dog, he ended up
in a slaughterhouse, gutting
pigs and skinning cattle,
up to his elbows in blood,
and the whole village understood
when he took to the drink
and his heart burst like a
blown blossom.

SWAMP

My grandfather's house
lay next to the village
swamp (marsh to be polite)
and every summer evening
a dozen squadrons of mosquitoes
squeezed through the cracks
in my bedroom screen
(big enough to accommodate
a mouse), and buzzed like chittering
chainsaws in either
ear, and I thought of vampires
gnawing at necks, blood
bulged and, when sleep
finally seized me,
drilling into my dreams.

BLUR

After January's thaw
Leckie's fallow becomes
one great lake
unlinked to any horizon
and soon glazed over
and metamorphosed into a
rink without beginning
or end, and we found ourselves,
under a menstrual moon
in a sky as black as Dracula's
glance, skating on the iced
curves of the world, and girls
and boys with mittened fingers
in tentative touch in their
seesawing glacial glide,
and I kept one prurient
eye on the freckled face,
wind-nuzzled curls
and kittenish grin of the blur
beside me, whom I had fancied
since I first learned
what amazement was.

WINCE

I remember Jerry and I
taking turns playing
Turk Broda with our Eaton's
shin-pads, abandoned
ball glove and a junior-
sized puck: Jerry
preferring the herky-jerky
style while I liked the gliding
gambit and quick kick,
but what I remember most
is the surprise in Gerry's eyes,
as black as berries in season,
as my best shot struck
him just above the knee,
and he grinned, wincing, as if
to say, "That's how it's done!"
Gerry is gone now,
like most of my childhood chums
and all our games are moot,
but we do not need
a reason to keep on loving.

TWELVE

I had just turned twelve
when my brother and I imagined
a whole menagerie of teddy-
bear beasts and bunnies,
and I began to spin tales
of their hobnobbing shenanigans,
forsaking elves and goblins
to feast on the foibles of bruins,
lion cubs and an elephant
or two, and I've often wondered
not how the adventures ended
but how they began, for we
had no books in our house
and only "Goldilocks" on
Grandpa's knee (with voices
and a wee wink, and me:
mute with expectation);
what urge tempted the trajectory
of my pen across the uninked
page to startle the world
with stories or propagate
a poem, dream-dreamt?

LEAP

While I was wrestling my way
out of the womb, the first stanchions
of the Blue Water Bridge
were driven in not a hundred
yards from my grandfather's house,
and this would be no
simple trestle-arch,
but the rectilinear leap
of an exoskeletal rigidity
above the booming St. Clair,
while my infant brow was bursting
into alien echelons
of air, and when I grew
enough starch in my legs
to reach my bedroom
window: there we were
together in the now, groomed
for life in the village I loved.

UPWARDS

Under a moon the colour
of a rusted chrysanthemum
and a sky pin-pricked
with stars, we skated on the
glazed face of Leckie's
field and the embers of Autumn,
and with the wind humming through
our tuques we soared on the hiss
of our blistering blades beyond
the grip of gravity, beyond
the gift of grace, and sallied
upwards through the yielding
lunar air towards
Jupiter or Mars.

BLUES

We ogled the curves of the girls
on Canatara's unbaulderized
beach, as round and swelling
as the underbelly of the moon
or an apple-dappled autumnal
"snow" or the swerved furrow
of a sun-glazed dune,
and prayed our gaze could creep
but an inch higher to the
plum prize just
beyond our reach, but in vain
did we grapple with the blind
fury of our desire: that left us
uncinched, blues-
blurred, mind-boggled.

BOUYANCY

Under a pale and translucent
moon and a sky scattered
with stars in their Grecian arcs,
we feel the bite of the ice
on our blades and cruise through the
hovering dark, glad
to be night-skating here
where the Earth has no edges,
and when Coop hits a shattering
of shale, we laugh at his pin-
point landing and his leveraged
leap upright,
and cheer when Marilyn spins
like a dulcimered doll, and Bonnie
and Sharon insist on doing
a duo as sisters, and Grace
and I come to the brink
of coy contiguity before breaking
asusnder, and the moon turns
as golden as a doting doubloon,
and we feel as a singular soul
the sheer joy of buoyancy.

ADDER

Butch and I combed
the meadow grasses
below our homes for garter
snakes or best of all,
a puffing adder, and we killed
one of the latter, slithering
through the stinkweed
like Lucifer through Eden,
with a massive blow to its devil-
inducing brow: "But snakes
don't die till midnight,"
Butch said with a knowing wink,
so we came back later
that day and the creature,
its eyes tight, was as dead
as the blown bloom in the
ruined Garden where Paradise
once lay; "We must've
hit him too hard,"
I heard Butch say.

SHINNY

The ice was always icier
on Foster's pond, even
if it was only an oval,
sun-glazed and wind-
thinned, among the cat-
tails and bulrushes
of the village swamp,
but we rallied and romped on
borrowed blades, gladiators
all in Maple Leaf
blue or habitant red,
breathing speed that sent
us sailing beyond
the breadth of our bodies,
nurturing a need we could not
leave to the morrow, and,
thumb-numbed, were lost
in the thrill of our blood's brief
burgeoning, while somewhere
above the Gardens the gods
of puckdom roll the dice.

SORTIE

I was dreaming of dreaming,
a pantomime as airy
as an fairy's elbow:
Grandpa mowing the back
forty, sweat gleaming
on his bared torso like a
gladiator's sheen in the Roman
sunshine, and me
winging along behind
like an airman's sortie,
and this seeming scene was so
real, so dauntingly deep
I turned it into rhyme
before it softened into sleep
and left me dream-bereft:
haunted by what might have been.

FIRST POEM

When I was just eleven,
my ink-dipped pen
nibbled at the white page
of my school scribbler, from which
emerged a set of rhyming
lines that seemed to write
themselves unassuaged
into the saga of Wolfe
and Montcalm and those
plains bloody with the mud
and grime of internecine
war, and two great
men who, conquering fear,
took their last breath
there, beseeching
Heaven, liberated by death,
and come alive again
in the linked couplets of a virgin
balladeer.

EDGE

At the first sign of frost
we waited for Foster's pond
to freeze over and the ice
to glow unrippled
among the cattails
and dog-eared bul-
rushes, where we sallied
forth on scything blades
with breeze-brushed cheeks
and tuques tugged low
under a mellow moon
and a sky stippled with stars,
lost in our thoughts
of blithe girls and love-
stunned boys while ghostly
galaxies spun far
above, hugging the edge
of everything.

WARTS

My village was a three-steepled
town, and at precisely a quarter
to eleven each Sunday
morning, the Presbyterian bell
outrang its Anglican
cousin, calling the faithful
to people the pews, swell
the stalls and come forth
in the name of Christendom,
singing hosannas to the
high heavens, warts
and all.

RIVET

It must have been the luck
of the draw when Bill McCord's
rink, jousting with a January
thaw and tucked succinctly
under the half-built
Bridge, was struck by a
rivet sizzling from the buckler
and, grazing the air's edge,
rousted the crowd and the
Point Edward All-
Stars below, before
taking a left-hand
pivot and setting the roof
ablaze, leaving the village
rinkless, and amazed.

PLAIN

Sharon was the plain sister,
Bonnie being bright-
eyed and courting curves
the boys ogled slyly
as she let her thighs show
doing Double Dutch,
blistering our walk with her
fevered toes and Bo
Jangles tactics, but I
don't put much stock
in high-wire acts,
and the radium of Sharon's smile
would set a room aglow.

OZONE

Coop and I wade into the
bone-chill of Huron's
waters, not particular
about the testicular shrivelling
going on below,
for our thoughts are lofty,
even though our girls
unfurl their wares
on Canatara's beach
(a millimetre behind us
and a mile beyond our reach),
cock-a-hoop over
two innocents trying
not to swivel too
hard in their direction or fret
about their stricken stubs,
still softer than the ozone.

INSTINCTS
*For Shirley McCord, my chum
and childhood playmate*

The first time I saw
Shirley grown gladly
into her new body, she lay
in the sun-furrowed sand
of Canatara, and my heart
burst at the view of her
nipple-stippled one-
piece bathing suit,
and her languorous limbs
(and the hint of something
dimpled burrowing higher
and beyond detection)
left me mad with desire,
until she smiled her simple
everyday Shirley-
smile, and I nodded in kind
to her and to the gods that sent
me rippling with a friend's
fulsome affection,
and wondering about the illogical
link between the propensity
of our senses and the instincts
of innocence.

DIFFERENCE

In wintertime with snow
sifting the sills and dozing
on the eaves, and the wind-chill
off the frozen Lake
and Canatara's smooth dunes
sweeping the schoolyard,
the boys on their side played
"warm beef", bodies
bunting bodies like box-
cars run amok
in an innocent parody
of the conjugal act,
while the girls on their side
huddled on the steps and practiced
the fox-trot with their freezing
feet, arms enlinked
in a communal cuddle,
lips lifting wide
in ceremonial song
and doing their best to ignore
the grunts and wheezing next
door, while their blood hummed
like a juggler's unblinking
heartbeat.

NOTE:
Warm Beef is a local children's
keep-warm game wherein boys,
in a line-up for school, form a
train and thrust back and forth
with their bodies against the
school door.

A WORLD AWAY

When I was young and whiled
the world away in the midst
of my innocence, I ambled
around the village that bore
me up like a propagated
poem, unbeguiled
by anything "other"
beyond its mothering boundaries,
breathing the incense of its easing
air as I rambled wherever
I pleased over meadows
where milkweed pods
unfurled to dust the breeze
with providential puffs
and the wild mustard
flamed as golden as the
lustrous sun ripening
the snows that hung from their trees
like the appetized apples of Eden,
and even the thunder was muffled
there and the rains renewed
the grasses' bedizening and all
roads ferried me home
where love bloomed so
flagrantly no god
could sunder it.

PELL-MELL

Under a mellow magical
moon and a sky stiffened
with stars and their pagan
pageantry,
we sweep, tuque-bedecked,
onto the ink-daubed
shimmer of Leckie's fallowed
rink, heading for a far
horizon, side-stepping
the shell ice as quick as a
riffing bassoon, and cruising
in mittened duos or singled
odds till our blood warmed
like a January thaw
and the gods who bequeathed us
this night and its awe,
guide us pell-mell
home.

DELLS

As Huron's waves, un-
hurried, caressed the belly
of the beach, we dove into the
swollen grooves between
the rolling breakers, and came
up spouting the good
news that we were young
and girls pranced in our wake
bare-limbed in the sun,
slung between the blue
shimmer of the Lake and the
heft of the horizon: emboldened
boys and pulchritudinous
girls doing the shy
dance of the duos in the watery
dells off Canatara's
voluptuous shore.

AWE

On our way to school we watched
in awe as Leckie's bull
Brutus, stiff pistil
a-throb, eyes bulging,
undeterred by the hesitant
heifer, and without a gee
or a haw, mounted his puckered
prize and furiously
furrowed her.

A KIND OF LIGHT

When the moon bloomed as bright
as a galleon ablaze in a sky
littered with stars and their diamond
dazzle, we took to the ice
like Eskimos to snow, following
the girls, enwombed in wool,
who became just pals
for the night, skittering skillfully
over the glacial glaze
of Leckie's fallow, in un-
gendered duos or improvised
threesomes, our bodies
boneless in the winter chill,
wondering what it meant
to be and looking for the kind
of light we cannot see.

ANOINTED

The sands of Canatara
(older than Adam's rib
or Methuselah's jumbled
numbers) adored the girls
of the Point, their breeze-easy
laughter, their sun-loved
limbs open to our guileful
gaze, and they were both
thigh-shy and bold-
eyed, and when they deigned
to toss us a beguiling smile
(while the libidinous swish
of Huron's breakers lavished
the shore) we thought ourselves
to be among the anointed.

TITHE

Shirley does the can-can
on grandfather's 'back
forty,' showing off
her long lithe legs
and, like the girls in France
who wear no pants,
she warbles, "And I lift
my legs so high
you can see my cherry
pie ay ay,"
and we all blush
like a mortified groom,
and promise
God to tithe till
Doomsday.

ROISTERING

Each summer morning
the sun boiled out of
First Bush and layered
our streets with luminous light,
and I greeted the coming day
with a gallop and a prayer,
aiming my brand-new
body towards the doors
behind which the friends
who drew me outside
of my centering self
awaited my hithering call:
Wiz Withers whose magical
hands could weave gizmos
and gadgets out of anonymous
odds and ends with a kind
of ledgerdemain even
the gods envied:
Butch McCord who had
no other name
but cushioned the blows of bullies
just for me, who trod
the voluminous girders of the Bridge
to show the world what daring
was and what it meant
to be a brother:
Jerry Mara who could swim
like a perambulating porpoise
and carried our daily play
to Canatara and beyond,
who gave full meaning
to the word loyalty:
Bones Saunders all
elbows and angles,
who let us stick him
with a nickname and hoisted
the friendship flag:
and so it was I learned
like Adam before the fall
what love was, its synesthetic
edge, its numinous glow,
and before the gloaming loomed
we all went out and royally
roistered.

CAMELOT

Nancy was a girl who belonged
in a Medieval romance,
a frail heroine some
Lancelot would give up
the Grail for, but alas
I was no star-studded
Knight and she was simply
a buddy among those
of us who clustered under
the glow of Mara's lamp
in the lustrous, moon-mottled
twilights to play hide-
and-go seek and do
our genderless dance,
un-duoed and a long ways
from Camelot.

GIRTH

Not even the moon could out-
do the amber glow
of Mara's lamp, bestrewing
its star-rich beam
into the antediluvian dark,
where we lay shrouded
in shadow, camped between
its ebony grooves, awaiting
the "All Free!" or pitching
woo whenever a calf
was lit by a stray ray
or a cheek's blush was un-
impeachable, but never manoeuvring
beyond the reach of that moth-
mothering light, that to us
outwitted the Earth's girth.

SPARK

On summer nights we gathered
under Mara's lamp,
like ants to heated honey,
safe in the glow of its ample
parabola: the girls letting
the shivers go slithering
thigh-high, while the boys
paraded a sly inch
from the shuddering shadows
ringed by our hexagonal light,
taking a chance on a
come-hither glance
or the sparkle in an opulent eye,
boys and girls in tight
tandem, singing hosannas
to the heterosexual dark.

POSSUM

One Spring day
we got a front-row
seat as the Holstein bull
(his flanks like a black and white
Mercator map) was up
to the hilt in a heifer in Leckie's
pasture, and there seemed no
pleasure, no rush of oestral
blood in this awkward,
stilted coupling (thanks
but no thanks, see
'ya later) that made
the girls blush blossom
pink and the boys wonder
whether to heckle or play
possum.

BRAVADO

Butch and I eye
the lowest girders on the Bridge,
me: I lay awake
nights worrying about heights,
but my chum clambers up
the nearest stanchion and, not
shy when bravado calls,
steps onto the first cross-
beam, wobbles like a tipsy
tight-rope walker
for a baffling second, then makes
his way ten feet above
ground, humming all
the while, letting me
(loving the gypsy in him)
do any shaking
on his behalf.

PRURIENT

The bone-chilling waters
of the Lake shrivel and stiffen
our male appendages, and Coop
and I walk awkwardly to the
change-room, where, stripped
down, we blush at our
trembling stalks, no bigger
than a gherkin, and wonder if
the girls giggling right
next door would perk
up at such a prurient
sight.

STORIES

In Ted Leckie's hay-
loft, we played kamikaze
pilots, bailing out
from the high beams and surprising
the sky before sailing
agley and settling, as soft
as a swan on water, upon
the dried fodder below,
where, divvied up into Allies
and Nazis we reenacted
the glories of the World War,
and I dreamed of piratical
poems and prize-winning
stories.

INCORRUPTIBLE

On soft summer mornings
the sun rises up out of
First Bush like a Phoenix
pouring Grecian light
on the village streets below,
and we are released like
Moses out of Egypt into
the airy outdoors,
and it's Move-Up in Withers
field, hopscotch
or Double Dutch with the girls
gliding aloft and a-glow,
or ring-around-a-rosy
with the little'uns in tow,
or, on a good day,
when bees hum to hear
themselves sing,
surprising Wiz in his cellar
with his magical gadgetry,
and we are as free as leaves
unleafing from the density
of the tree, and insulated from the
burst of the world by our
incorruptible innocence.

EMBODIED

After the double feature
at the aging Imperial, we race
home to re-enact
the action-packed matineé
and its six-shooter troubles,
and it was Hopalong
or Geronimo, Johnny Mack
or Crazy Horse in the late
lazy afternoons,
sagebrush sagas
(and Laurel and Hardy laughter):
these were stories I absorbed
and then honed into fictions
and poems, epic and otherwise,
that fired my fancy, stories
embodied by the bone.

FETCHING

Bonny and Sharon doing
Double Dutch, their lithe
limbs scissoring in a free-
fall dance without the
hint of a stumble, while the twinned
ropes lasso the air,
and there is something
in their fetching glance beyond
the edge of innocence, for in
the distance thunder rumbles
and darkens all gardens.

DAYS WORTH THE TELLING

Black Moss Press
2018

COP

Our village had but one
cop, few villains
and even less trouble:
Constable Pedan, whose principal
task was scouring the alleys
to get a bead on truants,
stopping the odd jay-
walker on our carless
streets, parsing the Pool
Room for underage
felons, rousting un-
ruly hoboes
from their afternoon snooze,
guiding to hearth and home
gentlemen who'd imbibed
too much booze,
or pursuing Butch and me
riding double and beating
his flat-footed trot
to the Bridge, where we hid
below its looping span,
pleased with ourselves
and basking in our own glow.

VILLAGE DREAMING

Rocking in my chair I dream
of the village where I was breathed
into being by the athletic lusts
of my hockey-heroing father
and the girl he deemed his paramour,
when my world was as new as a
chick picking at the shell
and a blank page I wrote
myself upon with words
wrestled from the womb, and a town
surrounded me with folks
to people my poems and startle
the stories I would create, in the
mortar and pestle of my imagination,
of their forgivable follies, the hustle
and bustle of their Dickensian lives,
and those childhood
chums I turned into combed
prose, who made my days
worth the telling and strummed
the strings of my memory, leaving
me to dream, rock and sing
the song of myself.

WORSHIP
For Grace Lecky

The gal I worshipped from afar
rode her roan stallion
like Dale Evans astride
her cinematic palomino,
her long-legged gallop
left me pale and alone
by the roadside, the dust
from the fuelled fury of hooves
settled on my punctured pride
like a penitent's pall: begging
my heart to stop its pulsing
thrust, and abide.

DEMUR

Joycee Clark was rumoured
to be promiscuous,
but not knowing for a fact
the meaning of the term, we had
to be content with wishing she'd
drop her pants and do
the hula-hula dance,
and then surprise us all
by showing off the tender
cleft between her thighs
(we dreamed the daylights
out of), but what we got
instead was a demur purr
and a furtive smile that left
the mystery intact.

EIDER

Billy Clark was a balletomane
on Foster's Pond, with the serpentine
strides of Gordie Howe
or Bobby's smooth moves,
and when the puck took
to his blade, it dazzle-danced,
swerved, torqued and twisted
its way to the distant twine,
while I, lacking my Dad's DNA,
stood on the sidelines
in the afternoon chill,
unable to find
the pluck to waddle on my ankles
like an eider on ice,
and prayed for dark.

NEW-FOUND

The wood-burning furnace
below heaves its heat
up into the classroom
above, where twenty-three
pupils in eight grades
sit rapt and waiting
for Miss Nelson to blow
into her pitch-pipe and tweet
a perfect "cee", after which
we all sing our anthem
to the King, and school begins:
that's me in the middle row
(good at reading but little
else) glancing across
two aisles at Grace
and indulging in the bulge
of her new-found breasts:
she fails to turn around,
and I am seized with some-
thing akin to despair,
uncaressed by hope,
watching her face pointed
straight ahead, her tresses-
enriched by the morning
light, at ease, alas,
with her womanhood.

PERFECT

My father and I fishing
for bass in Mitchell's Bay:
while I, wishing to be
elsewhere, disen-
tangle the knots in my line;
he tosses his lure with the
ease of a casual caress
and it welcomes the water with a
surreptitious splash,
and me hitching up
my pants and flinging my wobbler
after him, as we wait
yards apart for something
full-fleshed with a mouthful
of teeth to gobble what-
ever tempts its terrain
and tear at the bait, and soon
Dad is reeling it in,
playing it with practiced finesse
till it leaps moonward
into the air with a singing bravado
and I, nursing the net,
pass the catch triumphantly
up to him and watch as he smiles
at me as if I myself
had made the perfect pass.

STROLL

On sultry summer days
we'd take the ten-minute
stroll to the beach, up
Monck Street past
gabled cottages and the
Victory Gardens aflame
with flowers and across the old
Grand Trunk tracks
and their sun-bussed rails
in front of the lighthouse
with its lonely fog-foraging
beam and then it was down
to the sea-singing sand
just beyond the tightly
tucked knolls of The Slip,
and on to fabled Canatara,
where wavelets licked the shore-
line with lascivious lips
and Huron, as blue as a Jay's
wing, rolled west
to the far horizon, where the hulls
of steamers drifted and lazed,
and we, lake-fazed,
and never looking back,
let out a cheer for us,
exultant in our luck.

GLIDERS

Along the River Flats
in the big wind from the
belly of the Lake and in the
leavening light of early
dawn, we toss our jerry-
rigged gliders, rag-
tailed and slug-sleek,
up into the ripening sky,
where a benevolent breeze
blossoms and eddies them
with gratuitous ease,
and we feel the tug of the
kite-string from our heathen
hands all the way
up to Heaven's gate.

POISED

In the Lake's welcoming waters
Tom is as poised as a porpoise;
from the safety of the shore I watch
in awe as he dives delicately
under the shimmering surface
without the whisper of a splash,
and swims with the furious fins
of his out-turned palms
and comes up grinning,
shaking his hair like a
saturated Lab out of
its habitat, and unaware
as he passes me by
of the upwelling affection
in a grandfather's eye.

REGRET

Susan Coote, a sweet
six-year-old
who lived on the main street,
liked to cruise on her trike
around our block, scooting
past our front verandah,
but one day on an impulse
I stepped out, stamped
my foot and pulled her off
the sidewalk; it was more
than the act of an imp, rather
something set
deep and unmuzzled
inside that made me a bully,
and even now, all
the years later, leaves
me puzzled and rampant
with regret.

ENDURING

Gran was always good
for a nickel; I can still
hear the crisp click
as she opened her purse and lifted
a shiny five-cent
piece onto my outstretched
hand, and then it was off
to Harry Brand's (with his eighty-
year, tight-fisted
smile) for a Pepsi (sucked
till the straw gave up)
or a couple of grab-bags
or a pair of black-balls,
and I thought then, as I do
now, how lucky I was
all those years to have
such a grandmother and the enduring
gift of her love.

PEN

I took up my pointed pencil
at Grade Three, not
knowing what odd urge
took hold of me,
but I recall the surge of serenity
as the blank page came
alive in my eyes and the
surprise that stories were born
inside before they aged
and allowed themselves
to be written and read,
and I knew even then
it wasn't for renown or glory
but the release of words in their
anointed wonder on the chance
that someone disembodied
out there might understand
and give me the nod:
I can't tell you or God
when, but the time will come
when I will have lain down
my pen.

UNBRIDLED

In the place where I was born
the sun rose like a blown
bloom over First
Bush, inundating it
with lascivious light
that stirred the oak's sap
and whetted the thirst of its
root-thrust, then
with a lavish licking, scrubbed
the streets clean of the numbing
night's dust before
settling on the angular eaves
of each house like the blossoming
of a bride's veil, and lapping
at my window where I lay
awake, sun-stunned,
to hail the morning as if
it were the first un-
bridled day of my life.

SUMMERING

When my grandfather and I
walked out upon
the settled streets of our mutual
village, I talked a blue
streak and he listened,
unnettled by my boyish
insistent interrogation;
I wanted to know everything
about the place I was born to
and I wanted to love this
man whose hand I held
with a gentling gesture and strode
beside as we circumnavigated
our June town, while the
Sunday sun glistened
just for us in the summering
sky above.

COUNTRY SCHOOL

There weren't enough of us,
boys and girls, to keep
our games uni-sexed
or favour picking sides:
the girls hurled the rugby
ball with nary a wobble
and the boys did some fancy
footwork in Double
Dutch with nary a hobble,
and in between there was
Prisoner's Base, Move-up
and May I, and with all
the huffing and puffing there wasn't
much time for the perplexed
tickle of romance.

WIDOW

Mrs. Bray floats
among her flowers, swallowed
by sunshine, and glides
through her sea of petals
like Gaia on a good day,
doting on daisies or roses
and loving the way light
laps at the lips of poppies
or black-eyed Susans,
the way her garden grows
effusive, reminiscent
of that other garden
where there were no
wars and no widows.

ASTRIDE
For Sharon, Bonnie and Marilyn

The girls gather round
Marilyn and the pony she sits
astride, buffing the pommel
with her free hand, as Sharon
strokes the curling mane
and Bonnie giggles as Champ
pokes his nose into the
feed-bag, and the sisters
beg for a ride they will never
own, while in the fallow field
the stiff-legged hired
man hobbles homeward,
roughshod and randy.

SALVATION

When the fever finally broke
and I was me once
more, having come within
a decibel of Death, my mother,
relieved to see her boy
well and laughing at the pain
he did not remember,
brought along a toy
giraffe, bedecked with spots
and a cardboard neck
that soared as high as a giant's
thigh, so that I might forget
that the valves of my heathen heart
had opened wide and seven
long months buckled
in bed lay ahead
before I would again see
salvation.

SPIES

For Gran, in loving memory

It's Sunday morning and Gran,
no fan of apse
or aisle, is peeling apples:
spies for her Sabbath pies;
I watch her slowly exposing
the wimple-white flesh
below the skin, falling
away in perfect curlicues,
her moves habitual, simple,
filed unlapsed
in the muscle of memory, and I know
she will, through thick and thin,
be doing this labour
of love until the day
she dies.

TUG

The girls are hopscotching
bare-legged in the breeze,
skipping from square to square
with the elegant ease of an acrobat
on a tremulous trapeze, while the
boys
in the field beside them
are tossing a rugby ball
with the ardent thrust of a right
arm, watching its awesome
arc all the way
home, while the girls squeeze
their thighs tight in their high-
wire flight, and the boys
dream non-stop
of touchdowns and the tug
of desire.

STROLL

I stroll along Monck
Street under a marigold
moon, practising poems
still foaling in my mind,
and stories as yet untold
that some day may peregrinate
across the public page,
and I will pretend not
to care about all
that unctuous acclaim,
and take pains to look
rarefied and sage.

CERTAINTY

When we were too young
to know better, the spring
rains garnished my grand-
father's grass, and we skidded
bare-footed across
its green lush, only
vaguely aware the tulips
still tingled from the thunder's
touch and the daffodils
relaxed their dew-splashed
bonnets, and so, cheered
by the sun-varnished sky,
we sang sonnets to the gods
in their lush lingering: certain
in our hearts that the rains
would come again and again
and the world still revolve
on its axis.

BLISS

The first snowfall:
I feel the heave of the seasons
as flakes liberate the lawn,
soft as milkweed down,
as silk on a bride's gown,
as breath before a kiss,
they tremble on the last leaves,
they are tasted on the tongues
of the young, they stir memories
of a childhood undisturbed
by the Earth's bursting from one
solstice to the next, and freed
to know the bliss of their own
innocence.

NEO

When I was just ten,
I uncoiled my first
story: The Adventures
of Little Tiny Bingo,
hand-scrawled in a school
scribbler with oiled covers,
my protagonist a lion cub
thirsting for glory in the
bestiary I created for him,
where the characters were caught
between my fancy and the brio
of a rag-tag Animalia:
I was a neo-novelist,
not yet out of grade five
and unaware that the tales
would continue to flow un-
inhibited until the last
plot came to rest.

FAVORITE PHOTO

James and Tim, a year
or two from toddlerhood,
lean out of the Tempo's window
towards the camera, which captures
them unawares in their dimpled
innocence: Tim smiles
as if he understood
all he needed to know
about man or God, and James
flashes those imp's
eyes that are threatening to surprise
Grandpa by driving off
and leaving him bouche
bé on the sidewalk:
there are no boundaries
for pride and affection, built
on the foundations of love.

FIFTY
For Kate

Fifty is a nice round
number, but you took
some umbrage at turning
that age, even though
I recall each of your days
and the hope and happiness
they brought, the zest and spice
of your being you, the reason
for our rhyme: none of us
knows what lies in store,
but wise beyond your years,
generous and sage, you're
a prime candidate
for fifty more!

ART

This is me at nine
months, the photo craftily
coloured to bring out
the bloom in my cheeks and the sweet
green of grandfather's grass,
and who knew what plots
and stanzas lay behind
that unblemished brow
(the sorcerer's art
with words perhaps) or what
poet's passion I might
unfurl some day
and startle the world.

DEKE
Sarnia City Champions
1933-1934

I sit in my solitary study
and notice an eighty-year-
old plaque once
held in my father's hands,
and I see him skating
as sweet as a swan on the
magic mirror of a pond,
his dekes and yaws as smooth
as new ice on a raw
rink (he has the boy's knack
but the puck-wit of a pro)
and I can hear the applause
of the home-town fans
who made this slim kid
their hero, and what joy
it must have been to feel
every breath in your body
tuned to the grace of the game,
and no hint then
of the grim days ahead
when he was no longer
slim and, done in
by drink, couldn't out-
deke Death.

STRUCK

The things I remember:
five-year-old
Tom, tucked a-bed
and trying not to sleep,
his eyes still beaming,
alive with expectation,
and me alongside,
singing "O the great
ships sail through the
alley-ally-O
on the first day of September"
until, soporific with song,
he drifts into some dream
I am not privy to,
and I too begin to doze,
struck once again
by how deep love
goes.

MIRACULOUS

In the midst of my fever I saw
diaphanous-winged angels
fluttering like butterflies
just before bidding
farewell to their cocoons,
and singing a Siren song
as they gestured me gracefully
towards Heaven, where no
fevers thrive and there is
no need for the future,
but something gut-deep
and bracing in the bone drew
me back, and I awoke
to a welcoming, miraculous moon,
sweating and alive.

WELL

Sometime soon
the last person to recall
my name will have just
forgotten it. But
for all those at whom
I have hurled my misanthropic
thoughts and rhyme-riddled
dreams through the prism
of my poems (that promised
more than words are allowed
to tell), please, remember
me well.

HALLOWED

I look at this wedding
photo (a fading black
and white) with the two of us
in our Sunday best, staring
into each other's eyes
and sure there is a future
we will somehow
share, your beauty glowing
in your face I give you back
with my mile-wide smile:
so long ago
now, but an image
that still finds a place
hallowed in my heart.

NOT

I once loved Jesus,
but the thought of turning the other
cheek and loving thy neighbor
seemed too much
freight for a sinning teen
to bear, though I yearned
for something yielding,
some easing of the mind
and better than God glancing
straight into my crooked heart:
Jesus loves me still,
but, sadly, I love him
not.

DRIVE
For Doug McConnell
In Memoriam

Doug sweetened the air
above Hickory Ridge
with his long, gliding drives,
and if one should happen
to stray into the woods, he'd
stride straight for the
underbrush, where forsaken
balls were waiting in the gorse
for a friend to rescue them,
and emerge onto the fairway
with a grin as big as a
Shriner's heart, sharing
his cache with all and sundry:
a man's man, unmatched,
he will be missed on
and off the course.

KNACK
For Katie and Rebecca

If my girls were flowers they'd be
hollyhocks whose crimson
blooms, bride-bright,
grace a garden wall,
brushed by breezes summer-
sweet and perfuming the ambient
air: my girls have the knack
of affection, I love them
with a hallowed heart and they love
me back.

MEDAL

I cannot help but stare
at the lovingly-framed photo
of me at eight months, perched
like a proud prince on my
grandfather's lawn,
and appearing to glance down
at my President's Medal for a poem
I once penned, draped
over the picture at the end
of a bright red ribbon,
as if he needed convincing
that there was, beyond
the camera's edifying eye,
a world waiting just
for him, unflinching
and dancing with delight.

FOR ANNE

If you were a flower you'd be
a yellow rose sweetening
sunshine on June
afternoons, and at the edge
of evening mellowing moon-
light: we greet each
other in the morning's rise,
empowered by love in the
other's eyes, watching
as it grows and blooms
over the long years
we have been buoyantly
embowered.

GIFT
For Potsy: In Memoriam

Once again you slip
into my dreams with avuncular
ease: you and Arnold
Palmer are chatting about
the Vardon Grip, hitting
the ball flush and the dreaded
shank; then it's you,
me and Arnie on some
far gleaming green,
hushed over our putts,
you leave yours teetering
on the lip before calmly
tapping it in, and I
wonder who to thank
for such gratuitous gifts.

SKETCH
For Tom

It's no Van Gogh
but this child's crayoned
scrawl of Tom and me
fishing in Cameron Lake
is just as glowing (his caption
wishing me Happy Birthday),
and Tom, still six,
draws with the tangible clarity
all children possess:
there may be sticks for men
and a splash of green for the reeds
where the bass lie below
us together in that thick-
sketched boat, but each
line is limned with love,
and never to be feared,
Tom scribbles in
my bristling beard.

MAKING ROOM

We love to watch our grand-
children grow, galvanized
by their preordained ages:
infant, toddler,
pre-schooler and teen,
and so engaged are we
in the world we barely notice
the ticking of time, but each
year they add is one
less for us, groomed
for demise, making room.

MUPPETS

My girls are growing up:
no longer rosebuds
but fully flowered blooms,
their eyes now aimed
straight ahead at the future
and the thousand hours
that await them, but to me
they will always be,
above all else,
the curly-headed muppets
who found room in their hearts
for a grandfather's love.

VISIT
For Stan Atherton

When an old friend comes
to visit after an absence
of nearly two decades,
we soon fall into familiar
habits of speech, un-
surprised at how little
has changed, as if the yawning
years between had never
happened, and grateful that we
are more than the pawns of Time
and grateful too for the gift
it has bestowed upon us:
we end the day with a slow
hug, knowing we will not
set septuagenarian
eyes upon one another
again.

BURIED TREASURE

It's Sunday morning
and Tom and I are busy
at play: we are pirates
burrowing for buried treasure,
wending our way across
the carpeted sea from room
to room on rain-tossed
galleons, and I watched
your imagination bloom
in your blue-bold eyes
on those lazy Sabbath days,
and knew we would remember
those monumental
moments whatever
our futures might hold.

HARRY
For Katie and Rebecca

My granddaughters devour
Harry Potter, un-
daunted by the tome-thick
prose; they are at home
with the wizard and his
necromancing tribe,
absorbed by story itself
and its passionate action,
fuelled by just the right
flight of fancy, each
word newborn
in the mind's might: they
consume books with a
gustatory delight.

PREMATURE
For Tom

You were born premature,
a wee wrinkled thing,
encased in a glass hutch,
waiting to be un-
furled, breathing your own
oxidized air; we longed
to reassure you with a
tendril'ed touch, to curl
you in our arms and bring your
being into our loving gaze,
but you surprised us all:
you lay there unamazed,
your tiny heart embracing
the world.

THUNDERSTUCK

I wake with the morning sun
silking over my window
sill, and hop on my trike
to greet the street I've known
since I first remember
being me, both feet
pedalling away, I brake
for the milkman and pause
for Mrs. Bray, counting
every crack in the side-
walk, I circumnavigate
my block, my bike a bucking
bronco on a Roy Rogers
run, and I am filled
with the wonder of it all:
thunderstruck by joy.

GNOMES: 1944

When I went down with rheumatic
fever, I came within an inch
of dying, but the fever broke
and I was still alive,
and after seven months
my heart healed and I survived
another seventy years
or more, and I tried to repay
those gods or gnomes
who, with a pinch of pity,
let me thrive to compose
a thousand poems and stories.

GONE
For Alvin Gehl

I think now of those
good times when we were
teens in a friendship
so tight we rarely
noticed it, and I remember
again those games
of my invention you tested
with a keen eye and helpful
heart, and how many
hours did we spend in the
dusk-light of Orchard
Park, shagging balls
and mimicking Kaline
and Boone under a
marigold moon,
(you taught me to throw
a curve) and after dark
it was Red Rover,
Five Hundred and the
shy/sly manoeuvres
the girls ignored: what
a story we wrote together
so long ago,
and who would have thought
our lives would swerve apart
and fifty years would pass
before you called to say
"Hello," "How are you?"
and "Where have all the years
gone?"

ENCHANTED LAKE

It lies a jewelled blue,
this lake that fuelled
my boyhood imagination,
(I pictured lissome fish
and whales sailing) where
the uncle whom I loved
like a second father and I
trolled for trout or, on a
lucky day, a big-
mouthed bass who might spit
the hook and billow away
into the gleaming underworld
below, and on soothing summer
evenings we would swim
like breath-spent porpoises
in the shallows were a million
minnows mirrored the shrunken
sun as it shimmered between
the prisms of spruce and cedar
that circumscribed my Cameron
and endowed it with a shape
that glimmered through my dreams.

WHO WOULD HAVE THOUGHT
For Colm O'Sullivan: In Memoriam

Who would have thought that a man
who, as a lad, haunted
the heretic hills of Kerry
(where his kinfolk pestered
peat out of Irish bogs
eight centuries before)
would have landed beside me
at the College we shared and where
I grew to admire the Joycean
turn of his mind and a wit
whittled out of Yeats and Wilde,
who lavished literature upon
a generation of enthused students,
who took his last breath
without my permission:
what else can we do
when Death intervenes
but rejoice in his having been?

BLESSING

Stewart Geddes passed
at ninety-two in his sleep:
was he in the midst of a deep
dream when the darkness descended,
or did his breathing just cease
with the last, rhythmic stroke
of his aging heart, with the last
gleam of light? Who
can know? We are not
privy to what awaits
us on the other side,
and it's a blessing we will not
know that we have died.

PERPETUAL

As I waltzed around our block,
my first girl paraded
on my arm, the hawk-eyed
neighbours gawked, surprised
no doubt at such
an odd romance, but there was
nothing false about
the bold glitter that lit
up our eyes or the fetching
squeeze she gave my hand
as we serenaded one another,
locked in the old perpetual
dance.

CYCLE

A pair of robins bobbing
for worms, higgledy-piggledy
on my green lawn: one
surprises her prize
while the other fawns and preens,
then both fly home
to the stretched necks of their young,
too intent on living
to notice the worm is still
wriggling.

DUO

I was too shy to talk
to the girl I fancied,
but as luck would have it
she spoke to me first,
and, mouth-dry, I nodded
to her soothing smile, and we
strolled hand in hand
around our block till
I found enough pluck
to prattle my way into a
jewelled summer where we
danced as a duo.

END

When a poem percolates,
there is no end
in sight; meaning lies
not in the words, it flows
out of them towards some
timeless truth, and try
as I might I cannot
bend them to my will,
they are carried on their own
volition to the final, ruthless
rhyme.

DESIRE

When God ripped Eve
out of Adam's ribs, what
he saw was a mirror image
of himself: with breasts
unsuckled and an extra
cleft and hair that hung
like flung flowers; he felt
no fire in his loins
as hand-in-hand they strolled
the groomed sod, until
Eve purloined an apple,
and Adam, smitten, came
unbuckled with desire.

ITCH

When the words won't come,
teetering on the brink of my
tongue, I look to metaphor
to shore up my bard's
resolve, some trope
rich with unmentionable
meaning: it's then that I itch
to ink.

THRUSH

How rare to see a thrush
bouncing on my backyard
grass, so far
from his usual hangout
in the underbrush of some
guarded glen; he opens
his bill in a tawny yawn
and utters his tinsel
trill, then without a wink
my way, flutters off,
leaving me alone
and so envious, I give
the nod to God.

NON-SENSE

There is something of the
mad in every poet,
a tinge of intranquility
in the mind's dark density,
a dis-ease in the iambic
where the imp in impious
quivers the bardic quill,
and should pentameters flow,
they do so better
when radical, unhinged
from sense.

THIRST

I assume it was God Himself
who sent the serpent slinking
into the Garden to tempt Eve,
thirsting for knowledge,
to take the first bite,
and He must have known,
with a nod and a wink, that Adam
would cleave to his mate's side:
why then was Eden denied
and the transgressors doomed?
It must have been spite
or, unbelievably, a burst
of un-Godly pride.

THUNDER

I loved the loud sound
of thunder from the underbelly
of fast-flowing clouds
that cruised an inch above
the tree-tops of my grand-
father's house (and the abode
I called home) and then
the fresh sluicing of rain
replenishing everything
green, but I wasn't fond
of the lightning that cleft
our maples like carefree
kindling, and left
our verandah unshrouded,
open to the fiery festering
of the westering sun, and I
wondered whether anything
in this world really
lasted.

BOUNTIFUL

Adam and Eve had little
to do in their bountiful bower:
there was no garden to dig
or sod to turn, the crops
ripened on their own behalf
and fruit flowered within
a thumb's grasp (while God
blessed their joint-ventures)
nor was there any need
for clothing in the sun-
nuzzled afternoons
or nurturing nights anointed
by moonlight – until
Eve, gnawing for knowledge,
bit what was forbidden,
and Adam, no slouch,
shared in the blame as the
corrupted couple debouched
from Eden: fig-leafed,
Id-ridden and shamed.

TRUMP

They say you are a bully,
boisterous and bristling
with invective and innuendo,
unembarrassed by your
outsize wig,
but somewhere deep
inside the Donald's
body there sits a wee
boy, given to tantrums
when he wants his way,
kicking the cat when flouted
and begging the bigger boys:
"Pick me! Pick me!"

WROUGHT

A poem begins with a
thought hovering in the head,
willing itself into words
and surprising the black acre
of the page with raw
rhythm, a motion towards
metaphor and some
meaning I have no notion
of how it was wrought.

HURRY

When you're seventy-nine
there's no hurry left
alive, it's slow locomotion
all the way, the heart
thumps a thud or two
less per minute, the blood
flows as if it's on holiday,
there's no more hump
to get over except
the will to survive, and the best
we can hope for
is to beat the odds by a year
or two or spend our time
currying favour with the gods.

SKEDADDLE

It did not snow in Eden
until Eve, apple-
addled, tasted the fruit
of the tree forbidden,
and Adam, smitten, followed
suit, after which the flurry
of God's fury left
the sin-bitten bower
a wasteland of frozen roses
and withering foliage,
while chilling winds blew
hither and thither and the
paradisal pair
skedaddled.

JURY

It's been a long and satisfying
life, and I intend to go
gently into Dylan's Good
Night: after all,
I've had my day, weaned
my soul from strife and woe,
eased myself into age
like a lark lifting into air,
content with what has been
allotted me, but the jury's
still out: as the last lick
of light flickers in the dark,
I may shout "Nay!" – bent
by bravado, fuelled with fury.

OLD THINGS

We cling to old things
with the same passion we reserve
for the past that sings to our dreams,
and as the world renews itself
around us, we cling to what
is most familiar: a threadbare
sweater, a rumpled hat,
those friends who recall
the days when hope was un-
rationed, and most of all
we find solace in the woman
at our side, who has abided
there since love itself,
like Spring, blossomed and grew.

TROUBADOUR

Leonard Cohen is dead,
that sonorous deep-growled
thrum forever stilled;
he took a sound embedded
in the bowel and raised it
through his poet's throat
to haunting song (while
in his verse he played the minstrel
with a magic, whimsical wand);
there was always something
of the dirge or lasering lament
in the willfulness of his lyric,
in the tragic timbre of Hallelujah,
he gave us more than
we thought possible in the human
voice: this troubled,
talented troubadour.

COMING ON

Autumn is the time of leaf-
fall and root-rot,
and all the flowers whose bloom
scintillated Summer are petal-
seized and soon forgotten:
no robins sing
for their supper in the wormless
earth or the bare-breathing
trees, and there is a jinn-filled
chill in the pre-dawn
breeze as old men
contemplate their age
and rage at Winter's coming
on.

THE BREATH OF MY BEING

First Choice Books
2018

BREATH
For Anne in loving memory

I've suffered all the phases
of grief and am still stuck
on denial, for giving that up
would mean accepting your death,
and I want to carry on
loving you as you were when
luck was a living thing
inside us and just seeing you
in the mists of morning and gazing
into your anodyne eyes took
away the breath of my being.

EMBERS
For my grandfather in loving memory

The more I edge into my age
the further back the muscles
of memory flex, and I see
again the Celtic green
of grandfather's lawn
and dandelions blooming
like harvest moons and the sweet
sway of the lilacs on their hedge
and the fletched spray of the maples'
leafage, and I know a joy
felt in the ballast of my bones
and in the hum of my blood,
and I want to remember again
the eyes I loved more than
any other and forget the rage
that greeted their demise and left
me alone with the etched
embers of my grief.

GAZA

On Easter Sunday we wore
our brand-new shoes
and the Reverend Buchanan
told us the story of Jesus
pinned upon His cross
like a lepidopterist's moth,
and mentioned the magic stone
that rolled away, but all
the time I was thinking of Samson
with his locks lopped off
by the dazzling Delilah, blinded
by righteous rage and bringing
down the walls of Gaza
upon himself and the almighty
Philistines.

POD
For Anne in loving memory

We fitted together as snug
as two peas in the proverbial
pod, and we travelled in tight
tandem all the days
and nights of our long, enlinked
lives, seasoned with serenity,
and even now, with you gone,
I thank the gods who let me
feel the tug of love.

DYLAN
For Anne in loving memory

And so my beloved I refuse
to say goodbye as long as
you continue to haunt every
room I try to breathe in,
where your bright beaming smile
belies your having gone

BEGOTTEN

In Sunday school we learned
that God so loved the world,
but I had an odd thought:
why did our Lord have only
one begotten son,
who died to save me from my
mortal sins and Eve's ineptitude
in Eden, and whose birth
I celebrated with such Yuletide
carolling – when my humbly-thumbed
Bible was dotted with begots.

NUB

A poem is a thought in search
of words to give it room
to breathe, a feeling in need
of a succinct simile or two,
or perhaps a plot to be dubbed
in ink in pursuit of the numinous
nub we call meaning.

UNRHYMED

After the tears comes
the emptiness, the vacancies
you filled with such a graceful
presence for the years we shared
a shadow, and I am numbed
to the nub with the aching acre
of the grief I feel, and do
my best to find the will
to carry on without you
and the loving lustre of our life
together, remembering that Time
itself is the thief who robs us
of those we hold most dear,
leaving us empty – unrhymed

TRUTH
For Anne in loving memory

You loved Question Period
every weekday
at three on the dot, the cut
and thrust of debate where
no-one gave an inch
and thought gave way to
bombast; you were a political
junkie who loved the rumpus
of Trump and all his ilk, not
averse to venting your views
aloud and surprised when the
TV didn't flinch,
you despised the silken lies
he laced the language with,
and offered, in their stead, kindness,
everlasting love and the ruthless
truth.

KISS
For Anne in loving memory

You loved our house so much
you wanted to die in it,
and when your wish was granted,
I found you lying as if
softly asleep, the hand
I held in mine for fifty-
seven years cold
to the touch, and I raised it
aloft in singular thanks
to the god who gave you to me
to have and to hold, as I do
now in my mind's eye,
savouring the tingle of a deeply
remembered kiss.

DICKENSIAN

The Point was a place Dickens
would have died for, whose
Pickwickian characters massage
the muscle of my imagination
and wound their peripatetic way
into poems and stories: Ruby,
who tussled with rages and rattled
through the village on her two-wheeler and
Cap Harness the barber
who never saw the sea but charmed
us all with the latest tittle-
tattle and Silent George who couldn't
stop talking and Happy
Butler who plastered badly
but loved his Collie and his lime-
encrusted truck and Easton
Burgess who dubbed me the colonel
and doled out double-dips
and Harry Fisher whose front
yard was atilt with rusting
stove and failed fridges
just like his mind maelsromed
by Ypres and the Somme and Pussy
Carr and Rip Kemsley
and Long Tom Shaw
and all the other nicknamed
unanointed denizens
who tickled my fancy

GOLDENROD

It must be a September morn
because the sun is pouring
its molten halo over the
goldenrod fringing
the gravel-glinting road
we set out upon on our
wayward amble to a one-
room country school
unadorned by flora
or fauna, and we meander
past Leckie's farm
where Holsteins with Mercatur
maps on their bellies graze
lazily and in the meadows
sprays of sparrows are greeted
with "My wedding!" by the girls
we pretend to ignore, and soon
we come to hawthorn hedge
where Grace's colt cavorts
with his red-blooded erection
(our blushing bountiful) and beyond
is the edge of everything
and we are relieved when the school
looms into view, where we
will spend our days being groomed
for living.

FIRST KISS

I met her on the beach an hour
before we drove home
in the back seat of my pal's
fashionable Mustang, and before
I could flinch, her lubricious lips
were an inch from mine, and before
I could duck, her tongue lusted
after mine, and for the first
time it dawned on me
that girls possessed both
passion and pluck.

LUFF

When I was just pubescent,
I dreamt of the girls of Canatara
sweetening its sands in their one-
piece suits and lolling
Rubenesque in the libidinous
light of a midsummer
sun, and I felt the first
luff of lust all the way
down to my unmentionables.

POD
For Anne in loving memory

We fitted together as snug
as two peas in the proverbial
pod, and we travelled in tight
tandem all the days
and nights of our long, enlinked
lives, seasoned with serenity,
and even now, with you gone,
I thank the gods who let me
feel the tug of love.

EDEN

My village had just one
policeman: Constable Pedan,
whose only rouble in town
was Butch and I riding
double on the sidewalk
and daring him to catch us
with his two flat feet,
and oh the thrill we got
outwitting a cop
was greater than Adam's
landing in Eden.

NICK

Flaxen-haired Icarus
loved his waxened wings,
feathering the air above Greece,
riding higher than skylarks
and beaked eagles, until,
puffed by pride, he soared
into the molten sunshine:
jolted by joy but undone
by the nick of time.

WHY

Before the world weighed in
we danced through the milkweed
meadows below the Bridge,
casting a sideways glance
at pods like pugnacious peas
splitting open and letting fly
parachuting puffs that tickled
the sky with a silken tease,
and fractured stems milting
their unctuous ooze and a green
caterpillar tweezering a leaf
and a mottled Monarch tilting
a blue bloom, and we pranced
till our shadows shrivelled in the
noontide sun and never
once did we ask why.

BURLED

When I was young enough
to unremember the days
that passed between the sun's
rising and its feathered fall,
I tasted the tang of the newly-
groomed grass of grandfather's
lawn and let the odour
of burning leaves curdling
on the curb tingle my nostrils,
sweetened by the aroma of roses
blooming beside hollyhocks
hung on the fence like multi-
coloured moons and the dande-
lions'
breeze-blown fluff,
and my world was then always
a burled beginning, all feel
and sense and tendrill'd touch
without recall.

WINK

Shirley, the little mynx,
does the Can Can
on Grandfather's lawn,
trilling, "I lift my legs
so high you can see
my cherry pie ay ay!"
and my knees weaken,
while the
girl-next door
looks at me and winks.

BEING
For Anne in loving memory

I close my eyes and there
you are in all the brightness
of your being, surprised by joy,
and I long to sun my fingers
through your unbound hair
and sit you down for a cozy
chat in the language of love
we shared for fifty years
and more, and I wish you could smile
as if you were still alive,
while I stare at the urn that nurtures
your ashes and I am left
to grieve your absence as the world
moves on without your impassioned
presence.

FELICITY
For Anne in loving memory

You were not my first love,
but the last and most lasting:
there was Nancy whom I worshipped
from afar like Lancelot gazing
at the Grail and Shirley, the girl-
next door, whose eyes sparkled
like a moonlit star and Laura
who brought a tingling to my loins
and Sandy with our summer romance
and a heart briefly purloined
and Louise who taught me passion
that set my gong agley,
but you were all of my loves
fashioned into one, for whom
I dreamt a flawless felicity
and will carry on dreaming
as long as God lets my body
be.

STORY

When the world was new and I
grew straight and true
in the village that spawned me,
I idled my days away
whenever the sun sidled
out of First Bush and gloried
the grass of Grandfather's lawn,
knowing there would always be
another dawn, the Earth's
rebirth and the beginning
of my June-indued story.

LAST NIGHT
For Anne in loving memory

The last night that you lived
we sat together on the green
chesterfield we bought
fifty-six years ago
when our world was young
with the sheen still on it,
content to feel the perpetual
presence of our unalloyed
love: no need
to hold hands as we did
the time we strolled through the
feathered snow of a February
evening, the day before
I pledged my troth and you
delighted me with your nuptial
nod and we both thanked
the nearest god for the gift
of the other and a future un-
interrupted by anything
but joy.

GO

The Great Creator drew
Adam out of dust, just
to show He could do it,
and grew him a dappled garden,
rapturous with roses and docile
daisies, and when Adam complained
of being alone, Eve
was wrought from a rib, and all
was thought to be well until
the helpmate un-bibbed
and apple, and God uttered
an adamantine "Go!"

CEREMONIAL

In Sunday school at Christmas
time it was Hark the Herald
and We Three Kings, our voices
raised aloft like angel's
wings upon our Yuletide
breath, and we closed our eyes
and saw that little Town
and the mangered Babe, His sleep
softened by our ceremonial singing.

THE STAR-BRUSHED HORIZON

First Choice Books
2019

A BUTTERFLY FOR ANNE
For Gerry Parker

You send this exquisite
green butterfly in lieu of
a visit, perched poetically
on an amaze of lines,
alabaster moons and a dazzle
of dots fancied afresh:
a master's art that says
how much you loved my Anne,
that utters its grief through
its breathless beauty.

JURY

It's been a long and satisfying
life, and I intend to go
gently into Dylan's Good
Night: after all,
I've had my day, weaned
my soul from strife and woe,
eased myself into age
like a lark lifting into air,
content with what has been
allotted me, but the jury's
still out: as the last lick
of light flickers in the dark,
I may shout "Nay!" – bent
by bravado, fuelled by fury.

CADENCED

When Leckie's fallow froze
after January's thaw,
we took to the ice like ducks
on rudders, our blades scrolling
meridians we skimmed tenderly
under a moon hallowed
in the dark and a sky budded
with stars, boys and girls
together, hand-in-glove,
cadenced and going as the Earth
goes: we were all pluck,
ungendered, brimming
with hope and whatever
else comes before
the niceties of coupled love.

REACH

On sultry summer afternoons
we watched the wind-wafted
waves of Huron, as blue
as morning glories stroked
by lasering light, break
upon Canatara's
fabled beach, and we also
found time to cast
an unrighteous eye
upon the girls who once
were merely our chums
as they lay now full-
frontal on the sun-infused
sand, knowing all
along with our penultimate breath
that these creatures, lazing
there, feigning boredom,
would be forever beyond
our reach.

FURY

How many summers did we while
away the days on Canatara
Beach, where the sun hummed
on the heat-soaked sand
and girls, new-breasted,
smile-beguiling and thigh-
shy, stretched out
before our salacious gaze
(hoping to be pursued perhaps),
but all we could do was shout
something rude
and plunge, unfazed, into Huron,
where we stroked each wave
with mammillary fury.

GENDER

When Winter comes with its
numbing winds and crackling
cold, the swamp below
the village freezes tight,
and we on buoyant blades
are released from the vice-grip
of gravity for the seconds it takes
us to glide from west
to east like Vikings on a
silken sea, and if we,
emboldened, happen
to tumble backwards
into someone of the other
ilk (and inadvertently
tease a tender curve),
the ice will bear the blame
as we all surrender
to the pleasing ploys of the
gender game.

STRANGER

When our dog Moochie
fell ill with distemper,
my father drove him into the
countryside and dropped
him off, and I've always
wondered what dog-thoughts
went whistling through his head
as, confused, dazed,
abandoned, he started up
the nearest lane, hoping
some stranger would call
out, "Here, pooch!"
and show him more love
than we did.

BOYS AND GIRLS

In the dallying darkness
over Monck Street,
under a monsoon
moon marinating side-
walk and roadway
with a mellowing light
and beneath Mara's luminous
lamp, we played out
our ritual games: Red
Rover, May-I
and most of all Hide-
and-Go-Seek, sallying
into the shimmying shadows,
waiting for the "All free!"
boys and girls alike,
where a knee might accidental
another, triggering a rush
of blood and a smile as big
as the star-brushed horizon.

POVERTY

When Moochie was just a pup
we couldn't afford to have
him take the shots that would've
prevented the distemper
he suffered, but instead
of letting him die among
those who loved him, my father,
to my alarm, drove him to the
countryside and dropped
him off at the nearest farm,
where I was certain he would
crawl to the barn and let
his life slip away,
alone and shivering, and I thought
how hard my father's heart
must have been, but then
by and by I had
another thought: my father
couldn't endure watching
Moochie die: even
so I still couldn't forgive
him for being poor.

MILLENIUM

These dunes are as old
as Methuselah's sire,
washed ashore by a thousand
wavelets tonguing the beaches
of Canatara, dried
by a thousand wave sifting
and enthusing the sun-
drenched sands into hummocked
hills that shimmered in the light
of the midsummer moon
and where, in an afternoon
of Junes, we played pirates
and thought of the Attawandaron
long ago greeting
the gods and the dream of dawn
and pressing their bent bodies
against the dune's drift
and listening to the millennial
hum of heat below.

HAMELIN
For Jean McKay

You are a cross between
a pixy and the Pied Piper,
you move through the piebald
world
on tingling tip-toe
the better to sense the myriad
oblong objects you trans-
mogrify with your singing
flights of fancy and dainty
dioramas; there is nothing too
small to fit your exquisite
eye, and all the while
you toss out flute
tunes, frenzied cadenzas
and a poet's prose to those
of us who love you
and are happy to follow you
all the way to Hamelin.

UNRDEEMED

Above the hushed silence
of Cameron Lake, a menstrual
moon brushes the surface
with its tidal touch, and the woods
silhouetted with alabaster-
beaming birch are bereft
of birdsong except for Owl's
harmonized hoot, and the ink
of shadow within is sucked
shoreward to shrink
in the luminous wake where
loons abruptly rhapsodize,
and all seems tranquil
and true, while I stand
alone on the edge of everything,
fretful and unredeemed.

EXALTED

Loving you is an act
of remembrance, a recalling
of all those days when we
were
too young to be tempered
by tactful touch or the soft
collision of lips, when being
amazed was our common
fare,
when I knew such jolting
joy at a glimpse of your hair
haloed by juddering sun-
light or your eyes as blue
as crystallized cobalt
or the effortless allure
of your youthful gaze:
in truth our love was too
exalted to be nipped
in the bud.

STIPPLED

Nothing can retrieve
the aching days of my youth,
when I was unencumbered
by doubt, when the God I be-
seeched
to take my soul each
night before I slumbered
on safely through the night
routed my sins and follies,
and the sun unfurled
above First Bush
every morning and would do
so forever, and a
summering breeze strummed
the leaves of my grandfather's
maple with all the zest
of a jazz quartet, and I trod
the rippling streets of my village
ablaze with possibilities
of soothsaying and stories
stippled with truth, while Jesus,
pinioned and forsaken,
would rise again like Lazarus
and astonish the world.

ROAN
For Grace Leckie

I watched you galloping
across the fallow field
on your stalwart stallion
with a thigh-gripping ease,
and waited while you went
coursing by, your hair
bountiful in the breeze,
the roan tight-lipped,
nostrils a-flare, and I wasn't
sure whether I loved you
more, or the horse.

WAND

God, that great M.C.,
waved his magic wand
and Eden popped out of
the ether: a garden where tulips
and other blooms spawned
hither and thither until
Adam arrived, conjured
out of dust, to groom
the fruits and flowers and welcome
Eve, of whom he soon
grew fond, so that
when the slithering serpent,
in cahoots with Lucifer,
offered the Apple of Knowledge,
and Eve, grappling with temptation,
took a lusty bite,
Adam, pleased to assist,
and to spite his Maker, followed
suit, and the Lord, in a huff,
blew them both out of
Eden with a paradisal puff.

HOLY
For Gran: In Memoriam

In Sunday School we sang
as if God Himself
were keeping tabs, while
back home my Grandma
baked her weekly raisin
pies and watched her Jello
cool in its bowl on the side
verandah: I found it odd
that the Divine seldom visited
our abode, but there was affection
in those prized pies and more
love abiding there
than the Lord needed to keep
His Sabbath Holy.

NIGHT SKATING

We go night skating
on Leckie's fallow in a static
snow, the kind that drips
from the lip of Heaven and parachutes
to Earth as soft as a lunar
landing, and the only sound
to break the serenity of the silence
is the soft heave of our breathing
and the whisper of flakes ecstatic
on the cheeks we hold aloft
like pilgrims awaiting manna,
and even though we are numbed
by the Arctic chill, we feel
as hallowed as we will ever
be in Kingdom Come.

TWO FOR MRS. BRAY

WOUNDS

Bill Bray mowed
Grampa's 'back forty'
for fifty cents, half
of which he gave to his widowed
mother, whose clapboard
house was wombed with bloom,
and in there, amid
the daffodils and daisies
she grew happy, untouched
by war's wound.

CONSOLATION

Mrs. Brays' wide-
brimmed hat floats
above the flowers she dotes
on (amid the hum
of bees) and gives no
sign of the sorrow she felt
at the grim news that made
her a widow, for these
creations, daffodil
or daisy, will have to do
for comfort and consolation.

LUNAR

The moon gazed at itself
in the glazed mirror of
Foster's pond, and we zoomed
back and forth, shredding
our shadows, boys and girls
with tugged tuques and streaming
scarves, mittens just
shy of illicit touch,
and when someone yelled
'Crack the whip!' I found
myself tossed and flying
as sleek as a seal enticing
ice, while above all
the great Bridge loomed,
bisecting the sky
and arching towards the stars,
under which we skated
skittish and dreaming of
lunar love.

WHAT WE ARE CALLED

To be given a nickname
was our town's way of saying
"Hello, you belong," and those
so honoured could be seen
whistling down Michigan
Ave and nodding to their sobriquet
as if it had been quickened
at birth, whether it was Rip
or Butch, Cap or Wiz
made no difference,
for a village is the Earth writ
small, the heart's home,
where no one is alone
and what we are called is as
deep as a knowing in the bone.

IMPECCABLE

When Leckie's fallow glistened
like the mirrored pool of the Taj
Mahal under the auspices
of Venus and Mars, we take
to our skates and convene in ones
and twos beneath the jewelled
moon, the waltz of our wheeling
humming unschooled
in our heads, and the further we burrow
into the sheer shallows of the dark
we find ourselves listening to the
impeccable music of the stars.

CENTENNIAL

It wasn't the Santa Claus
Parade or even Macy's
Thanksgiving , but the brand-
new Fire Truck,
red as a raspberry,
led the way with the volunteer
crew hanging on
with both hands, followed
by the Boy Scout's
marching band, their bugles
blustering with all the zest
of a jazz ensemble,
and majorettes in their high-
stepping pace and twirling
batons glinting in the sunshine
the gods blessed us with,
and then came the vintage
autos, the Girl Guides
striding two by two,
a scuffle of ruffians from the
wrong side of the tracks,
and the Reeve in his rented limousine,
tipping his top hat
to the throng that lined Michigan
Avenue, and there was laughter
and tears amidst the merriment
and love for a town that had survived,
against the odds and with a little
luck, for a hundred years.

CHANCES

O the girls of the Point!
I see them now sifting
in the sunlight over
Canatara, their images
uplifted to my eighty-
year-old sight:
Nancy: as beautiful and un-
attainable as Guinevere
in some medieval romance
and I worshipped her from afar
like a lovelorn Lancelot,
and Shirley, just an inch
into her womanhood, stirred
in me feelings I later
learned were lust, and her sister
Betty, a big and bossy-
breasted Minerva who spun
the bottle and chortled at our
shy compliance, and Joycey
who longed to be Gaia
in her garden, but sported only
her underpants and puzzled
at the circumstances that left
her penurious and open to my
prurient glances: I see
them all again as clearly
as Huron's sky, re-anointed
by the years gone by,
and even now I'd like
to say: I like my chances.

ROISTERING

Each summer morning
the sun boiled out of
First Bush and layered
our streets with luminous light,
and I greeted the coming day
with a gallop and a prayer,
aiming my brand-new
body towards the doors
behind which the friends
who drew me outside
of my centering self
awaited my hithering call:
Wiz Withers whose magical
hands could weave gizmos
and gadgets out of anonymous
odds and ends with a kind
of ledgerdemain even
the gods envied:
Butch McCord who had
no other name
but cushioned the blows of bullies
just for me, who trod
the voluminous girders of the Bridge
to show the world what daring
was and what it meant
to be a brother:
Jerry Mara who could swim
like a perambulating porpoise
and carried our daily play
to Canatara and beyond,
who gave full meaning
to the word loyalty:
Bones Saunders all
elbows and angles,
who let us stick him
with a nickname and hoisted
the friendship flag:

and so it was I learned
like Adam before the fall
what love was, its synesthetic
edge, its numinous glow,
and before the gloaming loomed
we all went out and royally
roistered..

DOLLY

Dolly Gordon, after
an unfulfilling day
shovelling coal, liked
to quaff a beer or two
more than he should to ease
the pain and satisfy his soul,
but his good wife disapproved
of such indulgence, and when
he bent over, as far
as he was able, to clear
the cobwebs from his hobbled
brain, she tapped him once
on the skull with an iron skillet,
and when he woke, there was a
bulge on his bean, his head
was clear, and supper was on
the table.

STAMINA

When the ice glazed the fallow
of Leckie's fields like the
sheen of moonlight
on a mesmerized meadow,
we skated out under
the auspices of the stars, young,
callow and gendered by choice,
our scarves fleeing behind
us like the wisping tails
of Halley's comet, and we felt
in our glistened gliding the tidal
tug of the universe and something
deeper than the stamina of the stars,
something unyielding,
hugging the bone, and leaving
us dazed, cloistered
and inalienably alone.

AFFABLE

At the corner of Alexandra and Monk
Gran and Mrs. Bray
met most mornings
for their friendly chat and a laugh
or two, and the village being
both canvas and manuscript,
they talked about what
so-and-so said
to whom and other snippets
of this and that, tossed
out with a twinkle, until
the town grew round
and through them like a
dyslexic poem, pillaged
from the glossary of affable gossip.

FOSTER'S POND

In the summertime we waded
big-booted into Foster's
Pond in search of cattails
we wielded like furred
tomahawks, and dreamed
of setting them ablaze
in the final fading of the day's-
long light, but in the winter
our pond glazed over
and we skated the afternoons
away, sailing like balloon-
rigged schooners among
the reeds and goose-grey
grass, lost to all
but ourselves in the fury
of speed and the blur of our blading.

BUOYANCY

Under a pale and translucent
moon and a sky scattered
with stars in their Grecian arcs,
we feel the bite of the ice
on our blades and cruise through the
hovering dark, glad
to be night-skating here
where the Earth has no edges,
and when Coop hits a shattering
of shale, we laugh at his pin-
point landing and his leveraged
leap upright,
and cheer when Marilyn spins
like a dulcimered doll, and Bonnie
and Sharon insist on doing
a duo as sisters, and Grace
and I come to the brink
of coy contiguity before breaking
asusnder, and the moon turns
as golden as a doting doubloon,
and we feel as a singular soul
the sheer joy of buoyancy.

LOST

Mrs. Bradley's mad
chatter could be heard
across our half of the village,
bruising the evening air,
disrupting hopscotch
and marbles, we paused long
enough to let our blood
chill and feel the intimations
of what it is to be old
and lost somewhere
in the mind you used to have.

SHINNY

In the Winter on Saturdays
we played shinny on Foster's
Pond, with hand-me-
down sticks and a borrowed
puck, battered and burred,
and a goalie brandishing a broom,
like Turk Broda in his prime
(not even the catalogue-pads
so tenderly stitched
could undo his pluck)
as we skidded and slewed on the slick
surface in our galumphing
galashes, but we were young
and in the air above us
we could hear the skinny,
high-pitched voice
of Foster Hewitt urging
us on, while the crowd cheered
like Romans for the lions.

OTHER

Shirley spun the bottle
with a wristed twist and stood
above our boy-girl
circle with lips at the ready
and bug-eyed with anticipation,
while I watched the jug spin
like Cupid's arrow, dread
in my heart as it whirled
through my neighbourhood
and stopped stark beside
me, and the girls whooped
as their gendered mate gripped
me by the waist and planted
one smothering, unchaste,
tongue-tender kiss
on my startled gaze, and I sensed
something other,
some joy grazing
astride, unthrottled
and three miles wide.

A KIND OF LIGHT

When the moon bloomed as bright
as a galleon ablaze in a sky
littered with stars and their diamond
dazzle, we took to the ice
like Eskimos to snow, following
the girls, enwombed in wool,
who became just pals
for the night, skittering skillfully
over the glacial glaze
of Leckie's fallow, in un-
gendered duos or improvised
threesomes, our bodies
boneless in the winter chill,
wondering what it meant
to be and looking for the kind
of light we cannot see.

ANOINTED

Easter Sunday in the Point
was new shoes with the shine
still on them and pants
with a fine crease and ladies
bonneted and beribboned
and gentlemen in fresh habits,
and I remember staring at Christ
strung upon Golgotha (vinegar-
tongued, palms pinned
like moths on a lepidopterist's
display) just above
the altar where the Sabbath sun
limned His halo, and we felt
ourselves to be among
the anointed there, buoyed
by the yeast of prayer.

A WORLD AWAY

When I was young and whiled
the world away in the midst
of my innocence, I ambled
around the village that bore
me up like a propagated
poem, unbeguiled
by anything "other"
beyond its mothering boundaries,
breathing the incense of its easing
air as I rambled wherever
I pleased over meadows
where milkweed pods
unfurled to dust the breeze
with providential puffs
and the wild mustard
flamed as golden as the
lustrous sun ripening
the snows that hung from their trees
like the appetized apples of Eden,
and even the thunder was muffled
there and the rains renewed
the grasses' bedizening and all
roads ferried me home
where love bloomed so
flagrantly no god
could sunder it.

WARTS

My village was a three-steepled
town, and at precisely a quarter
to eleven each Sunday
morning, the Presbyterian bell
outrang its Anglican
cousin, calling the faithful
to people the pews, swell
the stalls and come forth
in the name of Christendom,
singing hosannas to the
high heavens, warts
and all.

INCORRUPTIBLE

On soft summer mornings
the sun rises up out of
First Bush like a Phoenix
pouring Grecian light
on the village streets below,
and we are released like
Moses out of Egypt into
the airy outdoors,
and it's Move-Up in Withers
field, hopscotch
or Double Dutch with the girls
gliding aloft and a-glow,
or ring-around-a-rosy
with the little'uns in tow,
or, on a good day,
when bees hum to hear
themselves sing,
surprising Wiz in his cellar
with his magical gadgetry,
and we are as free as leaves
unleafing from the density
of the tree, and insulated from the
burst of the world by our
incorruptible innocence.

COP

Our village had but one
cop, few villains
and even less trouble:
Constable Pedan, whose principal
task was scouring the alleys
to get a bead on truants,
stopping the odd jay-
walker on our carless
streets, parsing the Pool
Room for underage
felons, rousting un-
ruly hoboes
from their afternoon snooze,
guiding to hearth and home
gentlemen who'd imbibed
too much booze,
or pursuing Butch and me
riding double and beating
his flat-footed trot
to the Bridge, where we hid
below its looping span,
pleased with ourselves
and basking in our own glow.

NEW-FOUND

The wood-burning furnace
below heaves its heat
up into the classroom
above, where twenty-three
pupils in eight grades
sit rapt and waiting
for Miss Nelson to blow
into her pitch-pipe and tweet
a perfect "cee", after which
we all sing our anthem
to the King, and school begins:
that's me in the middle row
(good at reading but little
else) glancing across
two aisles at Grace
and indulging in the bulge
of her new-found breasts:
she fails to turn around,
and I am seized with some-
thing akin to despair,
uncaressed by hope,
watching her face pointed
straight ahead, her tresses-
enriched by the morning
light, at ease, alas,
with her womanhood.

PEN

I took up my pointed pencil
at Grade Three, not
knowing what odd urge
took hold of me,
but I recall the surge of serenity
as the blank page came
alive in my eyes and the
surprise that stories were born
inside before they aged
and allowed themselves
to be written and read,
and I knew even then
it wasn't for renown or glory
but the release of words in their
anointed wonder on the chance
that someone disembodied
out there might understand
and give me the nod:
I can't tell you or God
when, but the time will come
when I will have lain down
my pen.

ENDURING

Gran was always good
for a nickel; I can still
hear the crisp click
as she opened her purse and lifted
a shiny five-cent
piece onto my outstretched
hand, and then it was off
to Harry Brand's (with his eighty-
year, tight-fisted
smile) for a Pepsi (sucked
till the straw gave up)
or a couple of grab-bags
or a pair of black-balls,
and I thought then, as I do
now, how lucky I was
all those years to have
such a grandmother
and the enduring
gift of her love.

DEMUR

Joycee Clark was rumoured
to be promiscuous,
but not knowing for a fact
the meaning of the term, we had
to be content with wishing she'd
drop her pants and do
the hula-hula dance,
and then surprise us all
by showing off the tender
cleft between her thighs
(we dreamed the daylights
out of), but what we got
instead was a demur purr
and a furtive smile that left
the mystery intact.

ASTRIDE
For Sharon, Bonnie and Marilyn

The girls gather round
Marilyn and the pony she sits
astride, buffing the pommel
with her free hand, as `Sharon
strokes the curling mane
and Bonnie giggles as Champ
pokes his nose into the
feed-bag, and the sisters
beg for a ride they will never
own, while in the fallow field
the stiff-legged hired
man hobbles homeward,
roughshod and randy.

ART

This is me at nine
months, the photo craftily
coloured to bring out
the bloom in my cheeks and the
sweet
green of grandfather's grass,
and who knew what plots
and stanzas lay behind
that unblemished brow
(the sorcerer's art
with words perhaps) or what
poet's passion I might
unfurl some day
and startle the world.

STRUCK

The things I remember:
five-year-old
Tom, tucked a-bed
and trying not to sleep,
his eyes still beaming,
alive with expectation,
and me alongside,
singing "O the great
ships sail through the
alley-ally-O
on the first day of September"
until, soporific with song,
he drifts into some dream
I am not privy to,
and I too begin to doze,
struck once again
by how deep love
goes.

UNRAVELLED

Oh, Nancy Mara,
I loved you always and from afar,
dreaming of warlike
knights and chargers barging
with a will through a hail of arrows,
along untraveled paths,
going for the Grail I would bring
to you to have your lips
sip its holy ambrosia,
or in another sally save you
from a life in serfdom
or worse, your gratitude
a lissome look was all
I needed as the blue igniting
of your eyes redeemed and endued,
till we danced in duo
upon the glistening sands
of Canatara before the thrill
of the tale unravelled
as dreams ever do,
and I, back on the straight
and narrow, was left still
loving you from afar.

BLUR

After January's thaw
Leckie's fallow becomes
one great lake
unlinked to any horizon
and soon glazed over
and metamorphosed into a
rink without beginning
or end, and we found ourselves,
under a menstrual moon
in a sky as black as Dracula's
glance, skating on the iced
curves of the world, and girls
and boys with mittened fingers
in tentative touch in their
seesawing glacial glide,
and I kept one prurient
eye on the freckled face,
wind-nuzzled curls
and kittenish grin of the blur
beside me, whom I had fancied
since I first learned
what amazement was.

MIRACULOUS

In the midst of my fever I saw
diaphanous-winged angels
fluttering like butterflies
just before bidding
farewell to their cocoons,
and singing a Siren song
as they gestured me gracefully
towards Heaven, where no
fevers thrive and there is
no need for the future,
but something gut-deep
and bracing in the bone drew
me back, and I awoke
to a welcoming, miraculous moon,
sweating and alive.

SPEED

When the ice on Leckie's fallow
was just thick enough
to bear the brunt of our blades,
we went flying down the centre,
eschewing the shallow edges
that broke like brittle glass,
and stroke by stroke we garnered
speed in gusts of sheer
momentum, until at last
we seemed freed from our body's
ballast and took flight
utterly into the air, as winged
as Icarus speculating on the sun.

DEKE
Sarnia City Champions
1933-1934

I sit in my solitary study
and notice an eighty-year-
old plaque once
held in my father's hands,
and I see him skating
as sweet as a swan on the
magic mirror of a pond,
his dekes and yaws as smooth
as new ice on a raw
rink (he has the boy's knack
but the puck-wit of a pro)
and I can hear the applause
of the home-town fans
who made this slim kid
their hero, and what joy
it must have been to feel
every breath in your body
tuned to the grace of the game,
and no hint then
of the grim days ahead
when he was no longer
slim and, done in
by drink, couldn't out-
deke Death.

WELL

Sometime soon
the last person to recall
my name will have just
forgotten it. But
for all those at whom
I have hurled my misanthropic
thoughts and rhyme-riddled
dreams through the prism
of my poems (that promised
more than words are allowed
to tell), please, remember
me well.

FOR ANNE

If you were a flower you'd be
a yellow rose sweetening
sunshine on June
afternoons, and at the edge
of evening mellowing moon-
light: we greet each
other in the morning's rise,
empowered by love in the
other's eyes, watching
as it grows and blooms
over the long years
we have been buoyantly
embowered.

DESIRE

When God ripped Eve
out of Adam's ribs, what
he saw was a mirror image
of himself: with breasts
unsuckled and an extra
cleft and hair that hung
like flung flowers; he felt
no fire in his loins
as hand-in-hand they strolled
the groomed sod, until
Eve purloined an apple,
and Adam, smitten, came
unbuckled with desire.

TUG

The girls are hopscotching
bare-legged in the breeze,
skipping from square to square
with the elegant ease of an acrobat
on a tremulous trapeze,
while the boys
in the field beside them
are tossing a rugby ball
with the ardent thrust of a right
arm, watching its awesome
arc all the way
home, while the girls squeeze
their thighs tight in their high-
wire flight, and the boys
dream non-stop
of touchdowns and the tug
of desire.

WIDOW

Mrs. Bray floats
among her flowers, swallowed
by sunshine, and glides
through her sea of petals
like Gaia on a good day,
doting on daisies or roses
and loving the way light
laps at the lips of poppies
or black-eyed Susans,
the way her garden grows
effusive, reminiscent
of that other garden
where there were no
wars and no widows.

SEASON
After John B. Lee

We were all at ease with Autumn,
when everything green
in McPherson's orchard
turned as rosy as a bride's
blush, and we bit into the fruit
and let the exotic juices
glide chinward,
and dreamed of apple cider
and the acrid edge of its aroma,
and in the swamp that hugged
the Point, bulrushes and cattails
flourished, furred and dappled
in their dying, and the maples in our
yard reddened before
their fiery fall, and along
the road to our country school
the ditches were rich with golden-
rod that summoned sunlight,
and the mist-teased fields
festooned the air with the florid
fleece of wild carrot
and dilatory daisies, and later
on, the pungence of moon-
rounded pumpkins split
wide and oozing pulp,
and winter wheat whisking
furrows, like peach-fuzz
on the chin of those
seeking to leave behind
the tug of childhood:
being young we cared
not that Autumn was, at bottom,
the season of root-rot
and dank decay, for ours was a
world where hope had its say.

TROUBADOUR

Leonard Cohen is dead,
that sonorous deep-growled
thrum forever stilled;
he took a sound embedded
in the bowel and raised it
through his poet's throat
to haunting song (while
in his verse he played the minstrel
with a magic, whimsical wand);
there was always something
of the dirge or lasering lament
in the willfulness of his lyric,
in the tragic timbre of Hallelujah,
he gave us more than
we thought possible in the human
voice: this troubled,
talented troubadour.

GLOW

My girls are like the glow
that roses make when bussed
by the summering sun under
a moonless sky and no
clouds above to brush
the bountiful breeze aside,
with eyes alight and wide
with wonder they brighten every
room they sidle into,
like poppies blushing crimson
in June: I never grow
accustomed to their levitating
love.

GIST

Whenever Mara's lamp
blinked into the inked shadows
of Monk Street, we gathered
boys and girls together
like guineas round a fist's
throw of oats in the June-
lewd sun, savouring
its lascivious light under
a sky stamped with stars
and a monastic moon floating
in the black above, and we
re-enacted the age-old
rituals with ampled exactitude,
while thinking of our afternoons
on the dune-rich sands
of Canatara and its erotic
urges, and needing no
reason, purging or exotic,
to question our right to relish
the joyful gist of the seasons.

BOOGIE

At a quarter to noon we stood
breathlessly on our walk
and waited for Herbie Gilbert
to sail by in his almost
new Tin Lizzy
and waited for the grin as he
bassooned the ooga-ooga
horn and thrilled a neighbourhood,
leaving them dizzy with delight
and letting us know that being
happy was as easy as being
adult with a Model T,
and we dreamed there on our
home curbs of doing
the boogie-woogie until
the future failed us.

EASE

Shirley: lying on the beach,
and I try not to watch
as her thighs ease innocently
open, undeterred
by the tight tuck of her one-
piece bathing suit,
or, delighted with my luck,
stare in my boyish
bravado at the winking wrinkle
where her crotch catches
the luminosity of Canatara's
sun, and what I feel
is less than desire and more
than curiosity, for I am
the intruder, Eve's adder,
reaching towards something
teasing and untouchable,
impatient in my prurience.

APOSTLE
For Grace Leckie

My mother called it "Puppy
love," but what I felt
had nothing to do with dogs
before their dotage: my body
refused to breathe whenever
you glanced my way, oozing
some intimation
of romance that left me
utterly bereft of speech,
and when you and your stallion
stutter-stepped past
our house a mile beyond
my reach, my heart, jostled
ajar went hectic
at your angelic smile,
like an apostle at the Last Supper.

GERONIMO

The dunes of Canatara are infused
with the heat of a thousand suns,
tiny infernos festooned
with tufts of grass livid
since Adam left Eden,
and soon to be our make-
believe mountains where cow-
pokes out of cahoots with the law
take cover, waiting
for the adamantine dark
to cool their six-gun
itch and a moon above
pitching its glacial glow
upon a boy like me,
playing Geronimo.

HONEYCOMB

The bees in Mrs. Bray's
groomed garden tremble
on the tingling tips of stamens
tossed here and there
by a playful breeze, and probe
with their buzzing proboscis
deep into the nectared heart
of a tulip or rambling rose:
they've mastered the art of pollination,
and before cruising to their honey-
combed home, they leave
behind a dozen blooms:
bee-blossomed.

AT EASE

When I was young and free
and at ease with the world,
every morning was a superb
surprise, as the sun up-
rose above First Bush,
inking it with Apollonian
light, igniting the trees
elder than Eden and shimmering
shade where robins throbbed
with song, and Huron Lake
was wave-wakened and generous
enough to swallow Heaven
whole, and grandfather's yard,
laddered with lilacs, opened
to my impatient eye and welcomed
me into its paradisal precinct,
for there were no adders
slithering silkily through my garden
in search of Eves and apples
that hung like pendulous prizes:
for I was young and the world
had yet to be unfurled
and hence was I pleased to harbour
its hithering to-and-fro
with my incorruptible innocence.

BEAMING

Gran would take me to the
Band Tattoo in Athletic
Park because Grandpa couldn't
stand the tuba turbulence
or the trumpeting turmoil,
but we loved the skirl of the
kilty band, the tremulous
tooting of horns, the tinkle
of the glockenspiel, the glacial
glide of the trombones
and the smart marchers stepping
stride for stride: the teeming
maelstrom of music
I adored because Gran
was beaming at such guilty
pleasure and what-is-more
she was sitting beside me.

RANDOM

It was in Bill McCord's
rink that my Dad's story
was first written, where he skated
with the inborn grace
of a swan over the silken
face of a perfect pond,
where he thrilled his rabid
fandom with deft dekes,
brisk bursts and mad-
cap dashes – until the day,
while they were building the bridge
that would loom over the town
like a rectilinear moon,
a red-hot rivet
without a nod or a pivot
dropped straight onto
the roof of Dad's arena,
burning it to ashes,
and though I was barely proof-
read, I must have thought
there are things in this world
that are random.

GOODBYE

"I'm on the road to recovery,
Donny," were the last words
my grandfather spoke
to me, before the sutures
broke and he bled to death,
and to keep my spent spirits
lifted, I dreamt of a dozen
farewells when the future
we shared had come to a close:
breath on breath, our heads
held high, and savoring
the gift of goodbye.

TUFTS

On winter evenings when the snow
sifted down on Monk
Street like the silken tufts
from milkweed pods
and a hazy moon caressed
the flakes that kept our god-
less games aglow,
we thought of Bethlehem
and shepherds in the muffled
air over Galilee,
and we peered at the tingling
sky above, looking
for a single star to ignite
the larcenous night and cast
some bountiful blessing
upon our All Free!

ONLY

On the mile-long trek
to our country school, boys
and girls in a straggling gaggle,
we passed Leckie's pasture
and cast our eyes on the young
colt there, his roan
coat surprised by a morning
sun, set on the horizon
ahead like a gilded marigold,
and below the colt's belly
hung a bright red
erection, throbbing like a
bruised thumb, as the girls
went numb with shock,
looking in every direction
but Leckie-ward, and we
boys locked our gaze
on the proud protuberance
and considered something
other than romance and moons
on star-startled nights:
the furious fusion of that
amazing instrument with another
receptacle we couldn't quite
fathom, as the girls giggled
and Coop broke the spell:
"That's only his pecker,"
he smiled.

DIGNITY

When I was still young
enough to wonder at the world,
I would watch each morning
Ol' Cap Garvey
shuffle past our gate
en route to the mail
with his skipper's dignity intact,
and marvel that his hair had turned
snow-white after
the storm of 'thirteen when waves,
unmuffled by the seething
winds, sent dozens
of lakers under, and I thought
about what it would take
to keep that malignant
memory alive for seventy
years.

SWERVES

Shirley McCord was our
mate, flipping cart-
wheels on grandfather's
much-mowed lawn,
skipping Double Dutch
or playing hopscotch
May I? and, when a bit
risqué, Post Office:
we made the most of our joint
childhood, (our days
unbordered) but when,
after an absence of two
years, I spotted a girl
on Canatara, all
swerves and curves and pertinent
points, my heart hopped,
unsure how it
should feel, and when she said,
"Hello, Don," I wished
for a slow moment that Time
had stopped when we were young
and certain of the way the world
would go.

APPLAUSE

There I am seated on the
railing of grandfather's
side verandah, reading
my maiden "epic" to an audience
of three: the McCords and my pal
Butch: my words greeted
with only a touch of the skeptic
and more surprise than I
thought warranted, my voice
just failing to reach
the authorial tone I aimed
at (with a pregnant pause
or two), and I waited in vain
for the applause due to the
uninhibited, juvenile
scribe who dared to perpetuate
his plots on the pages of a
ten-cent scribbler.

ORPHAN

Aubrey Lyttle was adopted
by our elderly neighbours
after four bleak years
in an orphanage with no takers,
but his luck turned at last
and he found himself
with what he wanted above
all: to be loved, to be
entitled to a name he could
boast about, to have
parents who would see to
his niggardly needs (we welcomed
him into our gang as our mascot,
we admired his curls and boyish
pluck) and all was well
until his new father died
and his new mother sent
him back to the place where
joy was in short supply:
after all these years
I still think of Aubrey,
and my heart still bleeds.

COURAGE
For my Grandfather: in memoriam

These yellowed medical
records tell the story
of your suffering and affliction
(two wounds and dysentery)
but make no mention
of the courage it took to breathe
in the rat-riddled mud
of trenches or to pick lice
out of your fellows' hair
or fling yourself into
No-Man's-Land
singing with bullets and the cries
of the dying and the silence
of the dead (knowing there was no
glory in the blood and mire
of battle), or the courage to enter
sleep each night
not certain your dreams
might be your last, but
I like to think your final
thoughts before exhaustion
claimed you, were about
the possibility of a future
free of combat,
and one that included me.

SISTERS

Betty was the big sister,
boasting breasts and a blistering
tongue, Shirley was all
cartwheels and flexibility,
flipping hither and yon:
we hung about their yard
like puppies in need, playing
spin the bottle with chaste
kisses and hesitant hugs,
but when Betty loomed,
the air grew greedy
with something unthrottled,
slithering and serenely sexual.

BUNNY
Easter 2017

At Eastertime the magic
bunny hopped from room
to room depositing eggs
and other treats under beds
and commodes, where we,
pleased to be teased,
discovered them without
divine direction, and then
it was off to Sunday School
with new shoes and a heart
heightened by news of the Resurrection,
with Jesus somehow
finding the strength to roll
the stone away from his three-
day tomb and levitate,
turning a tragic story
into a tale primed with God's
glory and one honey
of a bunny.

CHAIRS

On cloudless afternoons
when the humidity allowed
or the sun didn't scorch,
you would sit on the front porch
with a good book and an extra
nook for a neighbor to stop
by for a friendly chat
about this and that or any
news stimulating the street:
there was no fuss
or fume about you, you spoke
your many kindnesses aloud,
you thought from the heart, and despite
my earnest prayers, I look
out now and what
I see is two empty
chairs.

SHY
For Bobby Cooper

Shy doesn't do justice
to the diffident dignity
you offered the world, but
there was a twinkle in your eye
that betrayed the elfin imp
inside, who kept Belgians
in a hutch next door,
while we watched their noses
dimple pink; we spent
long days on Canatara's
sands on the brink of Huron,
where westering winds under
the simple sun gusted
the waves we leapt in tumbling
tandem; here in your class
photo you stare at the ground
as if the camera might expose
more than you were willing
to present to us who loved
your humble humor and all
that friendship you bestowed
on me for four short
years, whether I deserved
it or not: we plotted
our future together
and dreamed, as the days went by,
that it would never end.

CLASS PHOTO: JUNE 1950

The sepia tones now
just a little faded
in this photographic sketch
that freezes time's fallacious
flow: the classmates
I knew so well:
Bobby Cooper who raised
rabbits in a hutch next
door and watched their noses
wrinkle pink, Ronnie
Young who tried to lick
the moon off the boys'
window, Bonnie and Sharon,
queens of Double Dutch,
Donnie Turnbull
who clutched our rugby ball
like a lover's squeeze, and his cousin
Moo Cow Margaret
we teased until we teared up
in shame, and front and centre
my dog Moochie posed
for his portrait, and Miss Nelson,
who taught us to love
what we learned, and all those
other faces I can name,
as if the years in their yearning
had not intervened:
I feel the tug of remembrance;
memories are etched in the runes
of our bones.

TRUE

When the world was young in my
infant eyes and the sky
was ablaze with blue and grand-
father's lawn was as green
as grass after a rain
and the lilac hedge that edged
my docile domain bloomed
like a bride's bouquet
and the spirea that hugged my northern
border feathered the air
with its flowers and every stick
and stone was a superb surprise
and I ventured warily into the wide
outside, tethered always
to the known and true: at home
in my bones.

CONTINUOUS

The geography of my village
is a memory-map lodged
in my mind's eye forever,
but when I venture back,
I am baffled by the distance
between by-gone and be,
puzzled by the chasm between
was and is, has-
been and hope, where the streets
are hodgepodge and the houses
awkward and askew,
and it's only when I come in sight
of the Lake with the sun hefted
upon its copious blue
horizon and the sinuous sands
of Canatara that I feel
upright, assured of a world
that is continuous, that will be
here long after me.

THE GIRLS OF CANATARA
For Nancy Mara

The girls of Canatara
cavort on my beach
like gazelles grazing
the grass-tops of some
vast savannah before
they sprawl splendidly
on the satisfying sand,
where we gaze on the curves
and swells of their bountiful bodies,
on the sassy swirl of their curls
and on the gifted grace of their
unpinched faces, knowing
full well we were not
the sort to raise an eyebrow
or solicit a sigh, or bring
a girl like Nancy Mara
one inch closer
to my ravenous reach.

BALLAST

You have only one home:
having weathered the womb
and the burst of birth, you greet
the village that envelops you whole:
first, there's grandfather's
lawn, lavished with lilacs
and foaming spirea with a yard
yawning enough for a dozen
LaSalles to explore, and soon
a street teases a granny-
cracked sidewalk and an ally
blooms where pals pop
up and fraternize, and both
of your feet touch the Earth
until a song sings
itself to your soul: of ballast
and belonging.

PEDIGREE

Out favourite cat, Peachy,
proud of her feline pedigree,
brings us a gift, a robin
tangled in her teeth, its red
breast still aglow with the
living sun, a song
no longer throbbing
in its throat, and the tabby looks
up beseechingly as if
expecting (above all)
a pat on the brow that would make
her purr like a sated lover.

THRUM

It begins with a thrum in the blood,
something marinating the mind
before becoming an itch
that hitches itself to a word,
perhaps even a kind
of phrase, fully framed,
that tickles and tantalizes
until it sticks in the rut
of a rhythm, surprised by
sense, a semblance of meaning
straightened by metaphor
and the sibilance of simile,
by the extravagance of stanza
and a line's elastic dance –
and thus does a poem give birth
to itself and the Earth tilt
an inch on its axis.

ASHES

Another Mother's Day
and still I think of you
as the callow girl who must
have fallen for a fellow who skated
with the grace of Gordie and the
panache
of Rocket Richard, who tingled
the air above the local
rink in front of you
and the adoring crowd, when I
was not yet thought aloud,
when love was all it seemed
to be, a plot to fix
the future's fate and your life
had not yet turned to ashes,
leaving me without
a day to celebrate.

HOPE
For Nancy Mara

I sit in the sand and watch
Nancy dive, in the air
elegant as an antelope
holding its breath, she whispers
the water with barely a ripple
stirred, her lissome limbs
vanishing, saying goodbye,
and leaving me, a non-
swimmer, crippled by shyness,
without hope.

DOTE
For Tim and James

I dote on this photo:
James and Tim rudely
nude, posing on my easy
chair and feeling quite
pleased with themselves,
their multiple cheeks as rosy
and cheerful as cherubim
in an angel's arms, and I thank
whatever god brings me
such gifts that raise
a smile and lift the farthest
valves of the heart.

GARDEN
For Beth Whitney

I walk by your garden
and there you are, encircled
by the blooms you talked into being
with the same syllables Eve
must have used on the first
flowers to flourish in Eden:
you've found room
in your gardener's heart for
daffodils and daisies,
roses and their cousins that tickle
the air with their technicolour
flair and bring the neighbours
more delight than a dozen
rainbows or stars
that startle the night.

CAREER

I try to imagine the day
when I'll write my last line
of verse on the uninked
page; will it be a simile
that sings like an oriole's aria,
a metaphor succinct
in its mirroring magic,
or perhaps a rhyme to startle
with its simple chime: in any
case I shall lay down
my pen with a Chanticleerian
cheer: calling it a career.

IN LIEU OF ROSES
Valentine's Day, 2006

Snow on Valentine's Day,
a hush heard in the heart,
but love blooms anyway
and we, separate or apart,
find room for each other,
summer on what we recall
of June and the seasons shared:
Spring and snow-free Fall
(and Winter, too, one supposes).

Oh, I need no rhyme or reason
to send you this poem's love
in lieu of a dozen yellow roses.

363

IT IS HARD TO BELIEVE
For Anne: Christmas, 1996

It is hard to believe
we are growing old:
June upon June the dark-
eyed daisies irrupt
jubilant and anew
from the wrinkled root you
long ago cupped
in your bride's grip and
persuaded into the earth.

Once again you stand
sturdy and watchful
among the tendril'd bloom
of iris, dahlia, sweet
william, who bend up
to your touch like children
anticipating praise or,
like you, listen merely
for the winter note under the
honey-buzz of pollinating
bees, the sound the world
makes when all the robins
hesitate…

But: mother,
lover, husbander of so many
green things that must begin,
you turn your face towards me,
lay a plucked petal
along your open throat,
and – as the shastas / blood-
root / cosmos / flox
shimmer at your sandalled feet
and bear you bodily aloft
like some remembered Persophone
in the hour of her element –
your smile brindles the aging
air as it did the first
day I beheld its burst
among the bursting flowers.

NOT ANY GIFT
An Un-Valentine Poem:

Sheaves of roses
stooked golden in
ersatz wintered
light will not do

(too often used to gild
your lover's guilt
or seal the wound of a
rued absence)

A Hallmark card
bobbing with hearts as
buoyant as the venerable
saint's pulled out and
offered undigested to
Jesus will not suffice

(our love in its bloom more
passionate than pilgrim
and in the cadenced elegy
of its ageing too domiciled
for the pink hyperboles
of rhymed romance)

And living as we now do
from room to arboured
room, breathing the same
nurtured silences / the
covert coincidence of
wink and conjugal
nudge, even a word too
edged or syllabic
could scribble the intimate
scansion of touch and just
caress
        between us.

So any gift of mine
(however emboxed as
Valentine or poesy),
any re-averral of our
love's long amaze,
must be transmuted
without rose or trope
thru the tender intoxication
of shared
February
days.

MARA'S LAMP
For Anne, on our 37th
And for Nancy and Jerry Mara

1

Between the last sting
of the solstice sun
and the unstarred dark,
gripped centripetal
by Mara's hexagonic
hide-and-go-seek
streetlamp, we voyaged
our burgeoning bodies
into the shudder of shadow
and out to the moon-pulled
elixir of edges – let
them visit and estrange
till the oh-li-oh-li-en-free
sings us aback
to the home-post…

2

After 37 anniversaries
(so much already examined)
we reconnoitre like infant
archaeologists fingering
with solicitous touch
what is still most strange
and tenderly hedged,
knowing, even as we dare,
our love is as steadied and starred
as Mara's lamp.

ODDS

If there's a Heaven you'll be
first in line, your kindnesses
are heroic in a wayward world
where they are few and far
between, and when good
deeds were assigned in some
celestial lottery, you took
your share and much of mine,
and most of all you chose
to galvanize your love
for one who hopes, against
the odds, that Paradise awaits
and there really is a God.

LOVING YOU
For Anne

Loving you is as easy
as breathing, and our long
lives have not diminished
the intricate dance of our
separate selves, and above
all else we touch
each other in ways
that have no need for
anything other than a
knowing nod or a con-
junctive squeeze
of the hand.

COUPLET

This life, such
as it is, (all tremor
and tentative touch)
may be summed up
in a single couplet:
we worship whatever thrives
and mourn the abrupt brevity of
our lives.

SMALL GESTURES
A Birthday Poem for Anne

Thinking me fast asleep,
you plant a kiss upon
one arable cheek,
do not wait for any
break in the faithful
rhythm of my breathing –

a small gesture, perhaps,
but in it much abides:

a room in Nuremburg,
bridal-bright and un-
dulant with sun-seethe
and lovers in their morning
urges…

a speechless jog
along some Huron dune
or Georgian prospect:
our hands deliberate/
solo in the awkward
afternoon – but, ah,
the electric embrace
of bodies consoling in the cottage dark…

or that evening (in our season
of evenings) when we forgot
to merely remember the
passion that presaged
and girder'd our lush
loving…

Later, dream-revived,
I ease up behind you
bent (ageless) over the
breakfast Globe
and lip-whisper a kiss
that is almost a word:

you do not turn
from the page, nor do
I expect you to.

THE POINT

For Anne
On Valentine's Day 2002

And you most at home
in fields fueled by flowers
and air loud with blue-
jays and bobolinks,
and random is your roaming
among blood-bright
poppies and marigolds
bronzed by bee-buzz,
the sun aflame in your hair
and milkweed-haze
silkens and hummingbirds
covet and Carolina
wrens anoint with song

(no wonder few can hear
your house-bound lover
proclaim, "I love you
in your element," or more
to the point
 "I love you")

KEPT WARM
For Anne: Valentine's Day 2007

The slow snows descend,
the knee-deep drifts
swallowing houses whole,
revising horizons,
the wind as thin and iced
as February's air:
we stroll the frozen land-
scape, hand in glove –
kept warm by love.

URN

It isn't Grecian but its bronze
and pleasing curves are beyond
beautiful because all
that remains of you resides
inside that bevelled urn,
your last repose, so
close beside me
I can feel your love as it glows
the room golden, and when
I run my hand over its
slender tenderness, I see
your graceful face and look
for the hope you bring, brighter
than the light of a thousand dawns.

LOCKS

I fell in love with the carotene
curls you brandished like a badge
of honour: swept up
like a nun's wimple or let
fall as lush as Rapunzel's
locks: you took a simple
girl's delight in their evident
loveliness, and I adored
the woman who sported them
beyond reason and rhyme,
not knowing such love
would last a lifetime.

WHATEVER GROWS

You were born with a green
thumb, and ever since
everything you've touched
has sprouted, budded or blossomed:
roses that tumble on their trellises,
petunia pots showering
our porch with a blaze of petals,
forget-me-nots
fringing the lawn with the
sprightliness of Spring:
you are a daughter of Demeter,
a dean of whatever
grows, and you are un-
amazed at your own delight

ENDUED

When you pulled up
in that brand-new
Volkswagon with the sun
roof, my heartbeat
abrupted, as the girl with the
clementine curls, a smile
festooned with freckles and a
glance that rhymed with romance
stepped into the autumnal light
in her lemon-yellow dress
and I was smitten breathless,
bitten by love's bite,
and needed no proof
for my endued delight or
my sublime obsession.

LOVE ITSELF
For Anne: Christmas 2001

I watch your hands in awe:
their filigree flair
on the chopping board,
the mothering moves they make
to soothe an infant's ache,
the way they coax roses
to illuminate a room,
the tints their instincts choose
to swatch and amaze a quilt,
their five-fingered grip
on a spade working the earth/
grooming its garden aglow,
and, ah, what strength they've drawn
from a thousand days of lending
grace to all they touched
with tenderness,
and when I hold them up
like this, as now I do,
love itself falls thru.

TEARS
*For Anne. In loving memory
and for Katie and Rebecca*

And you happiest amongst
your granddaughters, one
on either side (a triptych
Gainsborough would have adored)
on a chesterfield we bought
so many days ago,
where joy has abided in its royal
riches for fifty-seven
years, and it is harder to love
the world without you in it,
but you have given me girls
Heaven would be proud of
and so much more, and all
I can offer in return are these
tears.

WALKING TOGETHER
ON A SNOWY EVENING

Guelph, Ontario: January 1961
For Anne, on our 40th

In that first windfall winter
the evening snows nested
confessional on fluted limb
and bough (intimate as lovers'
fingers minting a caress),
their silence steepled our strolling
with mute music – we heeded
the hinting of hearts that had
no need for sense or season:
enlinked, we grew abreast,
waxed ecclesiastic
at the blizzard-burst
blessing our blood.

CADENZA
For Anne and our trips to Toronto:
Valentine's Day 2018

I try to curb my enthusiasm
as you sweep up to the curb
in your brand-new Volks,
you hair piled high
above the smile you flash me
with both of your Baltic blue
eyes, and when you step
down in your lilting lemon
dress, my breath is in
a frenzy, and I wonder what
god has blessed this day,
as we climb aboard and toddle
off to cadenza town.

MARIGOLD

Cameron Lake was our magical
place, where the sun bloomed
like a magnified marigold fully
ablaze, where the breeze off
the dimpled water feathered
our cheeks as we lazed on the
porch my uncle built
with his simple carpenter's craft,
and where the rooms were warmed
by wood-stove and the aroma
of weathered elm, in which
we tidied away the effortless
afternoons, perusing tomes
comic and tragic, and certain
that this was a home where love
abided.

COUPLED

For a long time now
we have lain side by side,
coupled yet still distinct,
our bodies each folded
into its own furrow, close
enough to be tantalized
by touch, and if by chance
a hand should brush a hand,
it is a moment to be prized,
and when we wake,
with eyes enlinked,
our breathing in rhythmic rhyme,
what is exchanged in look
upon look will last
a lifetime.

FOR ANNE

If you were a flower you'd be
a yellow rose sweetening
sunshine on June
afternoons, and at the edge
of evening mellowing moon-
light: we greet each
other in the morning's rise,
empowered by love in the
other's eyes, watching
as it grows and blooms
over the long years
we have been buoyantly
embowered.

A BIRTHDAY POEM

We have stopped counting
our birthdays, but the years
glide on without permission
or our say-so, but we have eased
into our age as gracefully
as Time and Earth allow
(your hand in my glove),
and whatever fears
we may have for the future
are flouted by our abiding love.

NOW YOU ARE GONE

When lilacs bloom again
in all their lilting loveliness,
I'll think of you when daffodils
dazzle and tulips tantalize,
for there has always been
something of the Spring
in you with its perpetual
budding of hope and happiness,
even as our years lengthened,
and so, with summer gone
and Winter come a-chilling,
I need only recall
the lilacs in your eyes to find
the strength to carry on
and, above all, summon
the will to keep on loving.

PATIENT

Tom and I spend
half a day fishing
on Cameron, baffled
by bass, spurned by even
the lowly perch, and so
it is a day of lassitude,
savouring the sun, and when
we putt up to Potsy's
dock, you are waiting
as patient as Penelope,
your eyes alight with love
and hopefulness, your smile
as wide as any horizon.

TOWARDS THE LIGHT
For Anne: June 10, 1998

The years of our coming together
roll into each other like the brave
waves tumble upon my boyhood beach,
the air above them passionate with day-burst
they lust at with their just-about reaching.

Even then, I willed my bachelor being
to that circular foamed fury:
to be spun numb in my young bones
while the hurry of a hale heart
curves to quiet
awake.

Even now, in the midst
of our eased intimacy
(our aging hours seasoned
with gesture and oblique delight)
I want to touch you everywhere
that's riotous with remembrance,
that's rollicking and Rubenesque
and stirred reminiscent
by waves
arching
towards light.

ALWAYS

For the past few years
of our long-intertwined
history, we resided in distinct
floors, me above
in the study, inking poems
or perusing inch-thick
tomes, while you were happy
to grace the home rooms
with your perpetual presence,
your free spirit, your filigreed
flair, and I found some
comfort in imagining your love-
lined face, content to know
you were there, and assuming
you always would be.

HARMONY
For Anne and for John Barnett, in memoriam

Some days before he died
Anne fetched her father
from the tedium of his nursing home,
put him in a taxi
(wheelchair and all)
and together they motored
back through the village
John had known for more
than half his life, each
house precisely familiar,
jogging memories as they flashed
by, and as soon as the Lake
came into view, they paused,
and easefully Anne manoeuvred
the chair down to the beach
and side by side they sat
and stared out at the
calming waters, father
and daughter locked
in mutual harmony,
sharing all that had passed
and what was left of their
future.

CRIMSON

This sumac that has graced
our yard for these long
years is now in it death-
throes: once filigreed
with birds of every ilk
in their Sunday suits: robins
and sparrows, cardinals
and chickadees, and how
you loved to watch them flutter
down like fretful ballerinas
to the bowl of water you so
faithfully provided (and there
below the ruined trunk
new shoots tickle the air),
and see now its final burst
of bloom as if it did not
wish to say goodbye,
garnished-green leaves
hanging like shredded silk
that will for one last
time glow crimson
in the Fall, and how I wish
you could be there to hear
the hymn I will sing to you,
even though your going
has seared my soul.

NEVER AGAIN

Never again will you sit
in front of the TV
cursing Trump and his candied
coif, your sense of fair
play outraged
by his demagogic gaffs,
his legion of lies that you,
who believed in truth with a
ruthless candor, despised
as we sat in tandem on the
chesterfield that served
two generations and watched
reality ruptured, loving
every minute because
our souls coupled. Never
again but still I wish
there was you and humpteen
Trumps.

EPITAPH

"Margaret Anne Gutteridge:
1935-2018": the simple
inscription on a granite plaque
in the tall-treed urn
garden, a triptych in cold
stone that will have to do
for a life lived between
that stiff brace of dates,
a life of joyous giving,
of self-effacement, enriched
by friends and family and days
of gratuitous grace in a world
often whittled to the bitten
bone: you will be remembered
long after the rains
have withered away the stark
reminder of our brief residence
here on Earth and memories
have begun to wobble, but lives
touched by such boldness
of being as yours will survive
in the hearts of those who loved you
until there are no more
hearts to throb.

HARVEST

We were not Romeo and Juliet
with a balcony to keep us apart,
we began as companions, trotting
off together to Big
Town to take in La Boheme
or the Bolshoi: you suave
urbanite, me the country
bumpkin, but something
grew between us
other than our passion
for the arts, and in time we flew
with a single featherage under
a moon-piping sky,
and love bloomed like a
slow lily until we were doomed.
willy-nilly to harvest
our ripening hearts.

ABIDING

You once told me that you
decided not to be
a professional grandmother,
but Fate stepped in,
as she often does, with six
grandkids, and when
you cut your flowing locks
and let your hair curl up
into a frenzy of maternal red,
you took them underwing
like flocks of chicks in a feathered
hug, and oh how they tugged
at your hopeful heart until
you confessed your affection
and sang them cadenzas of
abiding love.

ON HONEYMOON BAY

We make love under
a menstrual moon,
only the thin skin
of the tent between us,
the starlit dark
and the great aloneness
of the lake: we listen
to the rhythm of the waves echo
our own, and all we ask
is that the world in it stark
severity, for our sake, laughs
at lovers and lets their bodies
be.

PRESENCE

I can't believe you're gone:
nothing prepares us
for the anguish of absence:
you filled your world with a
perpetual presence,
I still see you blooming
every room you graced,
every word I remember
hanging on in the long,
consummate conversation
of our life; your face will be
a potent palimpsest upon
my harrowed heart, and I am
consoled by the thought of our
lilting love, even
though my grief leaves
me unmarrowed.

URN

It isn't Grecian but its bronze
and pleasing curves are beyond
beautiful because all
that remains of you resides
inside that bevelled urn,
your last repose, so
close beside me
I can feel your love as it glows
the room golden, and when
I run my hand over its
slender tenderness, I see
your graceful face and look
for the hope you bring, brighter
than the light of a thousand
dawns.

MISS BARNETT

When I first laid eyes
upon Miss Barnett,
I observed a home-ec
teacher with an archipelago
of freckles and a burst of up-
surging tangerine locks,
patrolling the halls of Elmira
High with all the vim
of a school-marm, and little
did I know that we would
both be surprised by love
and its witting charm, and that
one of us would soon
be a missus.

THEY SAY

They say that love is never
enough, but from the first
moment I spied you in that
vimming Volks with your un-
ruffled Rapunzellian hair
upswept in a tangerine burst
and those freckles like a spray
of Venusian stars upon
each cherished cheek
and those eyes blue
with sentient surprise,
I was smitten with Cupid's bent
bow and amorous arrow:
my fate thus already
written, and after all
what do "they" know?

GEYSER

The day-lily is as steadfast
as Old Faithful's geysering
plume and when the dawn-light
lifts the bud's lid,
the petals, seething with sun,
open slowly like a Mozart
adagio, and by noon the bloom
has burst as bright as an orange
comet burrowing the night
sky, and you watched this
diurnal pantomime
and its lilting lustre and loved it
as much as I have loved
you, unbidden,
and, in your perpetual presence,
made a little bit wiser.

BEATITUDE

Blessed are those who love
for they shall move mountains
and pacify the Seven Seas:
they are the ones who bring
each child out of itself
into the bright breeze
of the light, who nurture and nurse
and bind up the wounds
the world makes, who, like you,
do not rest until the last
suffering soul, above
or below, has come to loving
rest.

OUR LOVE IS MORE POTENT

Your love unhinges
my heart, releases
the breath of my being;
in a world gone awry
your steadfastness
never ceases. which is why
as we edge towards Death
our love is more potent
than poetry while tinged
with regret.

HUMBLE

You never cared much
for Heaven or its Holy Hope,
but the spirit that moved Jesus
to galvanize Galilee and bring
mercy into a numbed world
moved in you who exuded
such kindness, such
self-effacing grace,
who lavished love wherever
it was needed, who surprised us
with the ardor of your affection,
given so freely:
whom the gods extol
they first make humble.

APART

In our latter aging years
we inhabited separate floors,
you below, me above,
and we greeted one another
each morning like two
old friends meeting
in Gibbons Park, and treasured
those few moments
we shared during our day-
light hours, but I could
gauge your measured presence
three doors away,
and knowing you were just
there was all that mattered:
it would take more than walls
to keep out hearts apart
or stall our levitating love.

PROMPT

I sat in the neighbouring room
and listened in fascination
as you prompted your pupils
into relinquishing their terror
of the printed page and those
letters tangling on their tongues,
but you knew all
the pedagogic angles and soothed
your charges into hinting at the
slippery syllables until
words were weighed and smoothed
tactical in those tender
minds, and you, no
rookie at this age-old
act, capped off
each lesson with a home-
made cookie.

NURTURE

You always loved Spring
when purple crocuses coveted
the good ground recently
rinsed by rain, and you waited
patiently for a glimpse of the first
tulip shoots aereating the April
mornings, and then the budded
burst of our maple like baby's
fists clenching life
and their sudden exfoliation
showered us with shade,
and you breathed easier knowing
the world was coming back
with the salient sun, and soon
there would be daisies
and foxglove and I loved you
more for loving them:
your unquenchable nurturing urge
that made my heart sing.

EVENTUALLY

When we were young and easy
in our own skin, we let
our bodies be as they pleased,
happy to find a home
in one another's arms,
and as we grew wiser
we met thigh to thigh
and our love sprung anew
with each familiar sigh,
and when age surprised
us out of the blue,
we let ourselves be
content to sit side by side
in abiding repose, knowing
that everything kith
and kin eventually goes.

ABRUPT
After Emily Dickinson

Because you could not stop
for Death he kindly stopped
for you, making his solicitous
visit while you slept alone
(dreaming your last ecstatic
dream?) and interrupted
your thinning breath, while
the heart that loved the world
with all its flaws paused,
skipped a beat and stalled:
like your life, there was nothing
dramatic about your going:
you left us sleeping, peaceful,
mindful of the grief that would
surely seize us at your abrupt,
tender departure.

PENDULUM

My grief, like a pendulum,
comes and goes, the sight
of a yellow rose, emblem
of our long loving years,
can overwhelm or the chesterfield
where you lay during your last
days can amaze tears
I had thought forgotten,
but mostly it is the ghost
haunting these halls
above and below, but it's good
to mourn what we have lost,
for it tells us how far
love has come.

FOSTER'S POND

Borealis Press
2019

MOON

The glow from Mara's lamp
threw a pool of brightness
across Monk Street
where we played our ritual games,
but beyond it lay Darkness,
interrupted only by the moon's
patina over the puddled
pavement and starlight
stippled in a livid sky
like confetti on a bride's veil,
and whenever we ventured
too far at Hide-
and-Go-Seek or May I,
we huddled like lovers assuming
some assignation and sensed
something close by
that rippled like ripped silk,
nameless and shuddering
like a moon gone mad.

POOR

We called the Barker's shack
"the see-through-house"
because the intrusive sun
slithered through the cracks
in the teetered clapboard
siding and lay upon
the tattered sofas inside
like illuminated worms,
and in the dirt-ingrained yard
(where no flower would grow,
no grass would green)
the Barker kids of indeterminate
sex cavorted stark
naked as if they had just
exited Eden where hope
was not yet aborted,
and they flashed their gritty
grins as we passed on by
towards the pristine allure
of Canatara's sands, for we
had neither time nor pity
for the withered poor.

WHISTLE

When we were young the world
wakened anew each
summer morning and the grass
bedewn was greener
than it was the day before,
and we were freed from the clench
of our houses to sally forth
like eager Argonauts into streets
and alleyways bristling
with hop-scotch and jump-
rope and softball
games (all our arrows
notched and rhyming) and then
it was off to Canatara's beach
and its singing bee-stung
sands, and dunes that needed
no name, with a Lake
hovering beside as blue as
iris in liquid light,
and we were happy to be
wayfarers riding
the wave that never reached
the shore, untouched
by the stinging whistle of Time.

FOSTER'S POND

In the summertime we waded
big-booted into Foster's
Pond in search of cattails
we wielded like furred
tomahawks, and dreamed
of setting them ablaze
in the final fading of the day's-
long light, but in the winter
our pond glazed over
and we skated the afternoons
away, sailing like balloon-
rigged schooners among
the reeds and goose-grey
grass, lost to all
but ourselves in the fury
of speed and the blur
of our blading.

UNSUNG

The point of it all is the village
where the sun levitates over
First Bush and wakens
the robins from their drowsy, red-
breasted sleep, and casts
a celebratory sheen on the ordinary
streets and houses we anoint
with the impetus of our innocence,
and spreads
its numinous light across
the wave-lush tillage
of Canatara and the blue
voluminous lacquer of the Lake,
where fish fantasize about the
ebbing of oceans, and where
we swim young and yearning,
and dream of being alive
and furled in this unsung
paradise.

SYNCH

In the stiffening blow from the
Lake, our kites swoop
and swerve with the verve of cliff
swallows on a bender, like eagles
buffeted by a belligerent breeze,
or bucking broncos on oats,
and Jerry and I fly our twin
missiles, like our friendship
afloat in perfect synch,
and Coop's, between gusts,
droops like an unsolicitous
sigh, and mine abruptly
rises above the arc
of the Bridge and, no bigger
that a midget's cuspid, plucks
at the precincts of Paradise.

APRIL
*After e e cummings
and for Bonnie and Sharon Lauer*

It's Spring and Bonnie and Sharon
are doing Double Dutch
with the alacrity of acrobats
and robins sing and crickets
creak and Donny and Aaron
play catch with a brand-
new ball and no-one
notices the half-hatched
adder slithering the dew-
licked grass among crocuses
surging upward into the breeze-
bubbling air and the boys
go hither while the girls
go thither un-
titillated by touch or the ancient
urges of April.

LOOSE

Juicy Joyce we called her,
standing in the shambles of her yard,
sporting only a brace of bantam
breasts and soiled panties,
and when we whistled she dropped
the latter with a single lazy
droop, unperturbed
by the gutting of the male gaze,
and we felt no shame
or pity for the poor, just
the thrill of the rut let loose.

GUNNER

Jerry's Dad was a tail
gunner, suspended in a glass
bubble every Messerschmitt
tried to shatter, their bullets
buzzing about him like berserk
bees, and if fear seized him
buried to the bone, he gritted
his teeth and carried on
alone, surprised to be
alive at day's end,
and no-one in the village
that welcomed him home blamed
him when he took to the drink
to muzzle the memories of blood
and thunder flailing at the maelstrom
of his mind, and there was nothing
but grief when his heart shook
itself apart.

PERFIDY
For Grace Leckie

You go galloping on your roan
stallion across your father's
fallow, long legs
astride the pronged saddle,
your hair like Guinevere's
contorted by the conniving wind:
you are where you belong –
Venusian, unraddled –
cruising on by the bard
(all hope aborted)
striving to hone your perfidy
into a poem.

SONG

In Sunday School we sang
of the Lamb's blood and of Jesus
and His bejewelled love,
clapping lustily to the soaring
rhythms of the "Sweet By and By,"
and the Reverend Buchanan reminded
us of God's fallen sparrow
and the adamant fact that Adam
delved and Eve span
and Noah flouted the Flood
and thus escaped damnation
while Mrs Anderson thudded
on her proselytizing piano,
and the song we sang for her
with just a tinge of impingement
was really the song of ourselves.

DANIEL

Our next-door neighbour
on the Fourth Line had a
spaniel who discovered herself
in heat one Spring,
and we watched in awe as a troop
of scruffy males of every
ilk nosed her spoor
hither and yon, and when
opportunity arose
mounted her, bug-
eyed and quivering, thrusting
her rump asunder in the throes
of what we later learned
was sex, while a rush of blood
found our lower regions
and the girls blushed and began
to wonder, and we all stared
at the besieged female and thought
of Daniel in the lion's den.

AT HOME

The dunes of Canatara
may be as old as the Earth's core
and what is more they were here
the day God proclaimed
"Let there be light!"
and parted the seas from the land,
creating clays, loams,
limestone and granite
for dinosaurs to graze on
and when they did their last
three-toed dance,
Neanderthals roamed
the slopes and voluminous valleys,
and thirty thousand years
ago a galaxian glacier
gouged out the bowl
that seized the azure blue
waters of Lake Huron,
where Attawandaron drank
with cupped hands and drifted
to extinction, and where on a
summer's afternoon
Jerry and I paddled,
exulted in the sun-rinsed
wavelets, let the multitudinous
sands sift through our fingers,
and felt at home.

RHYME

Summertime in Canatara,
where we felt the soul of the sun,
hearkened to the lush brush
of breakers, and ogled the new-
breasted girls of the Point,
sashayed on the unsilted
sand and anointed with a lilt
of light as gentle as a June
moon, and we all dreamed
that such wholesome days
would come to us forever,
and rhyme.

TOO SOON
For Dave "Wiz" Withers, in loving memory

I read on-line
the obit for Dave Withers,
dead these many
years ago, and when you are only
eleven, someone
at thirteen, who is a wizard
with wood, a prestidigitator
of magical gadgets, derby
racers, white-knuckle
trapezes and dizzying odds
and ends, you learn what it is
to be moon-struck,
to call someone (shyly)
your best friend, to be
surprised that, if there is
a God in Heaven, He failed
to see my pal through the star-
tinted eyes that I did,
taking him tragically too
soon, and leaving me
to mourn from afar.

WILL

A mere breath of breeze
over the Lake's undulant
blue swell, licking
at the slick lips of Canatara's
sinuous sands, the sun
as high as the sky allows,
bathers statue still,
as if entranced by the lofting
light, the dunes doze
as they have for millennia,
while the ghosts of Attawandarons
amplify the air, and I listen,
like a soothsaying ear,
to a sea-shell, and hear
the heartbeat of something
more worldly than my will.

AFAR
For Nancy Mara

Nancy: you were my first
romance: I dreamed of being
your Lancelot, of saving
you from dragons or Satyrs
with ill-defined designs,
I would lay my cloak on mudded
walks as willing as Sir Walter
and tremble when your hand
breathed on mine, and in
the moonlit hours I would plot
our first embrace a hundred
times, but always I awoke
in the polyglot dark
before the consummation ,
your face fading like smoke
before my surprised eyes,
but when you reappeared
(like the morning star on Earth's
radiant lip), distant
on Monk Street, my heart
leapt in the oldest dance:
idolatry from afar.

TABOO

On sizzling summer days
we gathered in Hendrie's hen-
house and waited for Joanne
to lower her panties and expose
the hairless cleft between
her thighs and blush like a
ribald rose, while in addition
to staring we, in return,
dropped our drawers below
our boy-sized stalks,
and all of us thought
of Hendrie's rooster boosting
himself over some
compliant hen, and wondered
in our innocents' eyes what
taboos we had broken, what
further amazements might befall,
and what exactly we were to do
before our interest fizzled.

EMBRACE

There is a village of the mind
where we all go when the world
is too bellicose to face,
the place that bore witness
to our birth, watched us toddle
and teeter until we find
our sea-legs (and the Earth
unfurls again around
the sun), draws us
to the streets and alleyways
where every step is on
home-ground, on the familiar
turf of our native tillage,
and where every name is known,
lilting on our lips, and whenever
we roam too far
to the edge where the good gods
cease, love hedges
us in, as closely as a
mother's welcoming embrace.

PUSSY

No one seems to know
how Pussy Carr
got his nickname
and my village has not
divulged that tantalizing
tidbit, but I can surmise
that as a babe his mother
called him something
like "wee Snugglepuss"
and some erring uncle,
licking his lips, shortened it,
but "Pussy" it remains,
now buried in the bone
of his home town and,
for all I know, is carved
on his grave-stone

EMBODIED

After the double feature
at the aging Imperial, we race
home to re-enact
the action-packed matineé
and its six-shooter troubles,
and it was Hopalong
or Geronimo, Johnny Mack
or Crazy Horse in the late
lazy afternoons,
sagebrush sagas
(and Laurel and Hardy laughter):
these were stories I absorbed
and then honed into fictions
and poems, epic and otherwise,
that fired my fancy, stories
embodied by the bone.

ANOINTED

Easter Sunday in the Point
was new shoes with the shine
still on them and pants
with a fine crease and ladies
bonneted and beribboned
and gentlemen in fresh habits,
and I remember staring at Christ
strung upon Golgotha (vinegar-
tongued, palms pinned
like moths on a lepidopterist's
display) just above
the altar where the Sabbath sun
limned His halo, and we felt
ourselves to be among
the anointed there, buoyed
by the yeast of prayer.

BONDS

My girls make me as giddy
as gladiolas in August's sun,
as happy as hyacinths and their
whirling purples, as pleased
as poppies in their blood-red
glow, like the bonds that bind us
and grow like God's first
flowered bower: they make
my heart burst like lily
bulbs blooming in a June
breeze, they bring me the joy
of jonquil's yellows that would be
the envy of Eden: O
what bliss it is to be
the grandfather of such
glowing, gladsome girls!

CADENZA
For Anne and our trips to Toronto:
Valentine's Day 2018

I try to curb my enthusiasm
as you sweep up to the curb
in your brand-new Volks,
you hair piled high
above the smile you flash me
with both of your Baltic blue
eyes, and when you step
down in your lilting lemon
dress, my breath is in
a frenzy, and I wonder what
god has blessed this day,
as we climb aboard and toddle
off to cadenza town.

VET
For Tom

You are Orpheus with a lyrical
lyre, calming the beasts
of the field with your easeful
music, your hands on a steer's
flank as gentle as a lover's
tendrill'd touch, your fingers
on a horse's orphaned ears
inducing quietude,
for you have loved each
one of God's creatures
since the world welcomed you
in with such unyielding
joy, and now, with the thrill
of your heart's desire, you are
what you were meant to be:
shepherd, physician,
soothing surgeon and, above
all, man with a lyre.

LONGING
For Tim

The trumpets in Tim's school
band pontificate
with all the gusto of Gabriel
blowing his heraldic horn
in Gloryland, as sassy
as the brass of Dorsey or Ellington:
their cheeks swell with every
lusty breath, their eyes
squeezed shut by the pumped-
up tempo of the tune, their fingers
dancing delicate duets
on the vacillating valves,
and every one of them
longs to be Louis Armstrong.

FETCHING

Bonny and Sharon doing
Double Dutch, their lithe
limbs scissoring in a free-
fall dance without the
hint of a stumble, while the twinned
ropes lasso the air,
and there is something
in their fetching glance beyond
the edge of innocence, for in
the distance thunder rumbles
and darkens all gardens.

REPOSE
For Bruce Ashdown
In Loving Memory

You sent me a note to say
you'd been reading my poems
just before sleep,
and I was flattered that you,
who spent a lifetime
steeped in Shakespeare,
who solemnized soliloquys
with two generations of pupils
(knowing by rote each
palpitating pentameter),
who taught trochees and iambs
as if they mattered, as if
Dickens and Davies showed us
the wisdom of the world as it goes,
as if our lives were lived
through the prism of poetry:
I was flattered that my stilted stanzas
kept you awake and then
eased you towards repose.

FLUSH
For Ken Cooper and the gang

For more years than any
of us can remember (the mind
not as mindful these
days) Cooper's group
has meandered the lush meadows
of Hickory Ridge, striving,
against the odds and Lady
Luck, to strike a nine-
iron flush or stroke
a putt as smooth as a baby's
butt and go cock-
a-hoop when, on a sudden
whim, it trickles in,
but golf is a game of cozy
companionship, where the
good gods bless
us rosy with friends to console,
cheer or nip our hubris
in the bud.

TEMPO

More than once I've stared
at this picture of Tim
and James preening for Grandpa
in the front seat of my piping
green Ford Tempo
as if they own it and the world
they've grown into, leaving me
with these smiles tethered
to Time by my camera's preemptive
eye, but they are all
I need, ageing as I am
and weathering the years with an
old photo, ripe
with reminiscence.

ON THE DEATH OF MOTHERS
For John B. Lee

It's too bad we cannot
remember those dallying
days when we were enwombed,
when we were fed by our mother's
blood in that amniotic
room, moving with the rhythm
of her movements, our tiny
hearts, no bigger than a
robin's throb, beating
in tune with the more giving
one, nor can we recall
the hours when we were nippled
to the world, drinking affection
in our greed to be, but those
things we do remember
when she sends us out to live
un-umbilical are never
forgotten: the songs she hummed
to soften our sleep, the brush
of her touch when we were most
in need, the deep devotion
she brought to keeping us
steadfast as we grew
into ourselves and further
from her, and how sorrowful
it is to watch her age in the midst
of our thriving, to lose her grip
on those words she used
to soothe, her love no
longer spoken, and what a loss
there is when the cord
is finally broken, leaving
us alone with our grief and a dozen
empty tomorrows.

LABRADOR
For Jeff

My daughter married a man
whose laugh is as large as Labrador,
who plays the pixy when tempted
or whistles Dixie when exhorted,
he put the imp in impious,
dancing to his own tune,
and like the Pied Piper he entrances
everyone he touches
with his luminous love: carrying
kids, puppies, in-laws
and friends to Hamelin town
and its daffy delights; we adore
him because, like a June moon,
he shines brightest sitting
beside his bride.

GIFT
For My Son, John

You spent the better part
of your life in the school-
room, where you helped mentally
challenged children learn
to decipher their first word,
produce their first sentence,
you encouraged kids to reach
beyond the ambit of the self,
trapped in a treacherous body,
lifting them towards some
dream undeveloped,
you eased them out of the
anguish of autism, straightening
the maelstrom of dysfunctional
minds with your gentle, fostering
touch, your caring and your kindness,
you are one of God's
gifts to the world, an aficionado
of the mentoring arts: a teacher.

THE JIG

When my grandfather bled
to death on the surgeon's table,
I wondered how I could live
out the rest of my days
without his gifted guidance,
but living is what we do
as long as we are able,
and I have suffered a dozen
losses since: my mother
who died alone un-
praised, her heart
cleaved by love's demise,
my father whose whiskey-wizened
liver led him to die
without dignity, my Uncle
Potsy who tossed me my first
football and left me
without saying goodbye,
and the many others over
the years: friends, aunts,
uncles, companions — for whom
the jig was up, who let
themselves not be,
for we are second cousins
to death, bereft of all
but our bereavement.

RHYTHMS

How pleasing it is to visit
old friends, as Tom and I
parse the literary algorithms
of All in Good Time,
Bewilderment and Bus-Ride,
and my gentle questioner teases
out old and forgotten
truths about my long life
and my fiction, and resuscitates
the characters I drew out of the
belly of my breath as lucid
as a soothsayer's rune:
Wiz and Hutch, Gabe
Goodfellow and the risible
reeve and that voluptuous
village of the mind that started
it all, and here we are
now, coupled in this
cozy room and seized by the
rhythms of the heart.

FORTY-SIX
For My Mother

It's been forty-six
years since the day
I reached down to brush
your brow and found it cold,
your final face stiffened
forever, beyond surmise,
and I remember thinking,
"You're not old enough
to die," and wondering how
many hundred hours
it would take for my tears
to stifle my grief at such
a seismic sundering.

UNBIBBED
For Gerry Parker

You must have giggled at the
multicoloured mobiles
dangling above your crib,
something momentous
inside already saying
"This is how it ought
to be:" circles and swerves
and rainbow arcs in a
curved, unangled
universe, and soon a pen
and a brush magically fitted
your fingers and you nibbled
the alabaster page with wriggling,
dainty dots and blue
moons as big as Punchinello's
balloons: pointillist poems
Wallace Stevens would have been
proud of: you: painted the world
and its petite parts with a
bard's passion: ardent, masterly,
unbibbed.

OUT LOUD

My Uncle Bill was a young
bachelor and proud of it,
loved billiards and bluebloods
or, as he dubbed them,
"fillies on a fast track,"
and after slinging beer
at the St Clair for a froth-
filled week and, waving
goodbye to his cronies,
he would catch a cab and be off
two hundred or so
miles to the Fort Erie
Raceway (his natural
habitat) and tipping the cabbie
ten bucks for good
luck, he'd double down
on the Daily Double, caring
not that his redoubtable roan
finished last, for he was happy
to be here, the ponies
cruised apace, and he was
living his life out loud.

QUIP
For Alvin Gehl

My best friend Alvin
had a favourite quip whose bite
was legion in the neighbourhood:
whenever one of us
referred to our lower rear
region, Alvin would shout,
"Rectum? Damn near
killed 'im!" and once again
we would laugh because
we loved him and any witticism
that slipped his lips, and because
friendships are flavoured
with such delights.

LEAVENED
For Anne

Again and again I gaze
at this wedding photo,
now five decades
old: we are standing toe
to toe and face to face
on Lou's lawn: we seem
to lose ourselves
in the other's eyes, em-
boldened by the promise of a
bright embrace: me
in a borrowed blazer, you
all in white with your russet
hair swept up in a
heavenly haze, your smile
singing serenity, your gloved
hand squeezing mine
as if a breath might sever
it: we are caught in the camera's
miraculous moment
and cannot surmise
what the years might bring,
knowing only that our future
will be in tandem and leavened
by love.

CONVERSATION: A SUITE
For Tom

We sit in the tome-zone
of my study and quietly talk
books, only a microphone
dividing us and sipping
our words so effortlessly
exchanged: you
gentling the ageing author
with questions that stir the memes
of memory, me drifting
deep into the precincts of the
past, sharing our mutual
respect for the potency of a
poem, a lathe-gnurled
turn of phrase, a bare-
bones metaphor, a simile-
sibilant page or a sleuthing
whodunit, and linked
in ink-quipped conversation
by the leavening love of language.

AGES

Tom and I ignore
the summer sunlight
sifting through the study
windows, for we are too
focused on our monthly conversation
here in this cozy nook
about one man's
lifetime devotion
to books and the levitating lift
they bring to those who open
their hearts to the voices vespering
within the ink-prinked
pages, and we talk about what makes
a poet prick up his ears
at the words humming inside
or the impetuous pentameters
singing solo in his head,
and the need to strum the world
while reaching for the ages.

ONCE AGAIN

Once again Tom
and I on a June afternoon
with sunlight silvering
our book-bound room,
and words flow between
us as easy as a bard's
simile: it is hard to believe
that fifty years separate
our lives, as our minds mesh
with talk of plots and fresh
stratagems or what it is
that instigates a poem or story
or how an unvast village
could swallow a world whole
and glorify the presence of its past,
and we synchronize our souls
for the sake of literature
and its living lustre, with just
enough bravado to tempt
the Fates.

MUSE

In poems and stories galore
I have vented my voice on mine
and further generations
who might catch themselves
browsing my oeuvre, and I write
myself unmuted
to see how the plot turns
out, and to feel my soul
unhoused before
my betters, for words are
both missile and muscle,
they console and corrupt
with their lettered lunacy,
and I have lived in their midst
these eighty-odd
years, fearing no god
but the whimsicality of the Muse.

PERFECTION

God granted Adam
a garden of perpetual perfection,
a flowery bower where apples
were unmarred by blemish
or bruise and blossoms sipped
at sunshine but did not
move or bear fresh
fruit, for everything
was already ripened, doomed
to a sterile stasis, that is
until Eve brought the
odd news of her bountiful
beauty, the harvest of her hair
unberibboned, bursting
with breasts and a furred cleft
that left her mate disturbed
and thirsting for something
to change, something
to grow ungrappled,
some Tolman Sweet
too tempting not
to be eaten.

FOREBEARS

Cameron is as ancient as the
Neaderthals who, following
the ice-melt north, came
upon its pristine presence,
where they found the last
of the mastodons splashing full-
bodied in its shallows under
the lucidity of morning's light,
and they pelted the beasts with spears
until they fell in the hovering
dusk, tusks upright,
and then turned to have a gander
at the Lake gleaming beside them,
fish-blessed, clam-
clustered and as beautiful
as the gods who dreamed it calm,
and the marks of those forebears
still haunt the shadows
of our shoreline like a palm-
print or bright palimpsest.

BIDDEN

Another Sunday afternoon
and Tom and I sit in a
book-battened study
with the sun softening the air
between us, and talk
about the whodunits
I have penned over the years
and other works that matter
to both of us, as if
in some strange way
we have found the hidden flair
in each other's mind
and reached the rarity of common
ground, the gap of generations
postponed by the in-flow
of our intimate conversation:
bone-bred and blood-
bidden.

FORTY-THREE
For my father

It was just forty-three
years ago that I took
my last look at you,
the body I once admired
enmeshed in flesh-prolonging
tubes and hooked up
to a breathing machine
waiting for your last breath,
and I remember praying
that you would seethe against
the final ceasing, that you
would find again fire
in the belly, your old knack
for surviving, and hope in the heart,
which, against the odds,
I loved, even though
you favoured the gods of Bacchus
and drunk yourself to death.

GALLOWS

When Eve erupted from Adam's
ruptured rib, he kept
one eye upon her,
all curved and callow,
and something alien
leapt alive inside him,
and the blooms and blossoms
that saturated his flawless
garden loomed suddenly
shallow, and when his mate
consumed the apple, he soon
followed suit, listening
hard for God's laughter,
His gallows humour.

FURLED
For Katie and Rebecca

I watch my girls coast
through the room like swans
floating on the shape of their own
shadow: they have a dancer's
toes, moving willowly
winsome, and I gaze
in wonder at the bloom of their
young womanhood
with all the promise of a furled
rose, and I am un-
afraid to boast that some
day they will leave the world
amazed.

OLD MEN ON ICE

Our cry is "Hurry, hard!"
but it's hard to hurry
when your huff is greater than your
puff,
your rally rhythms are arthritic,
the hovering house is a blur,
your brush is governed by a rush
of blood to the brain, and the rock,
far from its neighbourhood,
ticks the guard for good
measure, but nothing beats
the camaraderie of old
men on ice defying
the odious gods of aging,
giving themselves
one more painful
of pleasure and another roll
of the dice.

PARKLAND

With a mind harrowed by hate,
a narrowing ego needing
something bigger than itself
to validate its being, and a finger
quickening the trigger of an AR,
seventeen victims were left
without breath for whom
there would be no more
dancing, no rippling
romance, no moving
into their living allotment,
and the grieving will go on
for those left crippled
with loss until they themselves
are relieved by death.

COUPLE

Did Adam in the nude show
God his gratitude for the
rib-wrought mate the Lord
dubbed Eve? And did
he give a thought to pouting
breasts and a furred furrow?
Or were they happy grappling
apples from the low-hanging
limbs and delving in God's
bloom-neutered garden,
content to be siblings
without sex, sensation
or the means of propagation?
Or was the peevish Commandant
expecting Lucifer so slither
supple towards the Tree
and its forbidden fruit,
undoing the uncorrupted
couple?

FAITH
For my Aunt Betty, in loving memory

One of the great pleasures
of Cameron Lake was spending
time with you, who were the first
to see in me what I hadn't
yet to see in myself:
the inklings of a writer on the brink,
and it was you who gave me
your prized Underwood,
upon which I typed my awful
apprentice novel and which
you praised as if you could see,
further on, the makings
of someone who, endued
with a kind of gift and a sense
of wonder, could turn a word,
surprising all but you:
there is no fair measure
of such faith nor any
limit to my gratitude.

BY AND BY

When Eve bit the apple
to spite her Maker and the corrupted
couple were naked to each
other's eyes, did Eve,
already worldly wise,
fetch the first fig
leaf to cover that part
of Adam she would grow
to covet, and did he,
mesmerized by his mate's
curled cleft, do a jig
for lechery, bereft of Eden
and its dappled domain, but able
at last and by and by
to understand the reason
why.

NAME

She was the cousin of my room-
mate, my first blind
date, and we sat side
by side at the football
game, holding mittened
hands and sipping surreptitiously
at a mickey of rye, and me
surprised at her kittenish
intimacy, grateful for such
a gift, and that evening
we danced cheek-to-cheek
and chest-to-chest to the sway
of Mart Kenny's orchestra,
and I felt the music move
through us, making us
more than strangers and less
than lovers, and when it came
time to part company,
we kissed as if the bliss
of it would never end,
and here, sixty years
onward, I recall that
magical night, the kindness
in her lips and my shy desire,
but cannot, alas, remember
her name.

CAREER

I try to imagine the day
when I'll write my last line
of verse on the uninked
page; will it be a simile
that sings like an oriole's aria,
a metaphor succinct
in its mirroring magic,
or perhaps a rhyme to startle
with its simple chime: in any
case I shall lay down
my pen with a Chanticlerian
cheer: calling it a career.

MARA'S LAMP

Black Moss Press
2019

MARA'S LAMP

Mara's lamp was only
a street light like a
crumpled cookie-cutter,
scattering its lambent glow
and luring us night
after night, like mesmerized
moths in a candle's flare,
to re-enact our ritual
game: hide-and-go-
seek: we became denizens
of the dream-dark, huddled
in nook and cranny, beyond
its radiant reach, we were
shibboleths of shadow
in the utter absence of light
until the "all free"
drew us running like shepherds
below a Bethlehem star,
whose bright beam
steadied our furled world.

EVERYTHING FALLS AWAY

Everything falls away:
the childhood we cherished
under Canatara's sultry
sun, exulting in just
being alive, with a Lake
as blue as a heron's un-
weathered wing, whose wavelets
tickled the shore and our toes,
but somewhere in the fickle
mists of our mind we realized
that those days singing
in our veins would not be
ours forever, that the world
is tethered to Time and the toll
it takes on what we, in our naivete,
trusted would never perish.

GLOW

There was only one lamp
along Monk Street,
its parabolic glow carving
the Dionysian dark
with a ring of light we gathered
in night after summer
night, caring not
that the Earth turned
on its amiable axis
or the amplitudinous stars
stained the heavens arched
above us or the moon
marshalled the tides
of oceans we would never see,
for we were havened here,
singing the song of ourselves,
safe in Mara's arms.

GIST

Whenever Mara's lamp
blinked into the inked shadows
of Monk Street, we gathered,
boys and girls together,
like guineas round a fist's
throw of oats in the June-
lewd sun, savoring
its lascivious light under
a sky stamped with stars
and a monastic moon floating
in the black above, and we
re-enacted the age-old
rituals with ampled exactitude,
while thinking of our afternoons
on the dune-dazzled sands
of Canatara and its erotic
urges, and needing no
reason, purging or exotic,
to question our right to relish
the joyful gist of the seasons.

FIRST
For Nancy Mara

Nancy, with your sloe-eyed
beauty and your girl's gamin
glow, you were the first
to stir in me feelings I later
learned where the inklings of love,
of an unglazed glance
under Mara's lamp,
a heightening of the heart's en-
raptured rhythm, while an image
of you intoxicated the dark
of my dreams with their furious fancies,
their lonesome yearning,
their dazed devotion: I could find
no word to embox
the seethe of my emotions,
but you were blood and bones
after all, and fresh
rivals appeared like pale
palimpsests to soothe and befuddle.

BREATHLESS

Mara's lamp was the beacon
that brought us breathless
to Monk Street on soft
summer evenings, where olly
olly en free echoed
all the way to the moon
marinating our play with its ghostly
glow, and we scampered, un-
hampered by thoughts of Time
or the dulcet Dance of Death,
from shadow to shuddering shadow,
our hopes aloft with the stars
that strafed our street as we
huddled as one, brightened
by their light, tickling our fancy.

BOOGIE

At a quarter to noon we stood
breathlessly on our walk
and waited for Herbie Gilbert
to sail by in his almost
new Tin Lizzy
and waited for the grin as he
bassooned the ooga-ooga
horn and thrilled a neighbourhood,
leaving them dizzy with delight
and letting us know that being
happy was as easy as being
adult with a Model T,
and we dreamed there on our
home curbs of doing
the boogie-woogie until
the future failed us.

TUFTS

On winter evenings when the snow
sifted down on Monk
Street like the silken tufts
from milkweed pods
and a hazy moon caressed
the flakes that kept our god-
less games aglow,
we thought of Bethlehem
and shepherds in the muffled
air over Galilee,
and we peered through the tingling
maze above, looking
for a single star to ignite
the larcenous night and cast
some beatific blessing
upon our All Free!

SEASON
After John B. Lee

We were all at ease with Autumn,
when everything green
in McPherson's orchard
turned as rosy as a bride's
blush, and we bit into the fruit
and let the exotic juices
glide chinward,
and dreamed of apple cider
and the acrid edge of its aroma,
and in the swamp that hugged
the Point, bulrushes and cattails
flourished, furred and dappled
in their dying, and the maples in our
yard reddened before
their fiery fall, and along
the road to our country school
the ditches were rich with golden-
rod that summoned sunlight,
and the mist-teased fields
festooned the air with the florid
fleece of wild carrot
and dilatory daisies, and later
on, the pungence of moon-
rounded pumpkins split
wide and oozing pulp,
and winter wheat whisking
furrows, like peach-fuzz
on the chin of those
seeking to leave behind
the tug of childhood:
being young we cared
not that Autumn was, at bottom,
the season of root-rot
and dank decay, for ours was a
world where hope had its say.

EASE

Shirley: lying on the beach,
and I try not to watch
as her thighs ease innocently
open, undeterred
by the tight tuck of her one-
piece bathing suit,
or, delighted with my luck,
stare in my boyish
bravado at the winking wrinkle
where her crotch catches
the luminosity of Canatara's
sun, and what I feel
is less than desire and more
than curiosity, for I am
the intruder, Eve's adder,
reaching towards something
teasing and untouchable,
impatient in my prurience.

PURE

In Sunday School we were all
washed clean with the Blood
of the Lamb and sang our gratitude
lustily, even though
no-one told us
why we needed such a
crude cleansing or who
exactly the Lamb was,
but we busted our lungs anyway
(benumbed by Kingdom Come)
just to be sure of being
pure.

CONFECTION

Harry Brand's Confectionery
beguiled us with penny
candies: like black balls
and grab-bags, two
cents each, crammed
with sweets for our delectation
and pretty-pink heart-
shaped lozenges that claimed
they loved us and licorice
pipes we smoked openly
in the brazen air and above
all the twinkling pause
in Harry's seventy-year
smile.

APOSTLE
For Grace Leckie

My mother called it "Puppy
love," but what I felt
had nothing to do with dogs
before their dotage: my body
refused to breathe whenever
you glanced my way, oozing
some intimation
of romance that left me
utterly bereft of speech,
and when you and your stallion
stutter-stepped past
our house a mile beyond
my reach, my heart, jostled
ajar went hectic
at your angelic smile,
like an apostle at the Last Supper.

DIGNITY

When I was still young
enough to wonder at the world,
I would watch each morning
Ol' Cap Garvey
shuffle past our gate
en route to the mail
with his skipper's dignity intact,
and marvel that his hair had turned
snow-white after
the storm of 'thirteen when waves,
unmuffled by the seething
winds, sent dozens
of lakers under, and I thought
about what it would take
to keep that malignant
memory alive for seventy
years.

WINK

Easton Burgess was grocer
to most of the village (not
counting the traitorous few
who slipped into DeJersey's
supermarket to enjoy the new-
fangled self-serve)
and he purveyed his goods
far into the country-side,
yet still managed to find
some sleepy hotel
that slung beer to those
addicted to the drink, but I
loved him because he always
made my cones double-
dip: with a small smile
and an alcoholic wink.

GERONIMO

The dunes of Canatara are infused
with the heat of a thousand suns,
tiny infernos festooned
with tufts of grass livid
since Adam left Eden,
and soon to be our make-
believe mountains where cow-
pokes out of cahoots with the law
take cover, waiting
for the adamantine dark
to cool their six-gun
itch and a moon above
pitching its glacial glow
upon a boy like me,
playing Geronimo.

LEAP

The moon was always bigger
over the Point, sitting
on the rim of our world like a
burnished marigold
and illuminating our ritual
games with its lascivious light,
as we catapulted from shadow
to shadow in the numinous night,
bare-legged and bright-
eyed, first among the
anointed, defying the odds
of the gods who furnished us
with pride and a fig-leaf
we couldn't wait to tear in two.

STRUT

Cooper's rooster strutted
across his wired pen,
with a wattle, sumptuously
plump as a berry's bulge
and twice as blooded, harrowing
his hens with a lust that never
tired, until the day
he flew the coop and we scattered
before his terrible talons
and that thrusting beak, letting
us know who was king
of the corral, cock of the walk.

HONEYCOMB

The bees in Mrs. Bray's
groomed garden tremble
on the tingling tips of stamens
tossed here and there
by a playful breeze, and probe
with their buzzing proboscis
deep into the nectared heart
of a tulip or rambling rose:
they've mastered the art of pollination,
and before cruising to their honey-
combed home, they leave
behind a dozen blooms:
bee-blossomed.

BLISS

On Christmas 'forty-three
my mother, "widowed" by the War,
couldn't afford a tree,
but the day before the event
Gran gave her two dollars
with which she bought a shrivelled
cedar, unendowed
with needles to hang our Santas
on and teetering where it
stood, but come the magic
morning we found under
those sagging branches,
just for us, a big
blue Greyhound bus
and a smile on Mom's face
as true as motherhood
and better than bliss.

STRANGER

A sunny summer day
and the Lake beckons us
as we slake our thirst for
adventure: at first it's Tonto
and the Lone Ranger with
Rustler's Roost in the dunes
and then Hopalong Cassidy
on the sun-saturated sand,
while ever westward
the unbreakable blue
of Huron fraternizes
with the far horizon, and we play
our galvanizing games and dither
a toe or two in the whispering
wavelets from time to time,
unaware that Time
itself lurks like a stranger
behind the silver moon
slithering in the noon sky.

BEAMING

Gran would take me to the
Band Tattoo in Athletic
Park because Grandpa couldn't
stand the tuba turbulence
or the trumpeting turmoil,
but we loved the skirl of the
kilty band, the tremulous
tooting of horns, the tinkle
of the glockenspiel, the glacial
glide of the trombones
and the smart marchers stepping
stride for stride: the teeming
maelstrom of music
I adored because Gran
was beaming at such guilty
pleasure and what-is-more
she was sitting beside me.

EXCURSION

Hide-and-go-seek
was our nightly excursion into the
summer's endreaming dark,
a chance to wreak both
speed and stealth and everything
tactical, to huddle in a shiver
of shadow and, for the lucky
few, pluck an occasional
cuddle or two, until
the olly olly en free
cry stunned the tide-
tugging moon that hung
in the star-jarred sky
like a silver dollar polished
to perfection, and although
our aim was to deter detection,
in truth we were merely re-
enacting the genes of the
generations abiding before us.

BLINK

Whenever Hoppy's pal
Johnny nuzzled his girl
on the screen, interrupting
our two-gun fandango,
the Imperial went a-buzz
(with the odd hoot or wolf-
whistle from the boys who knew
better): we didn't take
to our heroes going "sloppy"
or the least bit kinky,
and we waited for the scene to un-
tangle or, better still,
the arrival of the Durango Kid,
whose lips never bussed another's,
and who shot from the hip, abrupt
as a blink.

SPELL

Under the moon's magnetic
spell the shadows along
Monk Street shrivelled,
and shuddered all those
in the game hiding alone
in the grooves between
the shrubs, and our hearts swelled
with the frisson of fear we yearned
to feel in the ballast of our bone
and the bloat of our blood: ready
to howl in the owl-light
hectic hosannas to Heaven
and Hell.

BLADES

My grandfather sharpening
the blades of his lawn-mower,
guiding the whetstone
over the edges like a fretful
lover stroking a silken
thigh, and I never tired
of watching those workshop
rituals, even though I know
now that we are all
pawns in some god's
guileful game, indebted
to its wayward whims,
and that blades of some ilk
will be here long after
Grandpa's have been whetted.

GOODBYE

"I'm on the road to recovery,
Donny," were the last words
my grandfather spoke
to me, before the sutures
broke and he bled to death,
and to keep my spent spirits
lifted, I dreamt of a dozen
farewells when the future
we shared had come to a close:
breath on breath, our heads
held high, and savoring
the gift of goodbye.

RANDOM

It was in Bill McCord's
rink that my Dad's story
was first written, where he skated
with the inborn grace
of a swan over the silken
face of a perfect pond,
where he thrilled his rabid
fandom with deft dekes,
brisk bursts and mad-
cap dashes – until the day,
while they were building the bridge
that would loom over the town
like a rectilinear moon,
a red-hot rivet
without a nod or a pivot
dropped straight onto
the roof of Dad's arena,
burning it to ashes,
and though I was barely proof-
read, I must have thought
there are things in this world
that are random.

SWERVES

Shirley McCord was our
mate, flipping cart-
wheels on grandfather's
much-mowed lawn,
skipping Double Dutch
or playing hopscotch
May I? and, when a bit
risqué, Post Office:
we made the most of our joint
childhood, (our days
unbordered) but when,
after an absence of two
years, I spotted a girl
on Canatara, all
swerves and curves and pertinent
points, my heart hopped,
unsure how it
should feel, and when she said,
"Hello, Don," I wished
for a slow moment that Time
had stopped when we were young
and certain of the way the world
would go.

FESTOONED

It never occurred to me
that these child-friendly
dunes of Canatara
took millions of wavelets
nibbling the sibilant shore
and hundreds of thunder-thwarted
storms to hurl the sand
landward into grass-
groomed humps where we played
Comanches and other gun-
toting games, and now
I wonder which quibbling
gods imagined this
dune-festooned moon-
scape just for me,
and I can find no
word to sum up
its unblurred beauty.

APPLAUSE

There I am seated on the
railing of grandfather's
side verandah, reading
my maiden "epic" to an audience
of three: the McCords and my pal
Butch: my words greeted
with only a touch of the skeptic
and more surprise than I
thought warranted, my voice
just failing to reach
the authorial tone I aimed
at (with a pregnant pause
or two), and I waited in vain
for the applause due to the
uninhibited, juvenile
scribe who dared to perpetuate
his plots on the pages of a
ten-cent scribbler.

FIZZLE

Give me a July day
with a sun sultry and sizzling
over Canatara
and bare-backed boys
and long-limbed girls
at play, and I will grant
you that love lives
like an itch under the skin,
and in the distant thunder
lust lurks until
dark arrives to cool
the bejewelled sands
and all prurient thoughts
unhitch and fizzle.

ONLY

On the mile-long trek
to our country school, boys
and girls in a straggling gaggle,
we passed Leckie's pasture
and cast our eyes on the young
colt there, his roan
coat surprised by a morning
sun, set on the horizon
ahead like a gilded marigold,
and below the colt's belly
hung a bright red
erection, throbbing like a
bruised thumb, as the girls
went numb with shock,
looking in every direction
but Leckie-ward, and we
boys locked our gaze
on the proud protuberance
and considered something
other than romance and moons
on star-startled nights:
the furious fusion of that
amazing instrument with another
receptacle we couldn't quite
fathom, as the girls giggled
and Coop broke the spell:
"That's only his pecker,"
he smiled.

NO NEED

Grandpa and I strolling
through First Bush,
the tree-tops almost
touching overhead,
a sliver of blue between
where the utmost branches
inch upwards
towards the sun bursting
somewhere above,
and finches flutter in the
brief breeze, with robins
carolling their lush lyric
and butterflies dancing
in duo, feeding on lavish
leaves, and I am seized
by a feeling beyond love
and our coupled walking:
we do not hold hands,
there is no need.

NIBBLE

My first "novel" was pencilled
in my school scribbler, all
twelve pages of it and titled
"The Adventures of Little Tiny
Bingo," a lion cub
who must have been wee to merit
two quantitative adjectives,
but I sent him on his way
into my magical menagerie
(dredged up from my immaculate
imagination): beasts un-
daunted of every ilk
propagated plots galore:
stories of derring-do,
pratfalls, silken recitals
and belly-laughs heard
as far as kingdom come,
as I nibbled away at the edges
of authordom.

BRAND-NEW

Miss Nelson hands out
the brand-new scribblers
with vermillion, linoleum-
like covers, and I sniff
the oiled surface of the one
winking up at me,
open it to the first
virgin page, dip
my pen into the ink-well
and, trying not to spoil
the immaculate space
there, write "Composition,"
a word I hope will precede
the million more to come.

PIGGYBACK

When a wastrel wind blows
in from the Great Lake
and we wish a little March
madness, we rush right
to the River Flats and let
our jerry-rigged kites
go piggybacking
on the juddering breeze,
the joy-stick rigid
in our fists, and we are lost
in thought as our winged missiles
kiss the towering Bridge
before somersaulting
below and then levitating
like Elijah hearkening Heaven.

ORPHAN

Aubrey Lyttle was adopted
by our elderly neighbours
after four bleak years
in an orphanage with no takers,
but his luck turned at last
and he found himself
with what he wanted above
all: to be loved, to be
entitled to a name he could
boast about, to have
parents who would see to
his niggardly needs (we welcomed
him into our gang as our mascot,
we admired his curls and boyish
pluck) and all was well
until his new father died
and his new mother sent
him back to the place where
joy was in short supply:
after all these years
I still think of Aubrey,
and my heart still bleeds.

SISTERS

Betty was the big sister,
boasting breasts and a blistering
tongue, Shirley was all
cartwheels and flexibility,
flipping hither and yon:
we hung about their yard
like puppies in need, playing
spin the bottle with chaste
kisses and hesitant hugs,
but when Betty loomed,
the air grew greedy
with something unthrottled,
slithering and serenely sexual.

STALWART
For Grace Leckie

You rode your roan stallion
as robust as Rob Roy
haunting the Highlands,
your locks streaming behind
in the wind's whip-lashing,
your thighs gripping the saddle
with a lover's lust, your eyes,
as blue as cobalt in stunning
sun, staring straight
ahead, dashing, undaunted
with never a glance at the boy
on the roadside who dreamed
of stalwart steeds and Gaelic
romance.

BELLS

Whenever the bells tolled
for one of our own, Mrs.
Bray's flowers would light
up the room with a bold
spray of bloom for the bereaved:
a nosegay for the casket,
a glowing rose for remembrance,
a lily for love's loss:
life and death juxta-
posed, and widow Bray
growing and grieving.

LIVID

On steaming summer afternoons
we lingered in the livid light
over Canatara, the heat
bringing us to our knees
in the stinging sand, and in
those hazy days
we had time and rhymes enough
to dream of being something
other than ourselves,
some privileged, primal
insight we delved
deep down to see,
of what we might become
or hoped to be.

VIMY

Four divisions strong
under a borrowed flag,
you fought with the bravery
of boys becoming men,
you did not blench
at the muttering stutter of
machine-guns and bullets
craving a kill, you burrowed
below the unbridgeable
ridge like rabbiting animals
to face the enemy in their
intractable trenches,
until the day was finally
won and a country was born
out of maelstrom and mourning,
and the living felt the beginning
of belonging and the dead
would never know tomorrow's
joys.

PALOMINO
For Grace Leckie

It wasn't a palomino
like Trigger with Roy roistering
on his back, but the roan you rode
with such panache
was cinematic enough
for us, and you, bigger
than life or Saturday
afternoons at the movies,
sat high in the saddle,
far above the love
we tendered your way and the envy
we felt for being merely
boisterous boys.

TRUE

When the world was young in my
infant eyes and the sky
was ablaze with blue and grand-
father's lawn was as green
as grass after a rain
and the lilac hedge that edged
my docile domain bloomed
like a bride's bouquet
and the spirea that hugged my northern
border feathered the air
with its flowers and every stick
and stone was a superb surprise
and I ventured warily into the wide
outside, tethered always
to the known and true: at home
in my bones.

COURAGE
For my Grandfather: in memoriam

These yellowed medical
records tell the story
of your suffering and affliction
(two wounds and dysentery)
but make no mention
of the courage it took to breathe
in the rat-riddled mud
of trenches or to pick lice
out of your fellows' hair
or fling yourself into
No-Man's-Land
singing with bullets and the cries
of the dying and the silence
of the dead (knowing there was no
glory in the blood and mire
of battle), or the courage to enter
sleep each night
not certain your dreams
might be your last, but
I like to think your final
thoughts before exhaustion
claimed you, were about
the possibility of a future
free of combat,
and one that included me.

BUNNY
Easter 2017

At Eastertime the magic
bunny hopped from room
to room depositing eggs
and other treats under beds
and commodes, where we,
pleased to be teased,
discovered them without
divine direction, and then
it was off to Sunday School
with new shoes and a heart
heightened by news
of the Resurrection,
with Jesus somehow
finding the strength to roll
the stone away from his three-
day tomb and levitate,
turning a tragic story
into a tale primed with God's
glory and one honey
of a bunny.

SHY
For Bobby Cooper

Shy doesn't do justice
to the diffident dignity
you offered the world, but
there was a twinkle in your eye
that betrayed the elfin imp
inside, who kept Belgians
in a hutch next door,
while we watched their noses
dimple pink; we spent
long days on Canatara's
sands on the brink of Huron,
where westering winds under
the simple sun gusted
the waves we leapt in tumbling
tandem; here in your class
photo you stare at the ground
as if the camera might expose
more than you were willing
to present to us who loved
your humble humor and all
that friendship you bestowed
on me for four short
years, whether I deserved
it or not: we plotted
our future together
and dreamed, as the days went by,
that it would never end.

RHEUMATIC

When my temperature reached
one hundred and five,
I could hear the nurses discussing
my demise, their voices
barely alive, coming from
some unbreachable
gulf, but I was too young
and shy to die, so,
mystifying all,
I opened my eyes the next
morning, feverless
and emptied of sulfa,
and survived these many
decades, no longer
shy, and determined to resist
death with my penultimate
breath.

THE GIRLS OF CANATARA
For Nancy Mara

The girls of Canatara
cavort on my beach
like gazelles grazing
the grass-tops of some
vast savannah before
they sprawl splendidly
on the satisfying sand,
where we gaze on the curves
and swells of their bountiful bodies,
on the sassy swirl of their curls
and on the gifted grace of their
unpinched faces, knowing
full well we were not
the sort to raise an eyebrow
or solicit a sigh, or bring
a girl like Nancy Mara
one inch closer
to my ravenous reach.

PALS

Jerry Mara and I
summered on Canatara
beach, whooping it up
like juiced Geronimos
on the unimpeachable
beauty of the ancient dunes
after a swift swim
in the Lake as blue as a
heron's underwing
in a blur of sunlight,
and beyond the tumult of our
two-gun cries,
strummed on a tingling tongue,
our communion had no need
for the commingling of words,
and I still remember those
dallying days: good
pals are hard to come by.

CHARITY

Gran hadn't much use
for the goings-on in the apse
and nave of the Anglican Church,
a brief block from home,
but she always tithed and had a
blithe smile whenever
the Reverend Stone purloined
her parlour (every month
or so), and when she died,
at the committal he spoke with
little thought for clarity
of Paradise and Charity
for all those witting
enough to be among
the anointed (while Gran rolled
over in her grave).

HOME
*After a trip to Point Edward with
my grandson Tom, June 2017*

You can't go home again,
they say, but the home
you hugged when you were young
and the world was new and willing,
you carry with you all
the days you stray adrift
from its mothering moorings,
and it is more than mere
memory or the wallow of nostalgia:
it is a place of your own
married to the marrow,
embraced by the bone.

SIXTY YEARS
For Alvin Gehl

After a sixty-year
gap you phone to say
hello, as if we had just
finished a game of catch
and said our goodbyes
for supper; instantly,
your face sketches itself
across the miles between
us, your smile upper-
most in my mind's eye,
and we exchange
stories that run so deep
in the bone of our mutual
memory that sixty years
cannot erase them.

GRANDFATHER'S WAR

It was the noise that frayed
the nerves of you and the boys-
becoming-men beside
you: the sonic boom
of Big Bertha, the rattling
stutter of Tommy guns,
grenades bursting in a bloom
of shrapnel, and you, crouched
in your trench, wondering when
the next bullet would bore
to the bone, and so you dreamed
of balmy evenings on the verandah
and the tantalizing tonic of home,
while the world wound its way
thundering towards Doomsday.

DIZZY

As dusk settled down
on Withers field like a
hen feathering her hatchlings,
our game slowed: Wiz's
strike-out pitch
lingered, while Nancy's bat
was half its natural gusto
(the ball tethered to it):
and Butch, nettled by such
unhurry, appealed
to the invisible jury: it was
as if a world bigger than ours
had yielded to the thrust of the gloaming,
while the slithering dark
lusted for our bones, and drove
us, dizzying, home.

ALL

Potsy and I on the
manicured meadows of our
favourite course: I watch
in awe as he strikes a three
iron with the precise flick
of a surgeon's cut and the ball
quickens the arrowing air
and ingratiates the green
two hundred yards
away, where he will tickle
the cup with his patient, un-
flawed putt, followed
by his brief smile which seems
to say, "This is ordinary,
something understood,"
but my heart surges anyway
and my eyes narrow upon
this man standing tall,
standing good, whom
I loved above all.

PRAISE
For Aunty Betty, In Memoriam

You were a fan right
from the start, when I typed
my first disheartening dud
(Pass That Puck!)
on the portable Underwood
you donated to my cause,
and somehow found ways
to praise my maiden effort
with all its flaws, and when
my talent finally ripened,
you smiled winningly as each
new tale or poem
arrived, faithfully inscribed
to one who had understood
and nipped my naysaying
in the bud with this advice:
"Donald, there's no
such thing as beginner's
luck!".

PENDULUM

When we were young and free
from care, one day
was like another: the sun
boiled out of First Bush
like the slow explosion of a
rose and bathed the streets
in a lavish light where we
re-enacted our ritual
games: doing the hop-
scotch trot on the same
embroidered sidewalk
as the one there the day
before the world began,
swimming in the Lake whose
waves were repetitions
of the Eternal, while our River
flowed in roiling rapids
the Attawandaron reconnoitered
for Gitchimanitou,
we rounded the same bases
our fathers had plotted on Withers
field and skated improvised
filigrees on Foster's perpetual
pond: we played and played
again for all the days
to come: Time hung over
our village like a clock without
its tick-tocking pendulum.

DUD

Tossing my India rubber
ball against the shed
wall, I dreamed I was Dizzy
Dean with a mean curve,
but one day the curve
swerved off-beam
and took out the coal-bin
window with a crash that made
the village shudder: I hope
I took my punishment like a man,
but my principal goal was to find
my dud among all that
coal.

FIRST

The first stories I ever
heard came liberated
from the lips of my grandfather,
while I, perched on his knee,
absorbed by osmosis
the peregrinations of plot,
the contours of character,
and the lurch of suspense:
I rehearsed their rhythms
over and over in my dreams,
waiting for the day when a pitch-
perfect poem or some
scribbled prose would age
instinctive inside me,
then burst fully-formed
onto the uninked
page.

BRITTLE
For Grace Leckie

My heart hammered a hundred
beats per minute when-
ever Grace thundered
by on her roan stallion,
sitting one-handed
on the reins, the pommel pulsing
as she rode high in the saddle,
far above the ordinary
world, and I could only
stammer my admiration,
convulsed as I was by love's
bone-brittle pain.

DISRUPTION

When I was confined to a
bed no bigger
than a pup-tent, with no
breeze to tease my cheeks,
no lilac hedge
to stir my circumscribed
sight, my fancy grew
as fantastic as the dreams
that struck my nightly sleep,
and I drew into being
a whole menagerie of beasts
and tribes of invented souls
I infused with stories to match
their plucky personalities:
my imagination unfurled
with every beat of my flawed
heart, and I used its
awe-filled peregrinations
to disrupt the world.

MEMORY

In my memory the village
remains a perfect paean
to my boyhood: every
street as welcoming as a
teasing breeze on a
summering July day,
every home harbouring
a playmate who answers
my querying call with a grin
and an invitation to bat
some balls in Withers
field or propel
some pucks on Foster's
pond or bestrew ourselves
on the sun-struck sands
of Canatara, but memory
can mock us all,
and here again after
six decades away,
I try to recall an errant
eave or the lilac hedge
that edged my grandfather's
lawn, but the past has already
slipped beyond the heft
of our best remembering:
going home again
to unlock its embers
leaves me feeling
both joyful and bereft.

CONTINUOUS

The geography of my village
is a memory-map lodged
in my mind's eye forever,
but when I venture back,
I am baffled by the distance
between by-gone and be,
puzzled by the chasm between
was and is, has-
been and hope, where the streets
are hodgepodge and the houses
awkward and askew,
and it's only when I come in sight
of the Lake with the sun hefted
upon its copious blue
horizon and the sinuous sands
of Canatara that I feel
upright, assured of a world
that is continuous, that will be
here long after me.

EXULTED

I was lucky enough
to have a gang of pals
to hang around with
on sultry summer days:
Butch, Wiz, Bones
and little Jerry Mara:
with endless afternoons
on Canatara, ducking
rollers in the Lake, sallying
fin-first to the raft
or playing survival in the
derelict dunes under
June's luscious light:
we had no fear of Night's
Dark Dream or the moon's
ghostly glow: we loved
our life-on-the-go and most
of all we exulted in being
alive.

BALLAST

You have only one home:
having weathered the womb
and the burst of birth, you greet
the village that envelops you whole:
first, there's grandfather's
lawn, lavished with lilacs
and foaming spirea with a yard
yawning enough for a dozen
LaSalles to explore, and soon
a street teases a granny-
cracked sidewalk and an alley
blooms where pals pop
up and fraternize, and both
of your feet touch the Earth
until a song sings
itself to your soul: of ballast
and belonging.

SIGN

And me skating in my first
peewee match in the
cavernous city arena:
fully-padded with a brand-
new sweater (stick
poised in gloved hand)
to show my father who's
watching from the stands as I
wobble-walk on my ankles,
players from both sides
bursting past me
in rude moves, stalking
the puck, which, along
with everything else
eludes me and I am relieved
to reach the bench, winded
and wan: I look up
for a face in the crowd, some
sign of love: my Dad
is gone.

1

like outsize fleas
and monarchs teeter oddly
on the afternoon breeze
breathing on sand-burrs
and dried weed-stalk
and flocks of sparrows rise,
like a spray of flung confetti,
and a puff adder in the
undergrowth slithers
as silkily as Satan defying
his Maker, and further on
the marsh yields back-
combed cattails
and ruffled pussy willow
and somewhere by the water's
edge a weasel seizes
its prey and the Bridge arches
over all, serene
in its curvilinear rigidity,
and I feel my blood hum
and I am glad to have a
grandfather and hallowed
home where love abides.

HUM

I am walking through the field
below my grandfather's
house, where grasshoppers
leap from milkweed pods

INKING THE WORLD

First Choice Books
2019

VILLAGE DREAMING

Rocking in my chair I dream
of the village where I was breathed
into being by the athletic lusts
of my hockey-heroing father
and the girl he deemed his paramour,
when my world was as new as a
chick picking at the shell
and a blank page I wrote
myself upon with words
wrestled from the womb, and a town
surrounded me with folks
to people my poems and startle
the stories I would create, in the
mortar and pestle of my imagination,
of their forgivable follies, the hustle
and bustle of their Dickensian lives,
and those childhood
chums I turned into combed
prose, who made my days
worth the telling and strummed
the strings of my memory, leaving
me to dream, rock and sing
the song of myself.

COCK-A-HOOP

When I was almost eleven,
Joanne and I found ourselves
in Hendry's abandoned coop,
and as luck would have it,
she dropped her pants and exposed
the velvet pucker between
her thighs, while I, cock-
a-hoop, did my best
to close my eyes, until
she asked to view that part
of me only my mother
perused, and when I obeyed,
she brayed "That's quite
a surprise!"

ABIDE
For my father in loving memory

My Dad and I fishing
on Mitchell's Bay where the muskies
lay in the weeds like elongated
green behemoths with jig-
sawing teeth, and my father
teased his William's Wobbler
in their direction with a silken ease
that made my heart hum
with pride at sharing the genes
of this man who could master
a musky, strum a ukulele, and sing
like Bing, and when dusk settled
over our daylong bonding,
I looked into the angler's eyes
and knew that love, horizoned
there, would abide.

HOME

The day before morning
I was envowelled by my village,
and its syllables sang in my genes,
and I was allowed to roam
its alleys and leeways, enriched
in innocence, until I came
horizoning to the edge of
everything else, and dared
not move beyond the cunning
of my blood, shunning the
Doomsday tock till
something owl-wise
and sibilant drew me back
to the womb-warp of home.

VIVID

When I delve more deeply
into the past, undaunted
by Time's treachery, I see
myself vivid in the village
that spawned me, a lad
of eleven, his head humming
with poems and stories about
to be born when the right
words begin their rhyming
and something magical
urges their birth, and I am
soon walking on the Heaven-
hewn stretch of Canatara's
sands under the sun's
strum, livid with light
and dreaming of endless authordom,
while the Earth still turns
on its steadfast axis.

HEFT

Wiz Withers, our guru
of gizmos and gadgets, was not
one to dawdle or dither:
he'd wave his magic wand
and presto! a go-kart
worthy of the Soap Box
Derby would pop up
fully functioning on the
Main Drag and we left
the cheering crowd in our dust,
speeding as quick as Herbie
Gilbert's flivver; another
wave and lo! the circus
we dazzled the denizens with
that summer of forty-seven,
and I was intoxicated with such
effortless wizardry and bowled
over by his being bigger
than I had ever imagined
myself to be, under
the heft of Heaven

SPIN

If it wasn't Post Office
it was Spin the bottle:
anything to pin my lips
upon Shirley's cherub cheek
and watch her blush as the
rush of blood hit me
where I needed it most
and I thanked the Lord for the
gift of girls and the un-
throttling of male desire.

HUM

Shirley McCord was a drum
majorette in the Girl Guides
band, and she twirled her baton
with all the aplomb of a
Barnum-and-Bailey juggler,
and I watched her leading the parade
with a high-stepping, long-
legged stride, hugging
the pavement and making my heart
hum.

ALMOST

When I was almost young
and lilacs hung on the hedge
that hugged us snugly in,
I never ventured beyond
our homestead's edge
or roamed into the indelible dark,
content to squeeze my panda
bear and watch Grandma's
Jello cooling on the verandah.

VILLAGE

There was a time when my village
seemed to me to be
paradisal, where the lilacs
grew more lavender
and the sun bloomed on its horizon
like a slow rose opening
to the lick of light, where friendships
were made as if forever
would never end, where the groomed
grass of grandfather's lawn
was as green as the leaves of Eden,
where home was the place that eased
us into the diligent dark,
and where the days were metrical
and all my poems rhymed.

SPEECHLESS

In my seething imagination
these dunes were here
when the last Neanderthal
stood upright on Canatara's
beach, blinking into the
morning sunlight
and pandering to clams fresh
from the Lake's cellarage
(an age before Adam
or Eden were dreamed), not
knowing he would soon be
extinct, that all things
flesh must pass away
speechless so other
beings, sir or madam,
can be born and Mother
Earth renewed in her glory
and an octogenarian poet
can stroll past these mesozoic
mounds and tell their story
in a birthing of words.

RHYMES

Nancy Mara, I loved
you from afar: I was Lancelot
going for the Grail and I dreamed
you dulcet on Canatara's
singing sands and whenever
I closed my eyes I saw you
afloat on a star-brushed
horizon and I wanted to write
a dozen sonnets and dedicate
each one of them you:
scintillating with similes
and ringing with rhymes.

SOMEBODY ELSE

Strange what we remember
when old age creeps
alive into our capillaries:
the squeak of a rusted gate
when I strode out of my grandfather's
lot onto the welcoming
sidewalk and peddled my way
over granny-cracks
whose craqueleur I cannot
unforget, the squeal
of my trike's back wheel
and the heraldic honk of its horn,
startling Mister Robinson
and the banty rooster next
door, and thither I rode
past the immaculate lawn
of Bryant's groomed abode
(whose heart disassembled
from too much perfection),
and on by Gray's latticed
porch and the end of my designated
desmene: but try as we might,
nothing is born again,
the world withers away
without our saying until
we too are just somebody
else's memory.

SUCH A LONGING

I have such a longing
for the days that are no more,,
when the sun rose over
my boyhood town each
misted morning, hefting
light for my eyes only
as I circumnavigate the streets
(like LaSalle on the prowl
for gold and glory), looking
for the point poised between
the Lake and the River, greeting
each friend and rival
with equal ease, knowing
we shared this cozy
desmene, that ours was our own
story to tell, and that
we would never be bereft
of belonging.

BE

I have such a longing
to see once again
the lush lavender of the lilacs
that hugged grandfather's lawn
and to feel one more time
the brush of a breeze combing
the leaves of our Manitoba maples
and to know the warmth of a home-
kitchen, love-tugged,
and to tingle with the touch of fingers
so tender I could dream
only of being in their embellished
embrace and I have such
a longing to be born again
in the place where I could merely
be.

ROAST

Mrs. McCleister's cockerel
pulled the sun up
over the lip of the horizon
with his clawed beak and crowed
in the morning, his wattle waxing
as scarlet as a tanager, while
his hens feathered deeper
into their straw beds, wary
of his bottled fury, but the
widow next door didn't prize
his dawn song and threatened
to roast him for Easter.

TOLLING

Ours was a three-steepled
town, when, on a Sunday
morning the tolling of deep-
tongued bells and their tuneful
music drew the people
of the Point to their pews and the
weekly anointment, free
for the moment of Sabbath sins
and the impious whims of Lucifer
and his less-than-holy crew.

UNIVERSE

I wake and the world widens,
and just beyond the morning
dews the Lake swims
into view like a slow fuse,
so blue it would blind Zeus
or make Oedipus blink,
and a breeze quickens to wimple
the waves swallowing each
other and licking the silence
of the shore, and I reach the water's
edge and immerse one
simple toe in Cameron's
granite chill, feel
the immanent will of the Universe,
inked and abiding.

INSURGENT

The girls of my village sprawl
on the beaches of Canatara,
preening and prettifying in the
lilting light that prisms
off the Lake's face,
unaware that beauty
is its own grace, defying
all logic, all
reason, and these bodies,
embraced in biology, seasoned
by the noontide sun
and the sifting of silted sands,
leave the boys, beyond
reach on the nippled dunes,
un-willed, moon-
endued and prey to their most
insurgent urges.

WIDE

Eleven and still unable
to swim, paddling in the Lake's
shallows like a inflated dolphin,
while Nancy and the girls
disport on an anchored raft
fifteen yards away
(all that flesh caressed
by the afternoon sun),
flashing me a smile
now and then before diving
slim-thighed into the nearest
breaker as slick as seals
into a tumescent sea, as the raft
tilts and sways like Noah's
craft on God's turbulent
tide, breasting the waves
and waving at one who
could not stroke his body
across a heavenly divide
that might has well have been
a mile wide.

ALONE

My widowed grandmother
listening to the radio: soap
after soap carrying
from the dining room all
the way to the kitchen chair
where she sits knitting:
Helen Trent's romance
gives way to Pepper
Young's family – unless
the Tigers are playing at Briggs,
only then will she drop
a stitch or two with the crack
of the bat like wood on bone
or the thud of a pitch in the mitt
as the crowd cheers and she wishes
she could be anywhere
but here – unsung
and alone.

FOREVER

When you reach four score
and a bit, your mind moves
to those scenes of your childhood
where you were free to roam
the fraternizing streets and greet
Wiz and Bones, Jerry
and Hutch and where the sun
solemnized the village that whittled
you into the world, and a lake
awaited your wading in its beryl-
blue waves and a breeze
dizzied the trees in Canatara
and where Nancy Mara had eyes
for you alone, and where home
was grandfather's lilac-
lit demesne and we all
thought ourselves clever
enough to make it last
forever.

LUFFED

How many hours did we spend
speculating what lay between
Shirley's girlish thighs,
caught as we were in the first
flush of lust's lustre,
our consensus (from a single glance
at her one-piece suit)
being a tuft that tingled
and tantalized or a petalled pucker
that fuelled our fancy and tested
our masculine mettle, but alas
remained taboo, taking
the wind out of our sails
and leaving us luffed?

SMALL-TOWN BETRAYAL

When our neighbor Mr. Hart
offered to buy my grandfather's
house with its half-acre
groomed grounds, Where I spend
my happiest childhood
days, he pleaded poverty
and appealed to my uncle, who made
him a deal: reduced price
for a vow not to sever
the lot, to keep its lilac
and foaming spirea hedges
as they were, and so
the sunny haven I thought of
as home passed to others,
and a year later Mr. Hart
severed the lot and made
a pot of money

BACK HOME
On a visit to the Point with my son
John on June 15, 2018

For what may well be
the last time, I re-see
the village that vaulted me
into being, unumbilicalled
into its flawless world
that is both estranging
and familiar, where some houses
have same gee-and-haw
tilt they had when I first
tricycled past them,
and there is grandfather's
mansion, where I re-imagine
the trees that lightning levelled
and the lilacs now beyond
blooming, and my son nods
when I point to the room
where I lay a-bed for seven
months and lived to tell
the story, and the Lake lives
again here and in my mind
in all its blue-belled
bevelled glory, and we stroll
by Mara's place, unchanged,
and bid goodbye to the empty
space where the streetlamp
supervised our glorious games
and the June moon summered
on the horizon like an angel's smile,
and we stare at Canatara
uplifted by light, and sit
for a while under the Bridge
and watch the steamers go
slowly by like a dream
of themselves and like
the flow of Time itself
and this gift given
by the gods only once.

ANGUISH

The languorous-limbed girls
of the Point languish on the sands
of Canatara in their one-
piece suits, and long
to be ogled by boys
with impish grins and hurled
hoots, while the mustard sun
anoints their new-blooming
bodies and Huron's wavelets
soothe the shameless shore
and nothing stirs in the
blush of the afternoon
but lust's unfulfillable
anguish.

STARRED

Under the moon's gossamer
glimmer, we go a-blading
on Leckie's iced-over
fallow, the wind-chill
raw against our cheeks
as hand-in-hand we scribble
scrimshaws into the shimmering
surface, traceries
of our having been, here
on this hallowed ground
on such a night, limned
by light, tremored by tingling
touch, and all beneath
the unmarred wonder
of the starred firmament.

TIDES

It was the Ojibwa who gave us
"Canatara" for the "blue water"
of the big-bellied lake
that hugged the beach and its
mile-long stretch of
Saharan sand, a double
trochee rolling off
the aboriginal tongue
like the tunes of Orpheus, and I think
of those first peoples
offering a kind of birth
to those unbroken
sands and the cobalt swells
of a water-body wider
than half the seas on Earth
and mammoth enough to dwarf
their moon-tugged tides.

DOUBLE

Riding Double in the Point
was considered a sin akin
to eating apples in Eden,
but I was bike-free
and Butch's handle bar
beckoned, so we cycled
triumphantly through
the hodge-podge
of alleys and lanes, dodging
Constable Pedan (hapless
on foot), untroubled
by doubt, certain we were a
force to be reckoned with,
and wishing Eve the best.

WOOTSER

Mrs. McCleister's blood-
wattled rooster serenaded
each sunrise
with his lascivious aria,
making the mottled hens
tremble with trepidation,
knowing that, feast or famine,
they would be boosted one
by one, and at last a triumphant
cry could be heard all
the way to Wooster, Mass.

ZIPPER

While the great Lake's
wavelets lick the shore
with lascivious lips, the girls
of the Point bask in the fiery
sun above Canatara, and do not
ask whether they are being statued
by the stare of boys who would do
a jig to see them au naturel
or put a zipper on their whirly-
gigging desires.

HEATHEN

"Don't worry," Butch
says as he dispatches
the adder with a hectic blow,
"Snakes always come
back to life again
at midnight." "The little
heathen," my Grandma says,
"What a concoction!"
When we hurry back
next day, the creature
lies in the grass, unalive.
"It's okay," Butch says,
"I don't believe in the
Resurrection either."

SUNDAYS

On Sundays we sang of Jesus
and his glory and the precious blood
of the Lamb, our voices high,
as if we knew what it was
to be affixed to a cross
and have your highway
to Paradise paved,
or be strong enough to roll
that stone away and live
again – leaving us
to sing your story, and wonder.

BEING

We come into this world
unbidden; there is
no-one to applaud
our irreverent arrival,
so we irrigate the air
with our prodigal cries,
succumb to the need
to breathe, somehow
inhabit the broad
acreage of that space
Nature grants us –
and celebrate the birth
of our being.

RUTHLESS

And me composing poems:
inklings I tease
towards some sense
in words whetted upon
the wheel of memory
and swerving askance
upon the page where they lean
upright, enlinked,
ready to be swallowed whole,
raw and ruthless
in rhythmic pursuit
of the truth.

LIFETIME

My first story, cribbed
from the Grade Three primer,
garnered undeserved praise
from my teacher that not only
raised my spirits but made me
a believer, and so it was
no surprise two grades
later when I began filling
my scribblers with intrepid tales
of quibbling bears and duelling
rabbits with blinking blue
eyes, and finally my maiden
poem arrived, in rhyming
couplets, inked from a Muse
as demanding and she was un-
bribable, and soon the scribe
in me became habitual,
lasting a lifetime.

HOPES

Shirley was the first girl
whose elongated legs caught
my amorous eye as she whirled
and danced at Double Dutch,
showing us once in a blue
menstrual moon a thimbleful
of thigh and what we imagined
lay higher up
between the taut squeeze
of her glorious gams, but Shirley
took no notice
of the male gaze for she
was skipping in frenzied bursts
to entertain and amaze,
until the ropes sagged
like spent balloons and she flashed
us a smile that said,
"I'm no bimbo,
but this may be romance,"
or such were our hopes.

STRETCH

If you don't mind cattails
like badly brushed hair
and the odd pair of pussy
willows encased in the ice
like butterflies from the
Pleistocene age jewelled
in amber, you might
find yourself sailing
alone across a stretch
of ready-made rink
with the wind cherubic
on your cheeks,
fantasizing stanzas in snow
and sleek-paced poems
on a glazed page, etched
in indelible ink.

PROMISE
For Isabelle Macdonald
In memoriam

In nineteen seventy-nine
I travelled the byroads
of Lambton County, armed
with a film and an audiotape:
attempting to prompt poems
out of budding Purdys,
and the at one school,
there at the back of the class-
room, squeezed into an under-
sized desk, sat
Miss Macdonald. my Grade
Three teacher, come
to see if I had fulfilled
the promise she'd drawn from me
with her partisan praise
of my ink-squibbed scribbles –
we smiled at each other
across a forty-year
divide, linked by a love
of words.

THERE WAS A TIME

There was a time when I believed
that God inhabited the white
clapboard church
on Michigan Ave, seated
in the back pew, I could feel
His breath floating from the
sanctuary as light and healing
as a June breeze on my grand-
father's lilacs, I could hear
His unvoiced words and knew
that somewhere near
angels amplified the chancel
air, I said my rhyming
prayer each night before
I entered the slough of sleep,
begging the Lord to take
my soul if I should die
before waking, but oh
how relieved I was to see
the sun pouring through
my bedroom window
like a giddy doubter's dance:
yes, there was a time
when I believed, I really
did.

JOIE DE VIVRE

We heard the Tin Lizzie
three blocks away, the ooga-
ooga horn blaring
abroad, as we rushed to the curb
to catch Herbie boogying
on by at full
throttle, with a grin on his face
that would have impressed the Wizard
of Oz, fedora flapping
and a wave and a wink at his fans
and our raucous applause,
before he wheeled homeward,
erased in a cloud of dizzying
dust: we loved the show
so much we wanted to bottle it.

SUMMER
After John B Lee

What I remember most
are the sun-softened days
when we set out for the beach
like charlatan Champlains,
unhobbled by the heat,
out towels draped over
our fair-skinned shoulders
like cavalier's capes,
until we found the path
as familiar as our crease-streaked
palms and waved at the lighthouse
that stood alabaster and beckoning
at the edge of the wind-whetted
water, then welcomed the sands
of Canatara once again,
and let the waves flutter
over our unfettered feet
like tiny tongues licking
us lean, while we stood
stark in the free-flung
breeze, daring to be
the first to dive into the
cobalt, chilled undertow
and levitate like dolphins
flippered and flying through the
breakers, abetted by a north-
nudging wind, before exhaustion
claimed us and we flopped
like limp mops upon
the stinging, sun-stroked
sand, and wondered even then
how much of these doldrum.
summer-drifting days
we would always remember.

POP
For My Grandfather

We called him "Pop"
because all the real
Dads were away at war,
we trailed behind his corporal's
stride, hopping from foot
to foot to keep pace,
as if he were the Pied Piper
and we his willing worshippers,
until we reached the work-
shop where he wrought wonders
with wood and delicately shorn
steel (we watched it peel
away from the oiled lathe
in tiny girlish curls),
thence to be rendered into whirl-y-
gigs the whole town prized,
and while he stood there
with his wide, patient smile,
we peppered him with our child's
questions about the world
and its doings, like Socrates
interrogating the Wise, and wished
the war would never end.

NUMINOUS

I shall not rage at the
dying of the light: I've lived
too long under a luminous
sun to be at odds
with death; my days have been deft
with delight with just enough
pain to keep me ept
and witting; I've filled a thousand
pages with my word-scattered
scrawl, but I have left
my legacy in the brightening
eyes of my children's children,
and when the time arrives,
I will go gentle into that
numinous night.

SYLLABLES

I've often thought, penning
a verse, that it could be
my last, the inner voice
I've both blessed and cursed
for more than sixty years
muffled forever, but such
a loss would be nothing to your
leaving us: all the words
you used to lavish love,
kindle your million kindnesses
and make our house a home –
abruptly ended, but to me
you are worth above the thousand
poems I now send to you
in the syllables of your silence.

NIMBLE
For Rebecca and Katie

My granddaughters knitting,
sitting still as statues,
each stitch the itch
of a thought in the mind before
the fingers nimble it into
place: there is such serenity
in their faces as they re-imagine
this ages-old art
of women everywhere,
and carry it out
with loose-limbed grace.

LUCK

The Garden was so perfect
that Adam spent his days
plucking plums and pomegranates
(from trees rinsed
with rain and dried by sun)
and ogled the plump-thighed
creature he'd rib-delivered
(wondering what beauty was for),
while Eve eyed the apple
and prayed for something
lucky to happen.

LONG SLEEP

Sometimes I wish
there really was a Heaven
and a grandfatherly God
to hold you in His arms
and bring you comfort in your long
sleep, but most of the time
I realize the soul is what
the eyes give in the here
and now, and that you left
us the second your lids
shut out your last room
and me, and the soul is also
whatever lingers
of you in the air I breathe
and the memories we made
together in mutual delight,
when my world still turned
and my heart was leavened
with light.

RECALLED

I am reminded that you
are gone every time
I look at your photo on the
Free Press obit,
whose framed face smiles
down at me, and while
I can dream you alive,
I cannot fill the empty
rooms you graced with your perpetual
presence or erase the memories
that soothe and scald, coming
in waves that overwhelm,
and oh how I wish I could see
you sit in your favourite place
just once more,
reach out, touch you
and talk of a charmed life
recalled.

ALL THAT'S SAID AND DONE

The verses I scribble do not
change the world or move
the Earth tilting on its axis,
but nonetheless I carry on
as if my stilted stanzas,
coming as they do in dribs
and drabs, really counted:
for what else embodies
our longing for affection, our cry
at the demise of the light, our quarrels
with a fractious God, or the grief
I feel at losing you, scattered
across these raging
pages, where I find consolation
in the willingness of words,
knowing that, when all
is said and done, you were
the only poem that mattered?

SHY

You were always shy of the camera,
and whenever its intruding eye
took dead aim,
you hugged the nearest child
as a shield to share your smile
and let us know you were exuding
love, not a photo yielding
nothing but tugs of vanity,
and so, when we were searching
for a snapshot to grace
your obit, we had to crop
a family view, and, heart-
heavy, I sit staring
at it across this room,
even as I imagine you,
ever true to your own
tune, wince at my grieving
glance, amused at the world's
inanities.

AU REVOIR

I do not empty this house
of your presence: you are here
in every room we shared
breath in, your clothes still
hang where they belong
in their closets, and every painting
that adorns our walls is a reminder
of your artist's eye, and the chesterfield,
your bête noir, still
bears your imprint, and a novel
lies where your fingers last
lingered, nor am I made
forlorn on entering the space
now vacant of the woman
I cossetted and cradled with
love in its essence, for we are taught
that death is not an ending,
not goodbye but au revoir:
I refuse that platitude,
preferring your haunting hover
and the remnants of the things you
touched
with such tenderness.

PERPETUAL

My grief is a peripatetic pendulum
that swings from hard-
won resignation to sudden
bursts of tears that come
unbidden as I contemplate
the years I will have to live
without your love singing
to my soul, comforting
and ending these throbbing
sobs, while your fingers
brush my brow and sweep
the pain away, and your voice
reassures me of a perpetual
presence poised and ready
to reignite our love
and its fiery fiefdom.

PATIENCE

Patience was your password:
a hurting child, lad
or lass, in your arms was soon
soothed, embodied with love,
you waited out the minutes
while one of your pupils stuttered
over a letter until she got it
upright, and you smoothed
brows till the tears un-
uttered themselves
and your smile charmed them
into lilting laughter, and like Orpheus
the moving music of your voice
could tame the wildest canine
and make its tail wag
in grateful delight, but most
of all you suffered the way-
ward ways of the world
and tolerated God's oddities.

LINKED

For fifty-seven years
we occupied the same space,
sometimes rooms
apart, other times
side by side on the
chesterfield, where we cozied
in coupled harmony, the yellow
roses you so prized
winking from the window-sill:
you who were never thrifty
with your affection, me
your willing paramour,
and as we aged gracefully,
our lives, enlinked more
and more, were groomed with a bliss
the Heavens would envy: now
you are gone and I am left
with nothing to say except
I miss you.

LIFELONG

It will take me some time
to forget your final glance
as you lay rigoured by death
in your slack-jawed, breathless
body, your lids mercifully
closed, but I will try
by choosing to remember the freckle-
flecked, blue-eyed
beauty I first observed
across a schoolroom,
and saw that face again
each sun-burst
morning of our lifelong,
grace-bedewed romance.

UNDAUNTED

Our biweekly jaunts
to the big city did not go
unremarked by our town-
folks: tongues wagged
when we whirled up in front
of my boarding house in your brand-
new Volks like lovers
unafraid of their affair,
we shocked the gentry, as window
blinds sagged discreetly
and we essayed a chaste kiss
in the cheerful dark of the car,
but I wanted the world to know
I had found a girl with copper
locks who kissed me back,
who cared nothing for what
the locals deemed proper,
and we carried on undaunted
for fifty-seven years.

MUTTS

You led a dog's life,
surrounded by hounds, Scotties,
malamutes, pugs
and other ilk, they walked
you daily (one by one
or in twos and threes) through
Gibbon's Park, that manicured
meadow of silken grasses
and willowing trees, where
mistress and mutt could commune
in peace, for you spoke the lingo
of dogdom, and the love
they brought you was returned
ten-fold, singing
into their canine hearts,
with a little left over
for me.

EMBEDDED

It wasn't a fancy wedding,
a party of six including
the bride and groom in the county
courthouse with a courtly
judge who slipped me a lucky
dime to dance on for a lifetime,
but you lit up the room like a
bloom-burst of stars
in a night sky, the radiance
of your face leaving me breathless,
transfixed by your beauty,
and with thoughts of the romance
we confected, each of us
exuding joy at the other's delight,
our love abiding, embedded
with affection.

GRATEFUL

I was too shy to say
hello to you, so you
kindly said it for me,
and while it occurred to me
to ask for a date, I was
nonplussed by your smart
dress and sporty Volks
and that sophisticated up-
sweep of copper hair,
with eyes as blue as a heron's
April wing or the sky
when morning breaks upon
the world, but to no-one's
surprise you smiled me
supine and I offered you
my grateful heart.

OTHERWISE

In your last days you drew
into yourself, as if you knew
what was to come, you who
loved people and parties
at New Year's or any
time the spirit moved,
where we danced until the moon
abandoned its skies: you
with a smile as wide as the
lake we both adored,
and, ever outgoing, you made
fast friends that lingered
lifelong, and I watched
your slow descent with a stricken
heart, unwilling, though you
thought otherwise, to let
you go.

GIBBON'S

Oh how you loved Gibbon's,
the park where willows wept
elongated tears and grasses
swooned like wind whirring
through wheat, where dogs loped
leash-free and owls
with their cowled frowns
found treetops
to their liking, where you made
lifelong friends
and stroked their canine companions,
a meadow you loved more than
Eve loved Eden when she popped
out of Adam's rib.

DIXIE

This sumac, your favourite
tree, looms over our yard
and, once bristling with birds
and teetering with squirrels, is now
in its last throes, like all
those things we love
going in their good time,
and O how tickled
you were at a chickadee's
flickering flair, a cardinal's
scarlet calisthenics,
a robin's bashful bobbing,
and when I saw you in the hilt
of your happiness, I wanted to shout
Hallelujah or whistle
Dixie.

SACRED

Whenever I think of you in the
deep doldrums of my elongated
nights, I see Eve
in the glory of that dappled garden,
steeped in sunlight
that never unshone,
her naïve nudity haloed
to shape the suggestion of breasts
and the shadow where thigh
joins thigh, and set her locks
aglow like a nun's wimple,
and I think of that moment
when Adam first spied
his rib-ripped mate
and the blast that sight
must have made and eased
her story of an adder and an apple
into the conscience of his loins,
for beauty, like yours and hers,
with its simple sensuosity
hums in the heart and makes
remembering something
both aching and sacred.

PROPOSAL

It wasn't an elegant proposal
out of some fiery paperback
romance as we sat in your Volks-
mobile with the February snow
brushing the windshield
with feathered wispings, but you
said yes anyway, provided
there would be no bridal
showers, fancy engagement ring
or a fifty-plate wedding
supper, and I knew then
that you were your own woman
who knew life was no
bed of roses and would not
be rushed whatever the weather
or the stridency of my desire

HESITATION

Our home is exactly as it was
when your heart hesitated for the
last time: your clothes
hang in your closets ready
to be worn should you decide
to return, your coffee cup
awaits your nightly sip:
I cannot bear to part
with them any more than I can
bear the thought of losing you
as I roam from room to empty
room, stopping always
at the urn where you are resident,
relaxed in your final plot,
while the world and I continue
on our frantic axes, as doomed
as the yellow roses (you loved)
starved of slow light.

ANODYNE

I weep because tears are an
anodyne against the grief
that consumes me at odd
times of the day and night,
it rises up unannounced
and overwhelms as I think
of all the years your face
was the first thing I saw
wakening each memorable
morning, and your eyes unfurling
blue upon our shared
world, and I think of those
days when we were blessed
with the benediction of our bodies
and our belief in the gratuity of grace,
but most of all I weep
because somewhere
some malign god
has forsaken me.

HUNGERING

Each night since you've gone
I dream you alive: you are
a younger reflection of yourself:
your eyes as blue as flax
in bloom, your hair flowing
like cinnamon through my fingers
with a smile that says to the world:
I am thriving and together
we will dabble our days in delight,
O how wonderful
it is just to let our bodies
be, afloat in the Lake
of possibility, to take excursions
into felicity, babble our joint
joys and pray not to wake
as I now do, while the room
leaves me hungering after
any version of you.

HONEYMOON BAY (2)

I still remember that evening
we spent on Honeymoon Bay,
lacquered with starlight
and waves shallowing the shore
like my fingers lovingly through
your lingering locks and a
breeze that crooned to the
evergreens cupping
our little encampment,
and we watched the Night come
slowly down like a lover's
lids, and to no-one's surprise
our bodies met, mused
serene, and fraternized.

ABSENCE

Absence cannot be touched
or tasted: it lies in the
desmene of feeling when we yearn
for what cannot be,
it is the hollow where your head
lay, the room no one
like you occupies: I feel
its perpetual presence as the days
go on and on, I feel
it in the morning when I turn
and you are gone.

BATH

O how you loved your daily
soak, the tub filled
to the brim with boiling hot
water, suds-sudden,
into which you slowly submerged
like a lithe submarine, your flesh
afloat, weightless, tingling
in the sea-soft surround,
as if it were revisiting
the mother-womb that held
us bobbing in its warm amniotic
welcome: ands so during
your last days when you couldn't
make it up the stairs,
I knew I was going to lose you,
and never gain would I hear
a bath running without
a throb in the throat.

WHOLE

They say weeping is good
for the soul, but I find no
solace in the sobs that wrack
my body alive, and like
a man with an amputated limb,
I still believe the appendage
is there and thriving: I do not
wish to live amongst your memories,
as sweet as they may be:
I want you here – and whole.

PLEASURE

What pleasure I took in exploring
the boundaries of your beautiful
body, the tingling of touch,
the trepidation of lip on lip,
my face reflecting yours,
the sigh of thigh against thigh,
for it is in the meshing of flesh
that our souls sing to one
another, my breath breathing
the ept essence of your own,
our separate selves longing
to be, for the measure of a minute,
a single being, knowing
in our hearts that we all
are destined to live apart,
as I do, with your graceful
going.

RHYMED

This photograph
of my grandsons cavorting
in the front seat of my Ford
Tempo (as green as grass
garnished with rain) is a
frozen moment I cherish:
James looks as if he's about
to seize the wheel and mosey
off like an importunate imp,
and Tim's baffled grin
at this peevish possibility
leaves me laughing, and grateful
that some things beyond
the instigations of Time
can come to pass un-
varnished and perfectly rhymed.

FOR MY GRANDMOTHER

When grandfather died
your world was abruptly halved,
all those little rituals
that bound you one to one
now ended, you could not bear
ever again to sleep
in the bed you shared for more
than fifty years, your dreams
entangled through the long night
until morning woke you
with a new day, I remember
you best in the evenings,
you knitting in the kitchen,
Gramps snoozing through the news
a room away, but both of you
linked by love.

GRIEF

The night I first heard
my father cry: a single
anguished utterance,
the Earth tilted on its axis
half an inch or more,
and I thought of the oak
sturdy in our yard bent to
breaking in a tormenting wind,
and everything I'd known
and trusted was suddenly
as fragile as the life
of my dying grandfather,
and grief was a live being
with little time for childish
tears.

SOME THINGS

At precisely ten after six
every Saturday evening,
just past closing
time at the Balmoral,
Bob McCord staggered
past our house, singing
off-key and entertaining
the street all along his way-
ward route; we'd watch
him enter his front door
and stumble into silence,
after which came the slap
heard round the village.
And sometime later
Mrs. McCord would appear
on her front porch as if
nothing had happened,
smiling grimly at those
unashamed enough
to pass by, and young
though I was, I thought:
this is the way things are
in our town, and then:
there are some things
that shouldn't be.

MUSIC

On Good Friday we sang
of Jesus and His Precious Blood,
dripping from His hob-nailed
hands and feet on that
grim Golgotha, and dreamt
of an Easter morning when the sun
rose and solemnized
an empty tomb with the
stone rolled wondrously
away, and we felt a new
music throb in our throats.

REMEMBRANCE
For My Grandfather
In Loving Memory

Did you hear the sonorous
soaring of the Last Post
over your country's memorial,
the bugle singing as sadly
sweet as Gabriel's music
commemorating the brave in their
quiet graves, or the roaring
of the jets in salubrious salute?
Did you, my gloried grandfather,
come awake at such
concatenation, recall
your days doleful in that
far-away war?
No longer feel forsaken
by the souls you fought so
valiantly to save? Be
assured, we will remember,
though Time itself flies,
until the Earth un-
endures and the sun dies.

FORBIDDEN

Whatever was forbidden
drew us towards it
like moths to a mammoth moon:
we were warned against The Slip,
too deep for dog-
paddling neophytes,
or hoboes with their anguished
eyes, or the Pool Room,
where we were addled by the
slick click of cue
on ball and the thwack of the
struck pocket (hidden
strictly from view), and we
wondered what shenanigans
our parents got up to
when the blinds came down,
or what strange terrain
was squeezed between the thighs
of girls we worshipped
from afar, too shy
to say hello or goodbye,
we rode our bikes double
to tease Pedan, our slew-
footed cop, and most
of all we dared the indelible
dark that each evening
enveiled our village –
a long ways East
of Eden.

SWEET SEASON
For Anne in loving memory

When love bloomed in the sweet
season of lilacs and lilies,
we clung to each other
with such fierce felicity
that we wondered if love
could last and how the years
would treat the tendrill'd touch
of our embering affection, but then
you pierced my hectic heart
with your gifted glance, and we faced
the future free of fears,
remembering still the time
when lilacs bloomed like the
ungroomed gardens of Eden.

MOTIVE
Point Edward: 1948

The village that spawned me
and kept me cozy
for a dozen years, was pointless
(I searched for it one
day and came home
puzzled) and long ago
was a railway town
bustling with locomotives
and a switching yard, until,
like railroads everywhere,
they pulled up the tracks
and skedadelled, leaving
a single line to rust
away (and a village shrunken,
out-of-joint with the world),
a set of tracks we trod
our on way to Canatara
where the faithful
Lake was motive enough
for a day's play (while
the sun-nuzzled dunes
warmed us, where we clambered
on amber afternoons)
and the slow walk home
along those ties
where we felt the heft of history
and realized the point of it all.

DINNER

Mrs. McCleister's rooster
serenaded our street the moment
the morning sun tickled
his wattle, and then paraded
among his hens, crowing
over every conquest,
loud enough to make
a village wince, and boost
his gallic ego, till
my grandmother, losing
her legendary patience,
threatened to throttle him
and make him the principal
guest at her Easter dinner.

DELIGHT

When it was hide-and-go-seek
the girls of my village played
with all the pizzazz of Amazonians,
venturing into the virgin dark
beyond the umbrella-ed spray
of Mara's lamp to find
a cozy coign where many
a male purloined the swell
of a mislaid ankle
or a leg uncurling in the
shadows shredded by Mara's
light and at the All-Free
boys and girls together
emerged, outrunning
their breath, as if nothing
momentous had happened,
as if our un-Presbyterian
urges were our everyday
delight.

CHARLIE

Charlie was our neighbour,
a decorated vet who weathered
his nightmares with whiskey,
and, when that wouldn't do,
in beer binges at the Balmoral,
but nothing could unhinge
his image-riddled mind,
not even his three beautiful
daughters who doted on him
and us, and pretended not
to see that smile with the ache
in the middle.

INKED

Nothing could dampen our spirits
under Mara's lamp,
not the monsoon moon or the
stark startling of stars
in the dark of a brooding sky,
and always it was hide-
and-go-seek when we out-
ran our own shadows
along Monk Street all
the way to the village brink
where we conversed with the universe,
for we were young and free,
inked with innocence.

SUCH AN URGE

It might have been the moon-
light lacquering the black
length of Monk Street
or perhaps Mara's lamp
shrivelling the shadow around it,
but something in the air
that night drew us to the
farthest dark where an errant
knee might be harvested
by fingers a-tremble with touch,
or lips on lingering lips
in the grip of some desire
so fleeting we wondered
if such an urge could ever
be.

SOFT AND LOW
*For Anne in loving memory
and after The Bard and Dylan Thomas*

Like Cordelia's, your voice
was ever soft and low,
a lovely thing in woman,
and like Lear I could cradle
you in my aching arms and
shed a tear or howl
my grief to Heaven aloft,
for your sudden going has left me
bereft of all but the memory
of our iambic dance and a plighted
troth that budded and bloomed,
epic in owl-light.

ONCE AGAIN
For Anne in loving memory

Once again I stare
at our wedding photo (black-
and-white: we couldn't afford
colour), the only record
of our joyous nuptials, the two
of us on tip-toes
on brother-in-law's lawn,
nose to nose, our smiles
commingling, as if the future
lay before us, un-
ruptured, and I longed to swallow
you whole, grateful for the gift
of your self-effacing grace,
and knowing that you would always
sing to my soul.

TINGLE
For Anne in loving memory

I cannot hug a memory
or squeeze the image of you
detonating in my dreams,
for we are made of blood
and bitter bone, and need
the feel of flesh enmeshed,
lips ellipsing lips
and skin skittering on skin,
and so it is we are not meant
to be alone without
the singular tingle of love's
hug.

TOUCH
For Anne in loving memory

There was a time when we simply
let our bodies be, and found
solace in the other's touch,
(as tangled as a rhyming couplet)
and I let my fingers scroll
through your tangerine tresses
with such tenderness that my breath
abandons, and I know the feel
of you whole, hearken to
your lean heartbeat
and say "God bless"
to the dimpled dark.

FLAWS
For Anne in loving memory

I loved you because you were always
yourself and not an appendage
to my ego; I loved you because
you took my name and gave it
to our children to cherish; I loved
you because you made me feel
as if I could be whatever
the world offered; I loved you
because, above all,
you loved me, and now
that you are gone, I can love
the memories we made and let them
live on.

WALK

Every Sunday morning
my grandfather exercised
his heart, weakened by three
years in Belgium's maelstrom,
and me quick-stepping
a pace behind his corporal's
stride, firing questions
at him with Socratic aplomb
and waiting for his wise replies,
marvelling at his graceful patience
as we wended our way around
the home village - - a thousand
miles from the horrific hum
of Howitzers.

SATURDAY

Grandfather in his Saturday
morning workshop,
and me barely seven,
watching his steadfast fingers
soothing the lathe or nudging
a lozenge of oak through the
stutter of the bandsaw,
and I felt blessed to be
born to such moments,
to be enhoused by love,
to be utterly endeared
as I waited for his hand
to drift down and tousle
my hair.

MANY A NIGHT
For Anne in loving memory

Many a night I dream
you alive once again
and O how I want you to be
so much more than
a memory, for I need to feel
the warmth of your beguiling
 smile upon the cheeks
you cherished and know the dance
of delight in your Baltic blue
eyes and run my fingers
through the rippling rust of your hair,
as I strive to live without the loving
lustre of your glance.

BLESSED
For Anne in loving memory

Does anybody know how deep
love goes or how radiant
a rose can be in the luminous
light of a June morning,
for we are born to love
and beauty, despite the odds,
and we suffer heartbreak
and loss like heroic stoics,
and I have known it all
since you first flowed
into view and we fashioned a life
together, blessed by fortune,
embossed by the gods, passionate
and true.

THE LIGHT

I say goodnight to the
abstemious dark and drift
down to the dream-world
just below sleep,
whose images lift free
from their ordinary moorings
like prose poems without
rhyme or reason, dyed
deep with meaning beyond
the reach of mind or matter
which I may yet employ
in the daytime business
of iambicising, while I wait
for the chatter of robins saluting
the sun as it solemnizes the light.

BEGINNING
For Anne in loving memory

You were always your own woman:
I watched in awe, on those
days we fraternized in T.O.,
your cinnamon locks up-
swept in high style,
your lemon frock clinging
to every bow and curve,
your eyes ablaze with the vim
of a girl who promenaded
with pride through the Big City
beside a country bumpkin
like me, her smile dazzling
the denizens we passed on our way
to a beautiful beginning.

EXEGESIS
After Robert Browning

Approaching a poem should be
an act of love where one
soul opens itself
to another's textual touch,
where words are tasted on the tongue
and syllables sing us whole
again and tropes open
the heart to hope and similes
simulate in symmetries, where language
leaps alive with unredacted
truth and script is holier
than Scripture and exegesis
is ecstasy.

WITTING

With what witting wonder
did my ten-year-old
eyes watch my father's
every move? Mixing
concrete, its lime seasoned
with sand and a soupçon
of liquid, stroking back
and forth like a lover's caress
or a minstrel's metronome
and then his trowel pasting
the stew-rich mass
onto cinder blocks
he nudged into place row
by row, judging the precise
line with a taut string
that pinged against the perpendicular
and I thought I knew this man
and the things he could do
with his hands, making me
a house I would soon call
home, the struts of its roof
angled against the symmetries
of the sun's leavening light
like raw-boned ribs
and the beads of my father's sweat
bedewed his brow and garnished
that all-embracing smile
and I felt as Elijah felt
at Heaven's gate.

PAST

What I remember most
is the lake of grandfather's
lawn and lilacs lecherous
with light and bees inhabiting
the hollyhocks my grandmother
grew on the barnboard
fence and the lush pose
of the labyrinthine rose,
and I spent my days jousting
with joy and knew even
then that nothing lasts,
that what is present is already
past.

VILLAGE DREAMING

Hidden Brook Press
2020

VILLAGE DREAMING

Rocking in my chair I dream
of the village where I was breathed
into being by the athletic lusts
of my hockey-heroing father
and the girl he deemed his paramour,
when my world was as new as a
chick picking at the shell
and a blank page I wrote
myself upon with words
wrestled from the womb, and a town
surrounded me with folks
to people my poems and startle
the stories I would create, in the
mortar and pestle of my imagination,
of their forgivable follies, the hustle
and bustle of their Dickensian lives,
and those childhood
chums I turned into combed
prose, who made my days
worth the telling and strummed
the strings of my memory, leaving
me to dream, rock and sing
the song of myself.

SOMEBODY ELSE

Strange what we remember
when old age creeps
alive into our capillaries:
the squeak of a rusted gate
when I strode out of my grandfather's
lot onto the welcoming
sidewalk and peddled my way
over granny-cracks
whose craqueleur I cannot
unforget, the squeal
of my trike's back wheel
and the heraldic honk of its horn,
startling Mister Robinson
and the banty rooster next
door, and thither I rode
past the immaculate lawn
of Bryant's groomed abode
(whose heart disassembled
from too much perfection),
and on by Gray's latticed
porch and the end of my designated
desmene: but try as we might,
nothing is born again,
the world withers away
without our saying until
we too are just somebody
else's memory.

SPEECHLESS

In my seething imagination
these dunes were here
when the last Neanderthal
stood upright on Canatara's
beach, blinking into the
morning sunlight
and pandering to clams fresh
from the Lake's cellarage
(an age before Adam
or Eden were dreamed), not
knowing he would soon be
extinct, that all things
flesh must pass away
speechless so other
beings, sir or madam,
can be born and Mother
Earth renewed in her glory
and an octogenarian poet
can stroll past these mesozoic
mounds and tell their story
in a birthing of words.

FOREVER

When you reach four score
and a bit, your mind moves
to those scenes of your childhood
where you were free to roam
the fraternizing streets and greet
Wiz and Bones, Jerry
and Hutch and where the sun
solemnized the village that whittled
you into the world, and a lake
awaited your wading in its beryl-
blue waves and a breeze
dizzied the trees in Canatara
and where Nancy Mara had eyes
for you alone, and where home
was grandfather's lilac-
lit demesne and we all
thought ourselves clever
enough to make it last
forever.

UNIVERSE

I wake and the world widens,
and just beyond the morning
dews the Lake swims
into view like a slow fuse,
so blue it would blind Zeus
or make Oedipus blink,
and a breeze quickens to wimple
the waves swallowing each
other and licking the silence
of the shore, and I reach the water's
edge and immerse one
simple toe in Cameron's
granite chill, feel
the immanent will of the Universe,
inked and abiding.

INSURGENT

The girls of my village sprawl
on the beaches of Canatara,
preening and prettifying in the
lilting light that prisms
off the Lake's face,
unaware that beauty
is its own grace, defying
all logic, all
reason, and these bodies,
embraced in biology, seasoned
by the noontide sun
and the sifting of silted sands,
leave the boys, beyond
reach on the nippled dunes,
un-willed, moon-
endued and prey to their most
insurgent urges.

TOLLING

Ours was a three-steepled
town, when, on a Sunday
morning the tolling of deep-
tongued bells and their tuneful
music drew the people
of the Point to their pews and the
weekly anointment, free
for the moment of Sabbath sins
and the impious whims of Lucifer
and his less-than-holy crew.

WIDE

Eleven and still unable
to swim, paddling in the Lake's
shallows like a inflated dolphin,
while Nancy and the girls
disport on an anchored raft
fifteen yards away
(all that flesh caressed
by the afternoon sun),
flashing me a smile
now and then before diving
slim-thighed into the nearest
breaker as slick as seals
into a tumescent sea, as the raft
tilts and sways like Noah's
craft on God's turbulent
tide, breasting the waves
and waving at one who
could not stroke his body
across a heavenly divide
that might has well have been
a mile wide.

HOPES

Shirley was the first girl
whose elongated legs caught
my amorous eye as she whirled
and danced at Double Dutch,
showing us once in a blue
menstrual moon a thimbleful
of thigh and what we imagined
lay higher up
between the taut squeeze
of her glorious gams, but Shirley
took no notice
of the male gaze for she
was skipping in frenzied bursts
to entertain and amaze,
until the ropes sagged
like spent balloons and she flashed
us a smile that said,
"I'm no bimbo,
but this may be romance,"
or such were our hopes.

ROAST

Mrs. McCleister's cockerel
pulled the sun up
over the lip of the horizon
with his clawed beak and crowed
in the morning, his wattle waxing
as scarlet as a tanager, while
his hens feathered deeper
into their straw beds, wary
of his bottled fury, but the
widow next door didn't prize
his dawn song and threatened
to roast him for Easter.

ALONE

My widowed grandmother
listening to the radio: soap
after soap carrying
from the dining room all
the way to the kitchen chair
where she sits knitting:
Helen Trent's romance
gives way to Pepper
Young's family – unless
the Tigers are playing at Briggs,
only then will she drop
a stitch or two with the crack
of the bat like wood on bone
or the thud of a pitch in the mitt
as the crowd cheers and she wishes
she could be anywhere
but here – unsung
and alone.

LUFFED

How many hours did we spend
speculating what lay between
Shirley's girlish thighs,
caught as we were in the first
flush of lust's lustre,
our consensus (from a single glance
at her one-piece suit)
being a tuft that tingled
and tantalized or a petalled pucker
that fuelled our fancy and tested
our masculine mettle, but alas
remained taboo, taking
the wind out of our sails
and leaving us luffed?

BACK HOME

*On a visit to the Point with my son
John on June 15, 2018*

For what may well be
the last time, I re-see
the village that vaulted me
into being, unumbilicalled
into its flawless world
that is both estranging
and familiar, where some houses
have same gee-and-haw
tilt they had when I first
tricycled past them,
and there is grandfather's
mansion, where I re-imagine
the trees that lightning levelled
and the lilacs now beyond
blooming, and my son nods
when I point to the room
where I lay a-bed for seven
months and lived to tell
the story, and the Lake lives
again here and in my mind
in all its blue-belled
bevelled glory, and we stroll
by Mara's place, unchanged,
and bid goodbye to the empty
space where the streetlamp
supervised our glorious games
and the June moon summered
on the horizon like an angel's smile,
and we stare at Canatara
uplifted by light, and sit
for a while under the Bridge
and watch the steamers go
slowly by like a dream
of themselves and like
the flow of Time itself
and this gift given
by the gods only once.

SMALL-TOWN BETRAYAL

When our neighbor Mr. Hart
offered to buy my grandfather's
house with its half-acre
groomed grounds, Where I spend
my happiest childhood
days, he pleaded poverty
and appealed to my uncle, who made
him a deal: reduced price
for a vow not to sever
the lot, to keep its lilac
and foaming spirea hedges
as they were, and so
the sunny haven I thought of
as home passed to others,
and a year later Mr. Hart
severed the lot and made
a pot of money

TIDES

It was the Ojibwa who gave us
"Canatara" for the "blue water"
of the big-bellied lake
that hugged the beach and its
mile-long stretch of
Saharan sand, a double
trochee rolling off
the aboriginal tongue
like the tunes of Orpheus, and I
think
of those first peoples
offering a kind of birth
to those unbroken
sands and the cobalt swells
of a water-body wider
than half the seas on Earth
and mammoth enough to dwarf
their moon-tugged tides.

ANGUISH

The languorous-limbed girls
of the Point languish on the sands
of Canatara in their one-
piece suits, and long
to be ogled by boys
with impish grins and hurled
hoots, while the mustard sun
anoints their new-blooming
bodies and Huron's wavelets
soothe the shameless shore
and nothing stirs in the
blush of the afternoon
but lust's unfulfillable
anguish.

STARRED

Under the moon's gossamer
glimmer, we go a-blading
on Leckie's iced-over
fallow, the wind-chill
raw against our cheeks
as hand-in-hand we scribble
scrimshaws into the shimmering
surface, traceries
of our having been, here
on this hallowed ground
on such a night, limned
by light, tremored by tingling
touch, and all beneath
the unmarred wonder
of the starred firmament.

ZIPPER

While the great Lake's
wavelets lick the shore
with lascivious lips, the girls
of the Point bask in the fiery
sun above Canatara, and do not
ask whether they are being statued
by the stare of boys who would do
a jig to see them au naturel
or put a zipper on their whirly-
gigging desires.

DOUBLE

Riding Double in the Point
was considered a sin akin
to eating apples in Eden,
but I was bike-free
and Butch's handle bar
beckoned, so we cycled
triumphantly through the hodge-podge
of alleys and lanes, dodging
Constable Pedan (hapless
on foot), untroubled
by doubt, certain we were a
force to be reckoned with,
and wishing Eve the best.

WOOTSER

Mrs. McCleister's blood-
wattled rooster serenaded
each sunrise
with his lascivious aria,
making the mottled hens
tremble with trepidation,
knowing that, feast or famine,
they would be boosted one
by one, and at last a triumphant
cry could be heard all
the way to Wooster, Mass.

LIFETIME

My first story, cribbed
from the Grade Three primer,
garnered undeserved praise
from my teacher that not only
raised my spirits but made me
a believer, and so it was
no surprise two grades
later when I began filling
my scribblers with intrepid tales
of quibbling bears and duelling
rabbits with blinking blue
eyes, and finally my maiden
poem arrived, in rhyming
couplets, inked from a Muse
as demanding and she was un-
bribable, and soon the scribe
in me became habitual,
lasting a lifetime.

DUNES AT CANATARA

It took a million years
to sculpt these dunes,
grain by grain of wave-
washed sand whipped
by seasoned winds into
voluptuous curves
and bevelled runes.
It took my pals and me
an afternoon to put
our imprimatur upon
the shimmering concavities,
our bodies pressing
their wry signatures deep
deep into the sun-stunned sand,
feeling the heat of a hundred
centuries oozing through.

STRETCH

If you don't mind cattails
like badly brushed hair
and the odd pair of pussy
willows encased in the ice
like butterflies from the
Pleistocene age jewelled
in amber, you might
find yourself sailing
alone across a stretch
of ready-made rink
with the wind cherubic
on your cheeks,
fantasizing stanzas in snow
and sleek-paced poems
on a glazed page, etched
in indelible ink.

HEATHEN

"Don't worry," Butch
says as he dispatches
the adder with a hectic blow,
"Snakes always come
back to life again
at midnight." "The little
heathen," my Grandma says,
"What a concoction!"
When we hurry back
next day, the creature
lies in the grass, unalive.
"It's okay," Butch says,
"I don't believe in the
Resurrection either."

BEING

We come into this world
unbidden; there is
no-one to applaud
our irreverent arrival,
so we irrigate the air
with our prodigal cries,
succumb to the need
to breathe, somehow
inhabit the broad
acreage of that space
Nature grants us –
and celebrate the birth
of our being.

SUNDAYS

On Sundays we sang of Jesus
and his glory and the precious blood
of the Lamb, our voices high,
as if we knew what it was
to be affixed to a cross
and have your highway
to Paradise paved,
or be strong enough to roll
that stone away and live
again – leaving us
to sing your story, and wonder.

OLD WARRIORS
Juno Beach, June 6, 2014

Unable to stride with the
practised ease of their youth
(embers of age aglow
in the eyes of these old
old warriors), they
nonetheless shuffle
with proper pride on the arm
of a grateful niece
or elderly son, recalling
that plunge through the waves
and bold rush up the
shell-shattered beach,
comrades falling all
around them: they carried
on because courage is more
than just a word, and here
on this hallowed ground
they gather together, some
seventy years on,
to remember those
who cannot speak
their bravery from the grave.

RUTHLESS

And me composing poems:
inklings I tease
towards some sense
in words whetted upon
the wheel of memory
and swerving askance
upon the page where they lean
upright, enlinked,
ready to be swallowed whole,
raw and ruthless
in rhythmic pursuit
of the truth.

THERE WAS A TIME

There was a time when I believed
that God inhabited the white
clapboard church
on Michigan Ave, seated
in the back pew, I could feel
His breath floating from the
sanctuary as light and healing
as a June breeze on my grand-
father's lilacs, I could hear
His unvoiced words and knew
that somewhere near
angels amplified the chancel
air, I said my rhyming
prayer each night before
I entered the slough of sleep,
begging the Lord to take
my soul if I should die
before waking, but oh
how relieved I was to see
the sun pouring through
my bedroom window
like a giddy doubter's dance:
yes, there was a time
when I believed, I really
did.

JOIE DE VIVRE

We heard the Tin Lizzie
three blocks away, the ooga-
ooga horn blaring
abroad, as we rushed to the curb
to catch Herbie boogying
on by at full
throttle, with a grin on his face
that would have impressed the Wizard
of Oz, fedora flapping
and a wave and a wink at his fans
and our raucous applause,
before he wheeled homeward,
erased in a cloud of dizzying
dust: we loved the show
so much we wanted to bottle it.

SUMMER
After John B Lee

What I remember most
are the sun-softened days
when we set out for the beach
like charlatan Champlains,
unhobbled by the heat,
out towels draped over
our fair-skinned shoulders
like cavalier's capes,
until we found the path
as familiar as our crease-streaked
palms and waved at the lighthouse
that stood alabaster and beckoning
at the edge of the wind-whetted
water, then welcomed the sands
of Canatara once again,
and let the waves flutter
over our unfettered feet
like tiny tongues licking
us lean, while we stood
stark in the free-flung
breeze, daring to be
the first to dive into the
cobalt, chilled undertow
and levitate like dolphins
flippered and flying through the
breakers, abetted by a north-
nudging wind, before exhaustion
claimed us and we flopped
like limp mops upon
the stinging, sun-stroked
sand, and wondered even then
how much of these doldrum.
summer-drifting days
we would always remember.

LINKED
For Isabelle Macdonald
In memoriam

In nineteen seventy-nine
I travelled the byroads
of Lambton County, armed
with a film and an audiotape:
attempting to prompt poems
out of budding Purdys,
and the at one school,
there at the back of the class-
room, squeezed into an under-
sized desk, sat
Miss Macdonald. my Grade
Three teacher, come
to see if I had fulfilled
the promise she'd drawn from me
with her partisan praise
of my ink-squibbed scribbles –
we smiled at each other
across a forty-year
divide, linked by a love
of words.

POP
For My Grandfather

We called him "Pop"
because all the real
Dads were away at war,
we trailed behind his corporal's
stride, hopping from foot
to foot to keep pace,
as if he were the Pied Piper
and we his willing worshippers,
until we reached the work-
shop where he wrought wonders
with wood and delicately shorn
steel (we watched it peel
away from the oiled lathe
in tiny girlish curls),
thence to be rendered into whirl-y-
gigs the whole town prized,
and while he stood there
with his wide, patient smile,
we peppered him with our child's
questions about the world
and its doings, like Socrates
interrogating the Wise, and wished
the war would never end.

NIMBLE
For Rebecca and Katie

My granddaughters knitting,
sitting still as statues,
each stitch the itch
of a thought in the mind before
the fingers nimble it into
place: there is such serenity
in their faces as they re-imagine
this ages-old art
of women everywhere,
and carry it out
with loose-limbed grace.

SUCH A LONGING

I have such a longing
for the days that are no more,,
when the sun rose over
my boyhood town each
misted morning, hefting
light for my eyes only
as I circumnavigate the streets
(like LaSalle on the prowl
for gold and glory), looking
for the point poised between
the Lake and the River, greeting
each friend and rival
with equal ease, knowing
we shared this cozy
desmene, that ours was our own
story to tell, and that
we would never be bereft
of belonging.

NUMINOUS

I shall not rage at the
dying of the light: I've lived
too long under a luminous
sun to be at odds
with death; my days have been deft
with delight with just enough
pain to keep me ept
and witting; I've filled a thousand
pages with my word-scattered
scrawl, but I have left
my legacy in the brightening
eyes of my children's children,
and when the time arrives,
I will go gentle into that
numinous night.

THE VILLAGE WITHIN

We all have a village within,
a place where we go
when the world fails us,
the home-ground where every
face is familiar and child-
size, where the streets welcome
our walking and each house
is a variation of our own,
its idiosyncrasies known
and loved just for being
there from the beginning
when our eyes were as wide
as any horizon, when all
was new and unrehearsed:
O the tug of the town
that gave us birth is one
of the sweetest joys we know.

LUCK

The Garden was so perfect
that Adam spent his days
plucking plums and pomegranates
(from trees rinsed
with rain and dried by sun)
and ogled the plump-thighed
creature he'd rib-delivered
(wondering what beauty was for),
while Eve eyed the apple
and prayed for something
lucky to happen.

THE POINT OF IT ALL

The point of it all
was the village I was born to,
where each morning the sun
sizzled out of First Bush
on the eastern edge of everything
and eased me into its cushioned
arms, my pencil poised
to tell its stories, where village
characters startled the streets
with their Pickwickian ploys,
and I roamed the town with my pals
Butch, Bones and Wiz
in search of adventures I would weave
into plots-to-be, and where
the incandescent waters
(under a sky pricked
with stars) of Huron would engender
poem after poem, rhyme
after rhyme, where there was time
to savour the unjudged joy
of being among the anointed,
of making my point.

ETERNITY

O what a village
I was born to, where the
sun over First Bush
rises reinvented each
morning, layering its
lacquered light upon
streets fresh from a
hushed night's dreaming,
and I sally forth like a
sea-going Argonaut
for the ells and alleys where roses
grow umbilical on
barn-board fences,
ablaze in rhyming red,
and stiff-trunked trees
are surprised by breezes
breathing serenity, and I am
now Earth's original
cartographer, nosing
amongst the by-ways
and fractured shadow:
foraging for a future
unhorizoned by time
or eternity.

STONE'S THROW

The creek that links Cameron
and Cyprus meanders along
like an adder sodden with sun
slinking through the reeds
and water-lilies floating
flamboyant on the mirrored
surface, and from whose pads
bullfrogs leap
on their tantalizing trapezes
and land with a punctuated plop
in shallows no deeper
than an elf's ankle, and so
it is that we have to pole
ourselves from bend
to bowing bend, soaking
in the morning's saffron glow
and savouring the soul of this
perfected place a stone's
throw from Eden.

BEREFT: A Suite
For Anne in loving memory

FLOWER

If you were a flower, you'd be
a yellow rose, more rare
than pedestrian red or shrinking
pink: you would bloom on
your birthday every June
as faithfully as the moon
on her monthly quest about
the Earth, and I would build you
a bower where love mellows
the heart and affection flairs
and no-one has to die.

BEDIZENED

It began simply enough:
you asked me if I wished
to see an opera in T.O.,
and when I discovered what
that was, I agreed, and off
we went: two mates
on a big-town spree:
you the city sophisticate
with a roil of red hair
swept up like a nun's
wimple and sporting a lemon
dress a diva would die for,
me the country tyro, just
glad to be along
for the ride, and after Tosca
and Lois at the Massey,
when your blue eyes made
the moon glow golden,
and after the bliss of our first
kiss, surprising us both,
romance reared its bedizened
head, and from that time
on we danced as a duo.

BEREFT

A pair of mated robins.
their bobbing throats a-throb
with parental song, gather
twigs and stray leaves
to build a nest along
our flowering trellis, feathered
and egg-ready: there's
going to be trouble you say
as day after day the birds
double their efforts to feed
the newborn chicks
with their stretched necks
and jerking jaws, but sure
enough there is a hitch
in the wind and the nest teeters
undeftly to the ground
where the young perish alone,
and I wonder if the parents
mourn their loss as humans
do when a quirk in the world's
weather leaves us bereft.

LONG SLEEP

Sometimes I wish
there really was a Heaven
and a grandfatherly God
to hold you in His arms
and bring you comfort in your long
sleep, but most of the time
I realize the soul is what
the eyes give in the here
and now, and that you left
us the second your lids
shut out your last room
and me, and the soul is also
whatever lingers
of you in the air I breathe
and the memories we made
together in mutual delight,
when my world still turned
and my heart was leavened
with light.

SYLLABLES

I've often thought, penning
a verse, that it could be
my last, the inner voice
I've both blessed and cursed
for more than sixty years
muffled forever, but such
a loss would be nothing to your
leaving us: all the words
you used to lavish love,
kindle your million kindnesses
and make our house a home –
abruptly ended, but to me
you are worth above the thousand
poems I now send to you
in the syllables of your silence.

ALL THAT'S SAID AND DONE

The verses I scribble do not
change the world or move
the Earth tilting on its axis,
but nonetheless I carry on
as if my stilted stanzas,
coming as they do in dribs
and drabs, really counted:
for what else embodies
our longing for affection, our cry
at the demise of the light, our quarrels
with a fractious God, or the grief
I feel at losing you, scattered
across these raging
pages, where I find consolation
in the willingness of words,
knowing that, when all
is said and done, you were
the only poem that mattered?

PERPETUAL

My grief is a peripatetic pendulum
that swings from hard-
won resignation to sudden
bursts of tears that come
unbidden as I contemplate
the years I will have to live
without your love singing
to my soul, comforting
and ending these throbbing
sobs, while your fingers
brush my brow and sweep
the pain away, and your voice
reassures me of a perpetual
presence poised and ready
to reignite our love
and its fiery fiefdom.

SHY

You were always shy of the camera,
and whenever its intruding eye
took dead aim,
you hugged the nearest child
as a shield to share your smile
and let us know you were exuding
love, not a photo yielding
nothing but tugs of vanity,
and so, when we were searching
for a snapshot to grace
your obit, we had to crop
a family view, and, heart-
heavy, I sit staring
at it across this room,
even as I imagine you,
ever true to your own
tune, wince at my grieving
glance, amused at the world's
inanities.

LINKED

For fifty-seven years
we occupied the same space,
sometimes rooms
apart, other times
side by side on the
chesterfield, where we cozied
in coupled harmony, the yellow
roses you so prized
winking from the window-sill:
you who were never thrifty
with your affection, me
your willing paramour,
and as we aged gracefully,
our lives, enlinked more
and more, were groomed with a bliss
the Heavens would envy: now
you are gone and I am left
with nothing to say except
I miss you.

PATIENCE

Patience was your password:
a hurting child, lad
or lass, in your arms was soon
soothed, embodied with love,
you waited out the minutes
while one of your pupils stuttered
over a letter until she got it
upright, and you smoothed
brows till the tears un-
uttered themselves
and your smile charmed them
into lilting laughter, and like Orpheus
the moving music of your voice
could tame the wildest canine
and make its tail wag
in grateful delight, but most
of all you suffered the way-
ward ways of the world
and tolerated God's oddities.

AU REVOIR

I do not empty this house
of your presence: you are here
in every room we shared
breath in, your clothes still
hang where they belong
in their closets, and every painting
that adorns our walls is a reminder
of your artist's eye, and the chesterfield,
your bête noir, still
bears your imprint, and a novel
lies where your fingers last
lingered, nor am I made
forlorn on entering the space
now vacant of the woman
I cossetted and cradled with
love in its essence, for we are taught
that death is not an ending,
not goodbye but au revoir:
I refuse that platitude,
preferring your haunting hover
and the remnants of the things you touched
with such tenderness.

LIFELONG

It will take me some time
to forget your final glance
as you lay rigoured by death
in your slack-jawed, breathless
body, your lids mercifully
closed, but I will try
by choosing to remember the freckle-
flecked, blue-eyed
beauty I first observed
across a schoolroom,
and saw that face again
each sun-burst
morning of our lifelong,
grace-bedewed romance.

UNDAUNTED

Our biweekly jaunts
to the big city did not go
unremarked by our town-
folks: tongues wagged
when we whirled up in front
of my boarding house in your brand-
new Volks like lovers
unafraid of their affair,
we shocked the gentry, as window
blinds sagged discreetly
and we essayed a chaste kiss
in the cheerful dark of the car,
but I wanted the world to know
I had found a girl with copper
locks who kissed me back,
who cared nothing for what
the locals deemed proper,
and we carried on undaunted
for fifty-seven years.

MUTTS

You led a dog's life,
surrounded by hounds, Scotties,
malamutes, pugs
and other ilk, they walked
you daily (one by one
or in twos and threes) through
Gibbon's Park, that manicured
meadow of silken grasses
and willowing trees, where
mistress and mutt could commune
in peace, for you spoke the lingo
of dogdom, and the love
they brought you was returned
ten-fold, singing
into their canine hearts,
with a little left over
for me.

EMBEDDED

It wasn't a fancy wedding,
a party of six including
the bride and groom in the county
courthouse with a courtly
judge who slipped me a lucky
dime to dance on for a lifetime,
but you lit up the room like a
bloom-burst of stars
in a night sky, the radiance
of your face leaving me breathless,
transfixed by your beauty,
and with thoughts of the romance
we confected, each of us
exuding joy at the other's delight,
our love abiding, embedded
with affection.

GRATEFUL

I was too shy to say
hello to you, so you
kindly said it for me,
and while it occurred to me
to ask for a date, I was
nonplussed by your smart
dress and sporty Volks
and that sophisticated up-
sweep of copper hair,
with eyes as blue as a heron's
April wing or the sky
when morning breaks upon
the world, but to no-one's
surprise you smiled me
supine and I offered you
my grateful heart.

OTHERWISE

In your last days you drew
into yourself, as if you knew
what was to come, you who
loved people and parties
at New Year's or any
time the spirit moved,
where we danced until the moon
abandoned its skies: you
with a smile as wide as the
lake we both adored,
and, ever outgoing, you made
fast friends that lingered
lifelong, and I watched
your slow descent with a stricken
heart, unwilling, though you
thought otherwise, to let
you go.

GIBBON'S

Oh how you loved Gibbon's,
the park where willows wept
elongated tears and grasses
swooned like wind whirring
through wheat, where dogs loped
leash-free and owls
with their cowled frowns
found treetops
to their liking, where you made
lifelong friends
and stroked their canine companions,
a meadow you loved more than
Eve loved Eden when she popped
out of Adam's rib.

ANODYNE

I weep because tears are an
anodyne against the grief
that consumes me at odd
times of the day and night,
it rises up unannounced
and overwhelms as I think
of all the years your face
was the first thing I saw
wakening each memorable
morning, and your eyes unfurling
blue upon our shared
world, and I think of those
days when we were blessed
with the benediction of our bodies
and our belief in the gratuity of grace,
but most of all I weep
because somewhere
some malign god
has forsaken me.

PLEASURE

What pleasure I took in exploring
the boundaries of your beautiful
body, the tingling of touch,
the trepidation of lip on lip,
my face reflecting yours,
the sigh of thigh against thigh,
for it is in the meshing of flesh
that our souls sing to one
another, my breath breathing
the ept essence of your own,
our separate selves longing
to be, for the measure of a minute,
a single being, knowing
in our hearts that we all
are destined to live apart,
as I do, with your graceful
going.

ANOINTED

Easter Sunday in the Point
was new shoes with the shine
still on them and pants
with a fine crease and ladies
bonneted and beribboned
and gentlemen in fresh habits,
and I remember staring at Christ
strung upon Golgotha (vinegar-
tongued, palms pinned
like moths on a lepidopterist's
display) just above
the altar where the Sabbath sun
limned His halo, and we felt
ourselves to be among
the anointed there, buoyed
by the yeast of prayer.

MAGIC

Cameron Lake is a pellucid
blue, and Tom and I
cavort in its chill welcome
like tantalizing tortoises:
now lolling on our plastic
mattresses, now diving
like deft dolphins or orphaned
Orcas, and when we've had
our fill, we lie upon
the sun-saturated sand
and let the wind dry
us benign, certain
that this magical moment
will be everlasting.

RHYMED

This photograph
of my grandsons cavorting
in the front seat of my Ford
Tempo (as green as grass
garnished with rain) is a
frozen moment I cherish:
James looks as if he's about
to seize the wheel and mosey
off like an importunate imp,
and Tim's baffled grin
at this peevish possibility
leaves me laughing, and grateful
that some things beyond
the instigations of Time
can come to pass un-
varnished and perfectly rhymed.

FOR MY GRANDMOTHER

When grandfather died
your world was abruptly halved,
all those little rituals
that bound you one to one
now ended, you could not bear
ever again to sleep
in the bed you shared for more
than fifty years, your dreams
entangled through the long night
until morning woke you
with a new day, I remember
you best in the evenings,
you knitting in the kitchen,
Gramps snoozing through the news
a room away, but both of you
linked by love.

GRIEF

The night I first heard
my father cry: a single
anguished utterance,
the Earth tilted on its axis
half an inch or more,
and I thought of the oak
sturdy in our yard bent to
breaking in a tormenting wind,
and everything I'd known
and trusted was suddenly
as fragile as the life
of my dying grandfather,
and grief was a live being
with little time for childish
tears.

SOME THINGS

At precisely ten after six
every Saturday evening,
just past closing
time at the Balmoral,
Bob McCord staggered
past our house, singing
off-key and entertaining
the street all along his way-
ward route; we'd watch
him enter his front door
and stumble into silence,
after which came the slap
heard round the village.
And sometime later
Mrs. McCord would appear
on her front porch as if
nothing had happened,
smiling grimly at those
unashamed enough
to pass by, and young
though I was, I thought:
this is the way things are
in our town, and then:
there are some things
that shouldn't be.

MUSIC

On Good Friday we sang
of Jesus and His Precious Blood,
dripping from His hob-nailed
hands and feet on that
grim Golgotha, and dreamt
of an Easter morning when the sun
rose and solemnized
an empty tomb with the
stone rolled wondrously
away, and we felt a new
music throb in our throats.

REMEMBRANCE

For My Grandfather
In Loving Memory

Did you hear the sonorous
soaring of the Last Post
over your country's memorial,
the bugle singing as sadly
sweet as Gabriel's music
commemorating the brave in their
quiet graves, or the roaring
of the jets in salubrious salute?
Did you, my gloried grandfather,
come awake at such
concatenation, recall
your days doleful in that
far-away war?
No longer feel forsaken
by the souls you fought so
valiantly to save? Be
assured, we will remember,
though Time itself flies,
until the Earth un-
endures and the sun dies.

FORBIDDEN

Whatever was forbidden
drew us towards it
like moths to a mammoth moon:
we were warned against The Slip,
too deep for dog-
paddling neophytes,
or hoboes with their anguished
eyes, or the Pool Room,
where we were addled by the
slick click of cue
on ball and the thwack of the
struck pocket (hidden
strictly from view), and we
wondered what shenanigans
our parents got up to
when the blinds came down,
or what strange terrain
was squeezed between the thighs
of girls we worshipped
from afar, too shy
to say hello or goodbye,
we rode our bikes double
to tease Pedan, our slew-
footed cop, and most
of all we dared the indelible
dark that each evening
enveiled our village –
a long ways East
of Eden.

DINNER

Mrs. McCleister's rooster
serenaded our street the moment
the morning sun tickled
his wattle, and then paraded
among his hens, crowing
over every conquest,
loud enough to make
a village wince, and boost
his gallic ego, till
my grandmother, losing
her legendary patience,
threatened to throttle him
and make him the principal
guest at her Easter dinner.

MOTIVE
Point Edward: 1948

The village that spawned me
and kept me cozy
for a dozen years, was pointless
(I searched for it one
day and came home
puzzled) and long ago
was a railway town
bustling with locomotives
and a switching yard, until,
like railroads everywhere,
they pulled up the tracks
and skedadelled, leaving
a single line to rust
away (and a village shrunken,
out-of-joint with the world),
a set of tracks we trod
our on way to Canatara
where the faithful
Lake was motive enough
for a day's play (while
the sun-nuzzled dunes
warmed us, where we clambered
on amber afternoons)
and the slow walk home
along those ties
where we felt the heft of history
and realized the point of it all.

DIXIE
For Anne in loving memory

This sumac, your favourite
tree, looms over our yard
and, once bristling with birds
and teetering with squirrels, is now
in its last throes, like all
those things we love
going in their good time,
and O how tickled
you were at a chickadee's
flickering flair, a cardinal's
scarlet calisthenics,
a robin's bashful bobbing,
and when I saw you in the hilt
of your happiness,
I wanted to shout
Hallelujah or whistle
Dixie.

CHARLIE

Charlie was our neighbour,
a decorated vet who weathered
his nightmares with whiskey,
and, when that wouldn't do,
in beer binges at the Balmoral,
but nothing could unhinge
his image-riddled mind,
not even his three beautiful
daughters who doted on him
and us, and pretended not
to see that smile with the ache
in the middle.

DELIGHT

When it was hide-and-go-seek
the girls of my village played
with all the pizzazz of Amazonians,
venturing into the virgin dark
beyond the umbrella-ed spray
of Mara's lamp to find
a cozy coign where many
a male purloined the swell
of a mislaid ankle
or a leg uncurling in the
shadows shredded by Mara's
light and at the All-Free
boys and girls together
emerged, outrunning
their breath, as if nothing
momentous had happened,
as if our un-Presbyterian
urges were our everyday
delight.

INKED

Nothing could dampen our spirits
under Mara's lamp,
not the monsoon moon or the
stark startling of stars
in the dark of a brooding sky,
and always it was hide-
and-go-seek when we out-
ran our own shadows
along Monk Street all
the way to the village brink
where we conversed with the universe,
for we were young and free,
inked with innocence.

SUCH AN URGE

It might have been the moon-
light lacquering the black
length of Monk Street
or perhaps Mara's lamp
shrivelling the shadow around it,
but something in the air
that night drew us to the
farthest dark where an errant
knee might be harvested
by fingers a-tremble with touch,
or lips on lingering lips
in the grip of some desire
so fleeting we wondered
if such an urge could ever
be.

RECENT WORK

ROMANCE

They said it was just puppy
love, but what right
did "they" have to tell
the world what romance is?
After all, when we strolled
hand-in-glove or called
each other "dear"
or traded soulful glances,
I didn't know down from up
or if the moon still whirled
in its oracular orbit, but nothing
really mattered except
the feeling we shared: of sheer
unjaded delight.

OVAL

Under the amber oval
of Mara's lamp and all
along Monck Street,
lavished by moonlight,
we play our ritual game,
and Nancy and I contrive
to share a shimmer of shadow
and for a lucid moment
we do a duo's dance
and I, no Lancelot,
espy a careless thigh
and harbour thoughts of ravishment.

TIME'S TICK

On a sun-strummed September
morning we abandon our summer
cocoons and hit the high
road for school, passing
Leckie's farm where Holsteins
graze lazily and shorthorns
remember themselves
and on past Gunn's place
where hogs wallow like hippos
with snouts in the snuffling mud
and the pasture where Grace grips
her stallion with incising thighs
and the hawthorn hedge where this
year's colt burgeons
his brand-new erection
(and the girls blush lushly
and the boys sing inside)
and in the haze ahead
sits the brick-coat
box we will inhabit
until the sprouting of Spring
releases us and I shout
for the sheer joy of titillating
Time's tick.

INSIDE

Curly-haired Shirley
doing the can-can
on grandfather's lawn,
strutting her stuff and flinging
her lovely long legs
so high wide and handsome
we burst into prolonged applause
and Shirley grins her little-
girl grin as if
to say, "Seen enough?"
that leaves us singing inside.

CHUM

When Marilyn, my chum from
school,
in the first bloom of her girl-
hood (with curls as wisped
as winter wheat), sauntered
past the hired hand
and me, the latter thumbed
his crotch, grinned and said,
"Now ain't that a sweet piece!"
and I wondered what part
of her he meant and what
made it sweet.

WISH

My Dad and I fishing
on Mitchell's Bay, and I watch
in awe at the lazy, lofted
loop of his plug and its soft
plop on the weed-rich
shallow and when a pike
as big as a barnacled barracuda
strikes, he sets the hook
with an infinitesimal tug
and waits for the finned wriggler
to break the surface, its muscling
arc bent like Robin's bow,
defying the grasp of gravity,
but the fight is over, the game
won, and my father grins
at me as if to say,
'That's how it's done!"
and I wish the day would last
forever.

RUDE AWAKENING

And once again we're gathered
in Hendrie's crude coop,
boys and girls lusting
after something other
than the skin they were born to,
showing off our male
merchandise and hoping
for just one peek
at whatever the girls were squeezing
between their thighs and we were
all cock-a-hoop
and as nude as Eve when the leaf
fell away from the pout
of her pudendum and the world
was in for a rude awakening.

LEGACY

The widow Bray stands
there alone, bee-
deep in her tenderly-groomed
garden (with poppies bleeding
scarlet, roses as red
as a bride's blush and violets
as lush as lavender), watches
the drones, pulsing with pollen,
do their dizzying dance
to apprise the hive of her blossoms'
whereabouts, and thrives
in her flowered bower like a
bloom-inducing wizard
despite the legacy of her loss.

NEW BONES

When my chum Shirley
grew into her new bones,
the boys on the beach ogled
the rogue swerves and curves
curtailed by her one-piece
suit (too shy
to try their luck, too
boggled to breathe), but I alone
felt my heart hum
like a muted flute when she smiled
at me with a will, as if
to say, "The summer's come
and we are here, two friends
still."

BONDING

My father and I go hunting,
twelve gauges slung
over our arms, ambling
side by side, kicking
at every brush-pile
and bramble bush as the afternoon
wears softly on in hopes
that some prey would startle
and there was no need
for the warmth of words until
a cottontail leaps out
and zigzags away;
"Fire!" and I do, wincing
at the rough recoil, but the rabbit
keeps running and Dad says,
"It's only a rabbit," and I say,
"I'm glad I missed."

LUCK

As luck would have it, Bonny
and Sharon agreed to play
"Show me yours" and Bonny
lifted her skirts thigh-
high to expose the puckered
pink rose that lay there
winking up at us,
and when I revealed my stubby
stalk, Sharon said, "Donny,
what do we do now?"
and none of us knew what or how.

STORYTELLER
For Bob in loving memory

You were my first audience
as we lay side by side
in the comfortable dark, and I
spun my bedtime
dramas about meddlesome rabbits
and bumptious bears, and when
I added voices to my creations,
you murmured, "Ah, that's Bingo,'
or "Oh yes, that must be Peewee,"
and laugh in all the right
places and forgive me my flaws,
and I am so grateful
you made a storyteller out of me
and more so now you are gone
and I still speak into the welcoming
dark and listen for your applause

THAT'S HOW IT'S DONE

My Dad and I fishing
on Mitchell's Bay, and I watch
in awe at the lazy, lofted
loop of his plug and its soft
plop on the weed-rich
shallow and when a pike
as big as a barnacled barracuda
strikes, he sets the hook
with an infinitesimal tug
and waits for the finned wriggler
to break the surface, its muscling
arc bent like Robin's bow,
defying the grasp of gravity,
but the fight is over, the game
won, and my father grins
at me as if to say,
'That's how it's done!"
and I wish the day would last
forever.

MUSIC OF THE MUSES

I was born with a village in my genes
and the spillage of its sunshine
settled in my soul, and I walked out
each memorable morning
word-perfect and poaching
poems by any means,
the mettle of my mind simmering
with simile and tropes about Cobalt-
blue waters and meadows
suborned by milkweed
and dunes seething with silkened
sand and lilacs breathing
lavender light onto
grandfather's lawn as green
as the glens of Eden, and I grew
anew into each iambic
day, tuned to the music
of the Muses.

TILLAGE

Each Spring morning
I walk into the wakening world
with the sun haloed on the horizon
above First Bush
and strewing the streets and every
coign and corner with bedizening
light and I wend my way
across the milkweed
meadow below the Bridge
where tender-tipped shoots
upburst from their root
and I stroll along the blue-
hued Lake and its self-
renewing waves and on
past dunes as ancient
as Adam's entry into Eden
and I feel the heave of all
things living and spend
my day purloining poems
from the rich tillage of my home
ground and letting them sing
to my soul.

INKED

Under Mara's lamp
and a night-sky as black
as a jackdaw's paw,
blinking stars and lit
by a molten moon, we play
the games our forebears
played when their world was young
and innocence was inked in their genes,
and, boys and girls together
and jolted by joy, they have no
need to heed the disembodied
gods of the cosmos.

LONG-AGO
With a nod to Michael Ondaatje

I remember the long-ago days
of my youth, when every morning
was a rebirth and we were like
butterflies fluttering free
from their wombed cocoons
in the lucid air over
grandfather's lilac hedge
blooming voluminous and we had
no brink but the blue
embrace of Lake and River
and First Bush where the celibate
sun rose righteous
and I ambled iambic, past
Mara's lamp on is pilgrim
pole, prefacing poems
as I went, to the water's edge,
where I dipped my pen in Ink
Lake and wrote myself whole.

GOING FOR THE GRAIL

Under the amber oval
of Mara's lamp we gathered
for hide-and-go-seek
and in the marinade of moonlight
shadows shiver and loom
and I find myself huddled
with Nancy beneath Foster's
handy verandah and the rub
of a random thigh is like
a bruise in my blood and I want
to love like Lancelot going
for the Grail with thunder in his genes
while the Earth cruises in its universe
and we all abide.

SAW

When Shirley spins the bottle,
I will it to point my way,
praying for the pleasure of a
chaste kiss, but when
our bodies almost meet,
something akin to raw,
unthrottled desire seizes me
sweet and I think of God's
odd look and that old saw:
sin in haste, repent
at leisure.

WISH

My Dad and I fishing
on Mitchell's Bay, and I watch
in awe at the lazy, lofted
loop of his plug and its soft
plop on the weed-rich
shallow and when a pike
as big as a barnacled barracuda
strikes, he sets the hook
with an infinitesimal tug
and waits for the finned wriggler
to break the surface, its muscling
arc bent like Robin's bow,
defying the grasp of gravity,
but the fight is over, the game
won, and my father grins
at me as if to say,
'That's how it's done!"
and I wish the day would last
forever.

AS I WALKED OUT

As I walked out upon
the town that loosed me from the womb
and June enthused the morning
with serenities of sunshine
strumming the streets, and the green
Eden of grandfather's lawn
greeted me outright
and I meandered the village
verges like an Argonaut savouring
the sea and soon found myself
in the milkweed meadow
where tiger-tinted Monarchs
fluttered their two-mooned
wings and nectar-noshing
bees hummed a Polonaisean
tune and I came at last
and always to Canatara
with wavelets lipping the shore-
line intimate and the dunes
stood there as wind-stroked
as the day God uttered,
"Let There Be Light!"
and I opened my iambicized eyes
and the Muses spoke.

LAMENT

I wake and feel the luff
of the dark and when I reach
for you, you are gone and I am
alone in a bed big
enough for two, and our love
like a star fixed in the firmament
or a candle with twin wicks
still burns anew,
and I try not to feel forsaken

PENCHANT

As a teen I was less than dashing,
had no pimple-face bravado,
and when she smiled at me
on Rondeau beach, I gave her
a lop-sided grin,
in return, and I must confess
to surprise when we found ourselves
coupled in the back seat
of a Ford Mustang, where,
with little adieu, she essayed
a French kiss, our tongues
torqueing lustily in a full-
throttled embrace and for the
first time I thought:
even girls have a penchant
for passion.

CRY

Mrs. Bradley could be heard
in the far verges of the village,
setting tongues a-buzz,
and Gran and I watched her
solitary on her front porch,
uttering a bone-chilling
cry in search of some
word that would tell her
where she was.

VISE

Next door to Hendrie's
abandoned coop, a bantam
rooster with his quickening cockade
is harassing his harem, and the girls
decide to play Truth
or Dare and Jo-Anne, forgoing
Truth, announces "The proof
is in the pudding!" and drops
her pants, whetting our wicks,
and we can't take our eyes
off that velvet vise.

RHAPSODY

My village re-imagines itself
each morning when the sun
rises over First Bush
where robins rhapsodize
and the streets and alleys, etched
in the muscle of my memory, throb
with mist-mellowed light
and I greet them like Adam
dreaming in Eden's perpetual
day and I wend my way
iambic to Canatara's rapturous
sands where on-shore
breezes blow like the breath
of a loose-limbed bellows
and rustle the silken curls
of the sea-grasses and I want
 to capture such passing home-
grown mementoes in the rhymed
crucible of a poem.

WADDLE

My Dad on skates: as silken
as a swan mirroring a pond,
and me, just eight,
on my maiden blades, gliding
on my ankles in a desperate effort
to bond with a man I hadn't seen
for five years and more
than one war between us, and I tried
not to notice the surprise
in his eyes, the disbelief
that any son of his could waddle
like a duck on ice and handle
a hockey stick like a dazed
bassoon, and I was grateful
to the gods, whatever their ilk,
who let me wobble beyond
his wounded gaze.

SEVEN FOR ANNE in loving memory

GIFT OUTRIGHT
With a nod to Robert Frost

We couldn't afford a photographer,
so here we are on brother-
in-law's lawn in the only
black-and-white recording
of a moment beyond the nuptials:
the two of us on tip-toe,
leaning into the dream in the
other's eyes, your chin
up-tilted to capture my kiss
as I embrace the joyous geography
of your face, and I want to promise you
fifty-seven seasons
of uninterrupted love
my gift outright.

THE SEASONS AS THEY COME

Now that you are gone
summer skies are not
so blue, the demise of autumn's
leaves is more subdued,
winter's snow sifts
less softly and the bulb-burst
of spring brings no
relief from my bereavement pain,
and so it is I face
the seasons as they come, hold
aloft our having loved,
acknowledge the gift of your grace
and carry on.

TRUCE

We find ourselves on the Bruce
Trail, weaving our way
through sprays of spruce and cedars
and over denuded hummocks
where limestone protrudes
like nicotined teeth, and after
a while we hold hands
as lovers do when touch
is triumphant, and let summer's
celibate sun simmer
through the screen of trees
and brush us with such tenderness
I want to hug you from here
to Heaven and feel the rush
of our moon-lucid love,
knowing that our lives are always
and ever making a truce
with the gods.

GIFTS
For Tom

You and I jigging
for walleye wriggling
for prey in the weed-rich
underwater meadows
of Cameron's Baltic blue,
(and hoping later on
for a smallmouth or two)
and seated side by side
and savouring the sun on the gunwales,
we lay our rods down
and let the afternoon drift
by under a day-
time moon marooned
in the southern sky, and the happiness
we feel, the exultation
of these moments are truly
gifs from the gods.

GENESIS

For fifty-seven years
we fashioned our lives in the same
furrow, tilted the odds
in our favour, and I loved you
with a poet's passion, you who
came to me like the gracious gift
of a benevolent God, who redeemed
all things under Heaven,
you who were the doyen of my dreams
and the genesis of my joy.

ADIEU

In the midst of my grieving
I forgive you your leaving,
for ours was a love rooted
in passion that mellowed with the years
like a June moon and we grew
in unison like the rings of a slow
oak and I am comforted
at the last by the memories that linger
and loll and by the stalwart
sting of my tears as I bid you
adieu.

PERCHANCE

In this dream I stand
alone on Canatara, listening
to the slow inwashing of waves
and wishing you were no longer
unalive and we could share
our summers once more,
feeling the sun's beneficent
beam thrive on our upturned
faces (and speaking in code
like a bee-dance in a hive)
or blinking in the light from the arch
of stars above us or never
again having to query
the perchance of our brave love
or its whereabouts.

AURA

My first love poem
was an ode to Laura Haggith
whom I worshipped from afar until
the day she rode shotgun
in my father's thirty-nine
Dodge and I drove up
and down the main drag,
showing her off like a prize
rose or the aura of a new-
born star, her youthful
beauty unblemished
by my futile ogle or the rogue
feelings I fought to hide
or the hodge-podge of my hammering
heart.

CONTEMPLATION
For my mother in loving memory

You tell me you found your mother
cold to the touch, the morning
sun pouring golden
upon the shimmered sheets,
and you but a girl of thirteen,
contemplating death and all
it means and not knowing
of course that I would discover
my own mother without breath,
feigning sleep, and I longed
to feel you warm once
more, your eyes smitten
with a smile, but we are all
hostage to love and loss, to laughter
at our a-borning and weeping at our demise

IRONIC

It must have seemed ironic
that Abelard's feeling for Héloise
was deemed Platonic when every
letter of every word
of their chaste correspondence
dripped with the lust they were denied
and the abdication of vows
they swore in haste, but love
is love and has been since Eden
when Adam, apple-dazzled,
gave in to the fiery combustion
of desire.

                          FULL-BODIED

                  When Virginal Eve sampled
                  the apple from the Tree of Knowledge,
                  she knew her nakedness
                  and festooned it with a fig-leaf
                  and Adam felt the first
                  of several moon-induced
                  urges and everywhere
                  in the ruined garden tulips
                  bloomed before dying
                  and lilacs on the hedges withered
                  before budding again
                  and all things grew autumnal
                  after the seeds' seethe
                  and the un-Edened pair
                  soon found themselves
                  dithered and digging
                  but still cheering the god
                  who'd made them the perfect
                  example of the human hunger
                  for love and a full-bodied
                  world.

NO WORDS
For Tom

I remember the first soft
ululation from your crib
two rooms away
and how you danced into each
day and the absolute un-
bibbed joy aloft
in your eyes, O child of my age
who even now, many
years on, can tug
at my tenderness and I wish
you welcome in the world
with these leavening words
though no poem can grace
the page to picture you perfect
and my heart bursts with the love
it can barely contain and I long
once more to hug
you to Heaven.

TENDERNESS

Who would've thought that such
a summer's afternoon on Cameron's
sun-strummed, pellucid
blue, would find us, fishing
rods in hand, poaching
perch finning soundlessly
a fathom below among the reed-
breathing underwater
glades or if luck holds
a behemoth bass cruising
like a teeth-seizing barracuda,
and I'd rather be here than
anywhere else but Heaven,
touched by tenderness and loving
the plot of our never-ending
story.

ANYWHERE ELSE
For Tom

You and I trying our luck
once again on Cameron's
blue flume on a summer's
afternoon, strummed by sun
and a bashful breeze, and we ease
into the rhythm of your rowing
before the anchor is weighed
a full fathom below
where the big-bodied bass
furrow the underwater glades,
probing for perch lurching
to pluck at minnows shivering by,
and above us sits a quicksilver
moon and we are hugged
whole by birch and fir
ten thousand years
in the making, and I'd rather be
here with you and love's
hug than anywhere else
on God's globe.

JUST
For Sandy

I was just seventeen
when I caught you in my amorous
eye and fell in love
with your unbudding beauty,
the sudden glamour of your glance
and the way you forgave
my befuddled forays into romance,
and we spent a celibate summer
proving something other
than lust grows gracefully
this side of Heaven.

GRIN
For Alvin Gehl

As a non-swimmer I was warned
off the River, but you,
like Huck Finn on the swift
Mississippi, built
yourself a raft and tried
your luck on the mud-loving
Thames, while I stood
ashore like a landlubber,
wanting so much
to be your budding Tom
Sawyer, but you, like any
friend, waved goodbye
with a grin that said, "This
joy is yours."

GENTLE
For Tom

Gentle is the word I'd choose
to describe your principled probing
of my oeuvre in this room
where we confer over books
or remark on how a poem
grows like the rings of a slow
oak or how a character
springs to mind fully clothed
and in between weighty
discussions of plot or incidental
ironies I recount the foibles
of a near-forgotten uncle
or ornamental aunt,
and so it is the animating
annals of family and forebears
take reliable root and are passed
on through the genes
of the generations
and I will rest with ease,
knowing my work will come
alive again every time
you open a book bearing
our name.

BLUE MOON

Under Mara's lamp
and a sky festooned with stars,
we play our ritual game:
hide-and-go-seek
in the indelible dark where the
Bogeyman lurks, and we are
unafraid because we are armed
with our innocence and a naïve belief
in the old saws: "A stitch
in time" and "Once in a blue
moon."

I DREAMT A VILLAGE

Cocooned in my mother's womb
and at ease in its sea-warm,
amniotic surround,
I dreamt a village seasoned
with similes, and when I was ready
to be unfurled,
it welcomed me into its world,
where I infused its exotic
air like a bard en route
to his muse.

STRANGE

Coop and I adrift
in the goose-pimpling chill
of our Lake, riding the somer-
saulting breakers in the lift
and carriage of their endless
looping, and afterwards in the
change room, stripped
to our stitches, we gawk at our
stiffening stalks and grin
as if we had discovered something
rich and strange.

ELYSEUM
For my brother in loving memory

O how you loved your Ludwig
and the refined thunder of those
nine symphonies with their trembling
tympanies, the hemming and hawing
of violins and cellos, the forlorn
soar of the French horn,
and all this maelstrom of music
heard only in the soundless
bell of the maker's mind,
and I love how you hummed along
with the Ode to Joy and its frenzied
fugues and Daughters of Elyseum,
and drowned in cadenzas of feeling,
raw and rogue, and whenever
I listen to such monumental
music, I remember you
and how much we shared
before death suddened us.

ROGUE

When I was young and the world
was willing and the seasons passed
like dappled days in Eden,
and I, like a map-happy
LaSalle or an Eve annexing
an apple, explored the nooks
and crannies of the village that bore me
and seldom did I venture beyond
its enveloping verges where the Bogeyman
lay in wait for those
of us gone rogue
with our innocent urges.

WALKING OUT ON A JUNE DAY
Point Edward: 1948

As I walked out on a June
morning when I was young
and my days were easy, I gazed
upon the sun boiling
out of First Bush and seasoning
the streets with lacquered light
and I hearkened to the throb of a
robins' song and a jackdaw's
caw as I loped along
the River flats to the burnished
blue of the Lake and the celibate
sands of Canatara and the
wind-breathing dunes
where Attawandaron talked
to their gods and the Earth gave birth
to itself, and home again
down Alexandra Ave
to grandfather's lawn
where the Muses lay in wait,
and I papered my world with poems

SKETCHING ANNE

If I were sketching you
from an image etched on my memory
in pencill'd lines and filigree,
I would call on the art of the ages
to limn your loveliness and stencil it
on my heart.

SOFT AND LOW
For Anne in loving memory

Alone at night I sense
your presence in every room
and when I am down, I simply
recall the silken swerve
of your smile or your voice,
like Cordelia's, ever soft
and low or the way you brushed
a curl from your brow or held
horizons in your eyes, and these
small remembrances, these
sweet shudders of delight
touch my heart's core
while your love blooms in my bones
like a sun-rubbed rose.

ONCE AGAIN
For Anne in loving memory

Once again I'd like to feel
your lips close to mine,
to hear you whisper "We'll
never part," but now
that you are gone, I'm finding it
hard to love with a crippled
heart.

A TREE IN GIBBONS PARK
For Anne in loving memory

There are dozens of trees
in Gibbons Park: weeping
willow, birch, scarlet
maple and its many cousins,
but there is one you loved
where I will stop and linger:
a sapling that will continue to climb
as the years stretch on,
carrying in its lofting limbs
memories of you and all
the days you strolled over
Gibbons sun-softened
meadows, making your dear
dogs happy, at ease
with a world you forgave
for giving up on you,
and so I tarry here
because not even the grave
can sunder the brave love
we shared.

Donald George Gutteridge: A Short Autobiographical Story

I was born in Sarnia General Hospital on September 30, 1937, and named (but never Christened) Donald George Gutteridge (my second name after my Uncle George McWatters). My Dad, who did not graduate grade 8 spelled it Gorge, later corrected by my mother (Margaret Grace McWatters), who graduated high school in Special Commercial. Days later moved to Point Edward, soon to take up residence upstairs in my Grandparents house at the corner of 208 Alexander (Alexandra) Avenue and Monck (Monk) Street.

In June of 1939 my maternal grandfather, John Leonard McWatters, who began living with us, was murdered in Sarnia. No one was ever charged.

In September of 1939 my Dad joined the air force (along with my Uncle Tom Gutteridge), and was soon stationed in Ottawa, where I moved with both parents. My brother Bob (Robert William), who was born that March, stayed home in the care of his grandparents. When my Dad was sent to a Labrador posting (later Iceland), my mother and I returned home in the Spring of 1940.

During the war years I led an idyllic life as a spoiled first child. I started school at the Edward Street School (now demolished) in September 1943. In October 1944 I contracted rheumatic fever and was hospitalized for a week. The high fever opened the valves of my heart. My mother put me in the care of her gynecologist, Dr. Christie, who ordered complete bed rest for seven months. I was a precocious reader and spent my bedridden hours reading whatever I could find. I never left the bed once until May of 1945. My Dad was given leave to visit me shortly after I came home from the hospital. My mother was my faithful nurse. I returned to school to finish grade two with the support of my wonderful teacher, Mrs. Young, who brought me homework to keep me up to date. I wrote my first story for Miss McDonald, my grade three teacher, (and a poem about it in *God's Geography*). From that time on I found a group of fast friends in the village whom I have put into poems and novels. It was a great life (as the books show). I spent a lot of time in my grandfather's workshop, and adored him. In July of 1945 my Dad came home after almost six years away. We had a difficult time bonding: he was a superb athlete, I wasn't. My Dad got a job as a switchtender on the local CNR and we prospered enough for my Dad and Mom to build their own house on the Fourth Line of Sarnia. The move into the lonely countryside, away from my home village, was devastating for me. For two years my brother and I, every second week, walked to the train station and caught the bus to Point Edward, where we stayed with Gran and Gramps, and tried to keep up the fraying friendships that had been so much a part of my life.

Bob and I walked a mile and a quarter to S.S. #12, a one room country school, which I attended from Grade 6 to 8. Like most kids, I soon adjusted and found new fast friends, Bobby Cooper and Tommy Fahselt, both of whom I have written poems about. I became entranced by a grade 7 girl, Grace Leckie, who occasionally rode to school on a chestnut stallion. Miss Nelson encouraged me to keep on reading and suggested I write a Christmas play for the school. It was performed, with me as leading man (Santa, I think) in the township hall before an applauding audience. My novel, Winter's Descent is a thinly disguised account of one of my years there. I also wrote my first poem that year, about Wolfe and Montcalm (in rhyming couplets).

I entered Grade 9 at Sarnia Collegiate Institute and Technical School in the Fall of 1950. There I was bullied and unhappy, failing a subject (math) for the first time in my life. In June of 1951 my Dad was transferred to Chatham (in an effort to save his marriage) and I spent the rest of that month with my grandparents and finished Grade 9. (My chief accomplishment that year was to write my first completed novel, Pass That Puck, typed out on an Underwood borrowed from my Aunty Betty). Once again I was devastated at having to leave the friends I had made and a life I had begun to enjoy. (I have written many poems about life on the Fourth Line and friends like Bonnie and Sharon Lauer, Marilyn Matheson and others.)

I spent a lonely summer in our new Chatham house at 28 Kerr Avenue in the subdivision of Orchard Heights. In the Fall I entered Chatham Collegiate Institute where, in the smaller academic school, I soon found friends with common interests, learned to play chess and handball and did well academically (third in the class). My high school years were the usual fraught story of girl-trouble and false steps, but overall happy enough years. I had two very close friends in the school and one bosom buddy who went to the Tech school, Alvin Gehl, who loved to test out the games I invented (an obsession that lasted well into my life). Alvin has been duly celebrated in several poems, and we remain friends in our old age. During these years I wrote part of a verse play on ancient Greece, an unfinished mystery story and a similarly unfinished novel about Dutch immigrants (who peopled CCI). I wrote only one poem, a lament about the failed Hungarian Revolution. I saw myself then as becoming a novelist. For the last three summers I spent in Chatham I worked in the yard office of the local CNR and saved my money for college. On the darker side, my beloved grandfather died after a prostate operation. I was devastated. It was the first of many such deaths I would suffer over the course of a long life.

In the Fall of 1956 I entered The University of Western Ontario (UWO), registered in Honours English. I did not do well in English (an indifferent lecturer) (a B) but enjoyed college life, surprising myself by having several dates and living with five other fellows upstairs in a home on the corner of Western and Sarnia Road (a plaza now), two of whom became good friends. I joined the Hesperian Club (for English lovers), heard Northop Frye speak to us and fell in love with my minor, History. I did little writing (except for a controversial essay I wrote for Folio, the school literary journal, "Let's Destroy the Church."

The next year was wonderful. I had Professor Ross Woodman for Romantics and fell in love with Keats and Shelley. I started to write longish poems in homage to them (several were published in Folio and fortunately have faded into obscurity.) I also loved History and Geography and made the Dean's Honour List (after which, in following years, I made little effort to replicate). My partner and I came second in the university badminton championship. Don Hair and I became good friends (and still are). Alas, my parents' marriage was breaking up. My Dad moved my mother and brother to an apartment in London, promising to follow, and simply never did. My mother had to go to work to support Bob and me through the rest of our schooling. In the summer following second year, I had a chance to go north to Red Lake and work as a solutions man in the gold mine at Balmertown. I played softball for the mine's team (third base and right field) and hit over 300. My Dad would have cheered, but for us it was too late. My Dad quit the CNR (just before being offered a superintendent's job), moved to Calgary, took up both taxidermy and the drink.

I lived with my mother for my third and fourth year at Western and was both lonely and unhappy, for her and for myself. My grades suffered and I barely made it out of fourth year. But with summer approaching in 1960, the happy thought of doing the teacher training term and getting a job and having a life, I started to write again, some poems and the beginnings of a novel (about life in Balmertown). I got a job offered to me teaching English to Grades 11, 12 and 13 at Elmira District High School in Elmira, Ontario. My real life was beginning.

I instantly fell in love with teaching. I had found one of the things I had wanted to do with my life. I also fell in love with the Home Economics teacher, Margaret Anne Barnett. Anne and I went on platonic excursions to Toronto (where she had gone to school and had connections) and soon were fully in love. I proposed on a snowy night in February 1961 in Anne's new Volkswagon. We were married by a judge in Guelph and attended a small reception for us by school friends and my mother and brother. We rented the back half (servant's quarters) of a big house (the old Drew homestead) and began our married life, driving each day from Elora to Elmira District High School. Many weekends we drove to Toronto for musicals and plays at the O'Keefe Centre. It was a wonderful winter and spring. Over 85% of my Grade 13 students passed their provincial English exam.

I had to attend the second half term of my teacher education the following summer, so we moved back to London and rented an apartment on Waterloo Street (now demolished). In mid-course I came down with a serious bout of appendicitis and had my appendix removed. A week later I was back in class, catching up and determined to finish the training. I passed with honours, and we returned to Elora for another year of teaching.

1962 was an uneventful year, marked by my decision to go back to Western for a Master's degree. Since we had not had a honeymoon the summer before, we went to Europe for a nine-week excursion, visiting England, Scotland, Ireland, France, Germany, Austria and Italy. That Fall, we rented a lovely apartment on Grand Avenue, near Ridout, and I began my new degree, falling back on our savings and a fellowship that had me teaching English 20. I loved lecturing and could envision myself doing this for a living. I did well in my courses (As) but got stalled on my M.A. thesis, mostly because I had returned to my novel about life in Balmertown and didn't know which project to focus on, with the prospect of a failed M.A. or a further term in the Fall of '63 (which we couldn't afford). Moreover, Anne was expecting our first child in June of '63. It was time to forget about writing (thesis or novel) and go to work to support my family. I got one teaching English and acting as department head in Ingersoll Collegiate. We moved to a new townhouse development on Oxford Street across from Oakridge High School and I commuted each weekday. William John Barnett Gutteridge arrived a month late (July 10) but hale and hearty. I was a father. At Ingersoll, once again I loved the teaching but crossed swords with an erratic principal. I decided I couldn't stick it out (the snowy 50-minute commute and difficult superior) and applied for a job in London. I was lucky to be offered one at Beck Collegiate, one of the best schools in the City.

I stayed at Beck for two years as an ordinary English teacher (grades 9, 11, 12 and 13). My mother divorced my father. My brother was teaching elementary school in Point Edward. Sometime during those two years I finished my novel and sent it to Jack McClelland. He liked it but said the entire book had not one word of dialogue. I thought that if I were to become a novelist I had better learn to write dialogue. (I learned later in the decade by taking the advice of Alice Munro: that dialogue comes naturally from the creation of strong characters put in the same room.) Meanwhile I had had my first poem published in a real magazine: "This Maple in my Fallen Yard" in the Fiddlehead (1961 or 1962 and republished in *The Village Within*). Encouraged I started to write both short lyrics about Point Edward and several long poems about the Jesuits in Huronia, Champlain and LaSalle. In 1966 I moved to Westminster Secondary School as department head and Catherine Anne Gutteridge was born on June 10. I was having some success getting my poems published in the little magazines of the period (three narratives in The Fiddlehead). Again I enjoyed teaching and running a large department. Sometime in 1967 I read *Strange Empire* by John Kinsey Howard and got to work on a series of poems about Louis Riel, eventually finishing it as *Riel: A Poem for Voices*. I sent it off to Fred Cogswell at Fiddlehead and he agreed to publish 500 copies if I would subsidize the printing. Somehow, with a growing family and a new apartment in Inglewood Park, I squeezed out $200 and my first of more than 65 books was published in 1968. I was an author.

The Rest

1968 was a banner year. *Riel* was published and received two good reviews and Professor John Smallbridge went on sabbatical at the new Althouse College of Education and asked me to replace him. Earlier in that Spring we moved from Inglewood Park to a townhouse on Kipps Lane. I settled in to teaching English methods to English grads and travelling about southern Ontario following my students and supervising their classroom experience. I had found a work that I really loved. I was equally fortunate in that the next year the College expanded and I was taken on full time as an assistant professor in the English Department. That same year we moved to Victoria Street. Writing-wise I began to gather together poems I wrote about Point Edward, the first of what proved to be a lifelong obsession, and Fiddlehead Poetry Books published the collection as *The Village Within: Poems Toward a Biography*. (I will not comment on all of my books in this document, except when there is a story behind the telling. (A complete bibliography is available on my Wikipedia site.) My interest in historical figures continued with

Death At Quebec and Other Poems (Fiddlehead 1972) (I won the UWO President's medal for title poem).

In January 1972 my mother died suddenly and I wrote a poem for her: Saying Grace: An Elegy (Fiddlehead 1972). But earlier in the summer of 1970 I found myself free of teaching and able to take on a major writing project. I sat in the shade of my back yard and wrote, in six or seven weeks, the first draft of a comic novel, *Bus-Ride*, published in 1974 (Nairn Publishing) and well reviewed. I have no idea where the germ for this book came from, nor had I ever seen myself as a comic writer. But I had mastered dialogue (one of the book's strengths)!

Shortly after I began to search about for historical topics for future poems. I discovered and devoured Samuel Hearnes's Journal and wrote a book-length poem on him (*Coppermine* 1973), which turned out to be a finalist for that year's Governor Generals Literary Awards. Encouraged, I wrote two more book-length historical poems, *Borderlands* and *Tecumseh*, all published, like the first, by Oberon, the most successful small literary publisher in Canada at that time. I felt I had arrived as a poet (and a minor novelist). I continued to enjoy teaching at Althouse, which became a Faculty of Education at Western and was promoted to associate professor. I continued to publish papers on educational theory and practice in English throughout my twenty-five-year career (40 articles on both pedagogy and literary criticism: details are available in my Wikipedia entry..)

Family life continued apace. Anne and I took Kate and John on a number of camping trips, visited Canadian battlefields and Fort Henry. I was ready, author-wise, for a change of direction. I had written out my interests in aboriginal figures and started to look back to *The Village Within* for inspiration. Within a year I had produced *A True History of Lambton County* (Oberon, 1977) in which I used passages of "found" material from the historical record and interweaved them with the poetry. Again the reviews were good and I had found a subject I thought I could explore deeply. I was not prepared for the several years of writer's block which followed. Desperate to continue writing poetry, I conceived a project eventually published as *God's Geography* (Brick Books 1982). In it I incorporated excerpts from *The Sarnia Observer*, original and vintage photos, and excerpts from interviews with local residents taped by my Uncle Bob. For poetry, I dredged up parts of *The Village Within* and wrote a few new pieces. It turned out to be not only the mélange of a desperate poet but my best reviewed book of poetry up to that time.

In 1978 I wrote the first of my ten "academic" books and began teaching graduate courses in English pedagogy. Then I surprised myself with another comic novel, *All in Good Time* (Black Moss Press 1982). Then followed the driest period in my writing career. I joined The League of Canadian Poets, served on the executive, did public readings across the country, but wrote no poetry. I was dry.

Sometime in 1984 or early 1985 the germ of a new novel arrived. If I could no longer be a poet perhaps I could be a novelist. I wanted to write an historical novel (that abiding interest) from a woman's point of view and *Lily's Story* was born and pursued for two years (one of them a sabbatical). I decided to publish it myself in two volumes, *St. Vitus Dance* and *Shaman's Ground* (1986 and 1988). The books are set in Lambton County and Point Edward, continuing my interest in local history. (In 2014 Bev Editions published the two volumes as *Lily's Story*) Novel writing continued with another historical novel, *How the World Began: A Parable of 1812* (Moonstone 1991.) The highlight of 1985 was the birth of my first grandson, followed a few years later by the birth of three more grandsons and even later by two granddaughters and since then they have been the highlight of my life. Tom lived with us for six years until Kate married, and when he was old enough we travelled with him widely, and he has inspired a number of poems over the years

In 1991 Oberon published a slim volume of verse, *Love in the Wintertime*. But again I turned to fiction as my main focus. And returned to my home village. Out came two memoir novels, *Summer's Idyll* and *Winter's Descent* (1993 and 1996) In between them I wrote a children's/young adult novel, *The Perilous Journey of Gavin the Great* (not published until 2011 by Borealis). I published one other book of poetry in this period. But I was also coming to the end of a long academic career. I retired in October 1993.

Bored with retirement, I started in on what became a twelve-volume mystery series, *The Marc Edwards Mysteries*, with four publishers over a twelve-year period (2003-2015). These would be the last prose I would write. But I started writing poems again. The principal focus in these numerous volumes (12 titles over 20 years and three more to come) was Point Edward with many occasional poems added, on family life, the process of writing itself and aspects of my aging. My style also evolved. I began writing short poems that gradually were subsumed by internal rhyme, assonance, consonance and alliteration, unlike the more free flowing lyrics of the earlier period with "natural" line breaks. I continue to write these somewhat old-fashioned poems.

It's been a full life and I'm still writing.

An Essay on
Don Gutteridge's "Big Book"
Point Taken

M.Sc. Miguel Ángel Olivé Iglesias
Associate Professor Holguín University, Cuba
CCLA Cuban President &
The Ambassador Editor-in-chief

It was a pleasure writing this essay about Don Gutteridge's book that we nicknamed "The Big Book." Reading such fine poetry felt like I was making a full literary circle. My life has been filled with books since I can remember. My parents were avid readers, a gift they fortunately passed on to me during my childhood. I read almost everything they would put in my hands: stories, novels, poetry, biographies, historical treatises, etc. Teen age however saw me take a turn towards poetry reading – and writing.

Years after, my cup of tea continues to be poetry, a pleasure I have been able to expand and enjoy in more than one language. I have read poems in Spanish, English and French. I have reveled in their magic to expose the world to me; space and time compacted and served as no other genre has done for me. Canadian poets have largely contributed to the way I feel, especially during these last three years in which the Canada Cuba Literary Alliance (CCLA) and its Founding President, Richard M. Grove (Tai), have given me the opportunity to fall in love with their poetry.

The book I am reviewing here, *Point Taken*, by Don Gutteridge, is a huge, welcome undertaking that pulls together much of his previous work. I must say that those early years in his life when he was "*consuming the small library there* (at Point Edward and nearby township) *and writing both his first poem and his only play*," were a strong influence for his career. They also acted as a reminder of my own literary childhood. Those were actually career-defining moments: "… *he spent his first eleven years in a childhood enlivened by schoolyard chums and summers spent sunning on Canatara beach and paddling in the chill waters of Lake Huron… pristine days of his boyhood… There he spent three idyllic years…*" that furnished Don's budding formative period and left marks on what would be his exceptional style and ability to recreate the past and lay it down freshly, strikingly and kindheartedly. It also built a foundation for his gallant, brave and confident attitude towards today and his being at peace with tomorrow.

This book has the rare touch to make me travel. While on my spatial-temporal voyage, I have been led into my own soul, my own memories, dusting many of them out of an almost forgotten past. I thank Gutteridge for it. It unveiled gently, completely, a universe of shimmering words and images to replenish the soul. In Gutteridge's statement: "*poetry is both bliss and consolation, a way of speaking to the world that subsumes both shy and defy.*" (Taken from his poem "Defy" in the book *Home Ground*). Jack Magnus tells us of Don's craft "*in making his images sing…*" (Taken from back-cover comment on *Home Ground*, a previous book by Gutteridge also included in *Point Taken*)

The book is divided into self-standing yet mutually-cohesive titles and dates that are hand-guiding the reader across its over seven hundred pages. Despite its length, Gutteridge has succeeded in collecting poems that will stay with us long after we have finished the book. John B. Lee tells us about Gutteridge and his poetry: "*we might carry these poems with us where we go…*" (Taken from back-cover comment on *Home Ground*)

We will put the book down with a mixture of states and feelings wafting about us. First of all, a bit of fatigue from the long, edifying journey. Secondly, a generous pinch of satisfaction for being witnesses to the extensive high-polish oeuvre the author has compiled throughout his prolific writing career, magnificently displayed here. Finally, we will be prideful for sharing in the message and scope of his work, and will sincere acknowledge the merits of the book and the poet. The book will also leave with us a sense of belonging to that group of people who are now in possession of an extraordinary volume. On *Home Ground*'s back cover too, Jack Magnus's impressions about the poet's work cannot be more commendable: "… *instilled in me a sense of wonder and presence at his memories…*" and he goes on to say: "*the reader can't help but be affected.*"

In my view, this book is to be approached with spirit and an open will to walk down the roads Gutteridge paves for us. You will need time, which you can profit from alone, or in the company of fellow poetry lovers. The poems in the book are heartening, inviting and embracing. John B. Lee best coincides about the effect of poetry when he says: "*kissing the darkness / when the pages are closed / and silent / as a dreamer's mind…*" (Taken from Lee's poem "Kissing the Darkness When the Pages Close"). The book gives us a latent past, a defining present and a future that may well be anyone's future.

That is how I felt regarding this book and its lingering aroma after reading it.

The book's parts acting almost like chapters, are titles from his previous books: *The Way it Was, Tidings, Peripheries, Inundations, The Blue Flow Below, The Sands of Canatara, Inklings, Cameron Lake: a Suite of Poems, Home Ground, Night Skating, Days Worth the Telling, The Breath of My Being, The Star-Brushed Horizon, Foster's Pond, Mara's Lamp and Inking the World,* are included in the order that they were published as standalone books.

A review of Don's intense, colorfully-varied images and aesthetic proposal must aim at revealing his straight-to-the-heart poetic and stylistic precision, masterfully evidenced in the book. To this end, I will make reference to poems in some sections. It will help me illustrate my analyses and clarify my criteria for the readers.

Gutteridge presents this formidable book in a chronological arrangement of his literary production from 2014 through to 2019, fanning out his most intimate nexus rock-solid meanings and indelible metaphors, which are finely expressed in his poem to John B. Lee in *Home Ground*: "… *the inheld breath / before we say the syllables / to ourselves and dream / them onto the page.*"

In the section entitled, *The Way it Was*, the author embarks on a trip to his early reminiscences with a free ticket to follow him. His poem "Blue-eyed," for example, abounds in tender phrases that depict moments and scenes familiar to everyone, thus creating links that we cannot break: "*and me, / at five, hopping in a one-footed dance at her side,*" or "*we breathe easy in the April / air, crisp clouds / clustered above: her glance / a blue-eyed barometer / of her love.*" The two instances settle comfortably in our mind's innermost recesses, playfully activating our personal experiences, positively connecting us to the next pieces.

"Letters" follows up in the trail of the previous poem. Earnest lines worth quoting for the reader, where Gutteridge displays his seasoned skills as a writer to give us his grandfather – and bring us ours: "*I try again to catch / that fleeting face in the prism / of a poem, to see it / again with the clarity of crystal.*" The poet knows the role of poetry and the power of metaphors in eternalizing what is precious to us: "*and feel that benign smile / in the serendipity of a simile, / knowing that he will survive / as long as these letters / linger and thrive.*" I could not avoid recalling Shakespeare's lines "*When in eternal lines to Time thou grow'st.*"

The poem, "Dunes at Canatara" shows us a poet of deep thought, of concerned meditation about time and land, which he gracefully blends with his own life. The poet does not detach himself from the land; he rather admires such creation and paints himself, and peers, into it: "*It took a million years to sculpt these dunes, grain by grain / of wave-washed sand whipped / by seasoned winds into / voluptuous curves / and bevelled runes. / It took my pals and me / an afternoon to put / our imprimatur upon / the shimmering concavities…*"

I notice Purdy echoes in this poem ("*I lay with my ear flat against the monstrous stone silence…, listening to the deep core of the world – silence unending and elemental, leaked from a billion-year period before and after the season of man.*") (Fragment by Al Purdy taken from *Al Purdy. Essays on his Works*. Edited by Linda Rogers. Essay by Stan Dragland)

We enjoy sound humour in the poem "Career": "*Oscar and I boxing / in the home-built ring / suddenly my chin… / too close to the gist / of Oscar's toxic fist, / and down I go, sprawled / on the cellar floor, knocked*

/ here and everywhere / at once, and contemplating / the demise of my illustrious / career." We smile in half-closed-eyes gratitude with "Nightfall" as we roll back to our childhood: *"When night came down / upon the village verge, / we gathered around / the intergalactic glow / of the streetlight like / marauding moths ..."*

In *Tidings,* next section in the book, I was deeply moved by "The Way Home": *"The way home is thru / the heart, every blood-beat / hums with remembrance."* This is a recurring leitmotif with Gutteridge, sweetly handled and firmly setting in our minds. Then again in "Home-grown" those Purdy vibrations that speak of the land, when Gutteridge mentions places of special connotation during his youth: *"… the curve of Canatara's bountiful beach, / the infinite surge / of Huron Lake, the marshes / below the angular Bridge / spanning the blue cadence of our River, / while meadows bounced / with bobolinks near a park / where we played until / the evening evaporated / – these were all of God's / geography I would need / to track the terrain of a story / or the swerve of a poem / with my cartographer's eye…"*

This is continually signalized in the poems "The Lake of my Childhood": *"I cannot pass the Great / Lake of my childhood / without a nod and modicum of shudder,"* and "Pleasure": *"the sea-deep Lake / … under a simmering sun, / while Huron held us in its / wombed vise, twinned / in mutual pleasure."* In all three cases, the attraction towards places which seem to vibrate deep in the poet´s experiences.

One particular poem of endearment, for me, is "For my Grandmother." This poem reaffirms Magnus's statement I quoted in my second page: readers will be affected by Gutteridge´s words: *"When grandfather died / your world was abruptly halved, / all those little rituals / that bound you one to one / now ended / … both of you / linked by love."* Those are very close mementoes that may as well be part of any person's personal remembrances. So does his poem "Allies": "*Nothing abides like love: / for fifty-odd years / side by side… / satisfied… / riding out our last days, / we smile and, knowingly, / nod.*" These lines confirm my assertion about the poet's attitude in regards to what lies ahead, his confidence and mature stance. He portrays his life, poem after poem, his family, his fears and joys; and we gently ease into them and feel on our skin what he has felt.

Peripheries is a section of little jewels as well. "Letters" speaks about the emotions stirred inside the poet. He enumerates them slowly, as if to imbue all the homesickness they inspire, as if to re-live the past that now passes before his eyes: "*It's a long way home / to the place where the heart lies: / the village that superintended / my birth, that gave me space / in its eyes to grow under / its lavish light… / a place where the heart lives, / etched in perpetual Spring, / unravished by Time.*" The last line tells us of the durable bond between poet and place.

Gutteridge is loyal to the Canadian tradition of writing about nature and the elements. In his poem "Gloaming" he impresses us with a splendid, eye-caressing feat of images, similes and metaphors: "*… floated / like a drunken dolphin / … as the dark / deftly descended and the moon / lurked aloft, a-glimmer / in the gloaming…*"

This is equally valid for "Eternity", a brief, passionate and nostalgic poem I quote in its entirety: "*My Lake was bigger than the / salten seas with no / horizon but a blue blur / where the sun would sequester / each evening, with a / kaleidoscopic squeeze, / and when we dipped a toe / into its chilled solemnity / and felt its heavenly breeze / upon our chastened cheeks, / it was as if we were touching / Eternity.*" I praise the poet for his delicate, well-outlined images and epithets: "*kaleidoscopic squeeze,*" "*chilled solemnity,*" "*heavenly breeze,*" "*as if we were touching Eternity.*"

"Unsayable" closes this part with the poet's musings about poetry writing. John B. Lee seeks answers to the mystery of writing: "*… to feel the fertile germination / of a sentient breath / transforming / tight-packed syllables / of interlocking words…*" (Taken from Lee's poem "Kissing the Darkness When the Pages Close") whereas Gutteridge explores possibilities and offers explanations: "*I've spent a lifetime / seeking the reason for rhyme / in pursuit of the perfect poem / where dactyls dance until / they make indelible sense / in the midst of metrical meaning…*" He does not give up ("*I've spent a lifetime*") and certainly does persist in the act, "*in pursuit of the perfect poem,*" while his metaphors waltz: "*where dactyls dance…*"

Yet, "Silence" epitomizes this quest towards the why and the mystery of writing: "*For sixty-odd years / I've been a wielder of words, / my pen propelled across / the page, metamorphosing / into three-beat iambics / enmeshed in metaphor / and circulating into sense; / when I can no longer be / a purveyor of poems, / I shall leave it all / to God and silence.*" The deeply religious man, poised and assured. Few poets spend so much time and sculpt such excellent pieces of poetry in dealing with this topic, and few achieve such heights in their attempts.

Inundations is a section that recaptures the scenes the poet so adores: family, context, childhood memories, sprinkling these with poems to nature, seasons, places and experiences like falling in love. Seasons, for instance, reverberate miraculously in his poem entitled "Dappled": "*When I die I want / it to be in the Spring / when the crocus erupts, / tulips tantalize / the sun, my maple's / leafage abruptly / levitates and the hedgerows / are hung with berries ripened / by light, when apple blossoms / blow blizzard-white, / and I may lie in some / dappled shade and dream / of being young.*" A sense of belonging and a bond with nature are noticeable in this poem, as much as in "Birdsong," "September," "Why" – and many others.

The notion of poetry writing is re-visited by Gutteride in this section too. Here we find "Wit": "*Once more I sit / down to compose, / amazed again at the / limned linkage / between the ink-dark / word and the flush of feeling / induced... / dazed with knowing: words / are both weapon and wit;*" "The Game": "*I'd like to write a poem / to take your breath away / but words have a will of their own... / they may / be read in a dozen different ways...,*" and "Rhymes": "*In my advancing age / let me still be the one / wrestling with words to wield / the world anew, to send / them dancing on some / distant dais, sylvan / with simile: the page / where all my rhymes ring / true.*"

All of these stunning sections: The Blue Flow Below, The Sands of Canatara, Inklings, Cameron Lake: a Suite of Poems, Home Ground, Night Skating, Days Worth the Telling, The Breath of My Being, The Star-Brushed Horizon, Foster's Pond, Mara's Lamp and Inking the World will show the reader a Gutteridge nurtured by his past, charmed by his present, and in concord with what the future holds for him. We must heed John B. Lee's observation on the back cover of *Home Ground* about Gutteridge: "*... he gives us the gift of something we might well carry with us into the future.*"

A more detailed analysis of Don´s skill as a poet can be understood with a look at *Home Ground*. He opens this section with "Black Lake." There is light in the poem, quietness and peace: "*unruffled, silvered surface,*" "*ravishing red dot,*" "*a pair of loons undulated,*" "*sunny butterfly fluttering.*" The poet praises the painter, Gerald Parker ("*so you added...,*" "*to subvert the scene you...,*" and adds his personal poetic "strokes" by meticulous descriptions for the reader. While the title includes "*Black,*" there is overwhelming beauty beyond blackness achieved by painter and poet.

As a professor of Stylistics, I could not help but notice flashes of the device known as alliteration: "*lustrous light to lavish on Black Lake's…,*" "*silvered surface, so,*" "*loons ululated on the cusp of lust and the little stream…*" Alliteration builds a melodic effect into the utterance and creates an emotional atmosphere, in line with the poets´ purpose.

"Moon Over Monk" shows instances of alliteration: "*Mara's lamp… mellowing its light along…,*" "*gently gendered,*" among others, plus other stylistic devices that embellish and give emotional connotation to the poem: a simile, ("*the moon sits in the horizon*") "*like a serene replica of Mara's lamp.*" The moon is a theme in Don's poetry and imagery, and it accompanies his memories. This time it reminds him of Mara – both lights will now show the way, together or alternately. The poet reminisces of his childhood games and "*the sacred place where we play.*"

My father smoked a pipe and long cigars when I was a little boy. He quit many years ago, more than forty-five, but I still remember the aroma of cigar and smoke and I still keep one wooden box where he placed his cigars. It is deeply registered in my emotional memories. "Helm" made me remember how essential and transcending scent, or sound, is for people. In reading "*a lozenge of elm or oak*" I instantly felt wood scents coming from a carpenter's work-shop. I was transported back in time. Gutteridge then blends scents with sounds: "*through the burr and bite of the band-saw.*" There is a floating sense of onomatopoeic echoes, direct and indirect, in the combination of the sound "b" in "*burr… bite… band.*" Alliteration escorts the scene: "*a particle of the puzzle he was perfecting piece by filigreed piece.*"

I realized of the gentle balance between the heavy work carried out in a work-shop: noise, sawdust, probably the logical mess of a place like that, and the child's full involvement ("*I nuzzled in closer*") with his grandfather's work, finely ended with "*knowing I would be cherished and thrive here with this man at the helm*" and preceded by "*the unspoken tousling of my cowlick.*" It was a heart-caressing memory where the poet does not remember his exact age; but he does remember wood names! An unforgettable experience.

Gutteridge skillfully serves us fond memories in "Apostasy." Feelings and human values are kindled in the furnace of human connection. From there emerge convictions and attitudes for life. Gutteridge praises his grandmother for her devoted undertaking of pie preparing and baking. As I read, I feel like I am *right there*, watching her "*put all her love and out-sized ardor into the gentle kneading of her dough… while we feasted on her pastries and praised the Lord.*" Gutteridge relives two experiences: unique home-made food and religion. One is a body-provider; the other, a soul-provider.

"Rare" offers another touching memory for us, and awakens our own. Alliteration is present ("*on the sand in his Sunday suit,*" "*even dove under like daring dolphins*"). Gutteridge leaves behind no memory /experience/anecdote to be forgotten. This time it is the beach, a place most children adore. I understand the sensation of water, of being "*perfectly safe*" in the hands of my own father, of "*venturing up to our waists and even dove…,*" of "(he) *smiled at us and we smiled back at him.*" Don translates happiness into ripples, splashes and adventure in the beach.

I have gone back on my own life, as I have been mirrored, so closely, in Gutteridge´s *Point Taken*. This wonderful collection of poems has brought happiness and homesickness to my mind. Even when Point Edward was taken, it was me, as a reader and admirer, who was taken too into the glorious poetic interweaving Gutteridge has done for us in this book.

As he hoped in his poem "Eternity," I can state Don has been able to memorialize his life in this "Big Book" and leave for us a recorded legacy thus touching eternity. This book is poetry and autobiography, one that will reach out to many and resemble their own. John B. Lee has said that Gutteridge's poems *"partake in the light."* I agree without hesitation.

Gutteridge's *Point Taken* should be among the top most recent poetry books a reader must have and hold, go to for inspiration, for enlightenment, for pleasure, for the sheer elation of reuniting in time and space with family, friends, remembrances; and then place back on a treasure-keeping bookshelf feeling fulfilled and complete. However, always willing to return to the book for feedback and spiritual enrichment. Thank you, Don Gutteridge for *Point Taken*. This is a work of art – point taken!

www.ingramcontent.com/pod-product-compliance
Lightning Source LLC
Chambersburg PA
CBHW080021130526
44591CB00036B/2403